D1426590

THE ASHES '77

THE ASHES '77

Greg Chappell
David Frith

Photographs by Patrick Eagar

ANGUS AND ROBERTSON
PUBLISHERS

ANGUS AND ROBERTSON · PUBLISHERS
London · Sydney · Melbourne · Singapore · Manila

A RICHARD SMART PUBLICATION

First published by Angus and Robertson (UK) Ltd
16 Ship Street, Brighton, in 1977

Copyright © Greg Chappell and David Frith, 1977

ISBN 0 207 95792 4

Printed by John G Eccles Printers Ltd, Inverness

CONTENTS

ILLUSTRATIONS

FOREWORD

The Ashes '77 is a six-stranded story. Its original theme was the tour and matches of the 1977 Australian team to England; but events forced it also to deal with the progress of the "Packer affair", which overshadowed even the Test series in importance. It is told by Greg Chappell, the captain of the Australian side, and David Frith, British-born, Anglo-Australian cricket editor and historian: so it is seen from both sides, the inside and the outside; and it is set in perspective by the combination of close contact and historic awareness.

The relationship between writer and cricketer has by no means always had a happy outcome; "ghost" writing has generally been unsatisfactory if only because, all too often, the player has been named as the author only to boost sales. This, though, has been a genuine collaboration, each writer assuming his own distinct kind of authority.

Brought up in Australia and subsequently living in both countries, Mr Frith is as nearly unbiassed as can reasonably be hoped in a field which compels such fierce loyalties as Anglo-Australian Test cricket.

Greg Chappell, second of three highly-gifted cricketing brothers, indicated the power of his character by the undemonstrative but firm fashion in which he refused to be overshadowed by, or moulded into an imitation of, an extremely strong-willed elder brother who captained Australia before him. The two have always had a mutual respect and a willingness to compete as well as co-operate. When Greg succeeded Ian he adopted an altogether less extrovert method, yet he was instantly successful to the extent of beating an outstandingly strong West Indian side by five-one. He handles a team coolly but with unshakable dignity. That quality, too, is apparent in his account of the development of team and tour. He is not afraid to give full credit to opponents who beat him, nor to admit errors.

He had announced his retirement before the series began or the Packer news "broke"; but presumably he merely anticipated the ban announced by the Australian Board. However that may be, he is an immense loss to the world game. His mere approach to the wicket, slim, erect, purposeful, is enough to identify him as a natural athlete. He was — indeed, is — one of the three finest batsmen in the world; probably the best onside player of modern times; quick in reaction, superbly poised, an immaculate stylist. His true successor is not in sight; and the applause when he came out to his last Test innings at The Oval was a measure of the respect for him in England.

He is one of the first cricketers to afford a clear close-up of a Test tour in which he is taking part. In such a case there must be a tendency to lose the shape of the wood in the weight of trees. He probably was wise, since he was so closely and emotionally involved, not to go too far in evaluating the progress of the matches. That has been done most capably by David Frith, who has already written studies of A. E. Stoddart and Archie Jackson, histories of fast bowling and the Tests between England and Australia; and is currently editor of *The Cricketer*. He watched every day of the series with unwavering interest.

The account of the Tests is absorbing; and especially pleasing to English supporters who had gone long on short commons of success — nine wins from 51 matches since 1956 — against the "old enemy".

1977 saw the establishment of Brearley as England's captain; an immensely successful return by Boycott with the "impossible" performance of his hundredth hundred scored in a Test against Australia, and on his native heath of Headingley. Woolmer, too, at Lord's and Old Trafford seemed to set foot on the threshold of eminence. The historic English strength in seam bowling was paraded by Willis, Hendrick, Lever, Old and Botham and it proved successful. Above all, it was supported by surely the finest of all English fielding sides. The exciting brilliance of Barlow in the covers was lost after the start but there remained Randall to cavort gloriously in the country; and the finest set of close catchers ever brought together in an English team in Brearley, Hendrick, Botham, Old, Greig, Willis, Roope, Miller, Woolmer, plus the high efficiency of Knott behind the stumps, with the safe and efficient Underwood and Boycott away from the wicket.

It is tragic that the Packer affair should so have overshadowed the series. When the tour was finished, Len Maddocks, the Australian team manager, who endured some terrifying stresses quietly, said that he believed the affair produced considerable strain among the players.

That now seems a trifling matter beside the fact that, as appears certain, twelve players who took part in the Oval Test — perhaps more by the time this appears in print — will never again take part in an official Test match. The repercussions of this sorry business cannot be clearly foreseen. It is more than possible, though, that this book will be seen by cricket historians as a contemporary view of the end of an era.

Alresford, September 1977   JOHN ARLOTT

1. SHADOWS ACROSS THE FIELD

David Frith writes:

In the minds of cricket fanatics, the fall of a government is as nothing compared to the winning or losing of the Ashes, which have been fought over by England and Australia since 1882. As a trophy, the tiny urn dwells only in the mind, for it never leaves Lord's. It is not held aloft by the triumphant captain at the end of the series; it is not put on display in Harrods of London or Myers of Melbourne; indeed, its very existence has been questioned by the uninitiated, its purpose by those who have had to sit through series during which retention of the urn has preoccupied captains' minds to degrees of paralysis.

"This is England's year. We must win the Ashes," was an exclamation heard often after England's creditable if unsuccessful effort in the Centenary Test match at Melbourne in March 1977. The sentiment sprang not only from certain heartening individual English performances — notably Derek Randall's innings of 174 — but also from Dennis Lillee's announcement that he would not be available for the tour of England, as his back trouble, sustained in 1972 and magnificently overcome in 1974, was threatening to bring him down again. The rumour of his non-availability had been rife for some time before the announcement, but it was a shock all the same. Dennis Amiss, the England opening batsman who had been Lillee's pet victim, expressed sympathy — with just a flicker at the corner of his mouth. As for the rest, scepticism prevailed. The tough West Australian had just saved the Centenary Test, taking 11 wickets for 165 runs in 385 balls. He simply wanted to make a financial killing, they said.

Yet two of England's leading runmakers at Melbourne told me that of his 385 deliveries, probably 380 were bowled at less than his top pace. Fred Trueman told of Lillee's anxious session with him one evening, when his despair about his ailing back was beyond conceal-ment. Thus, to some, the great fast bowler received the benefit of the doubt, even if fresh doubts arose when his association with Kerry Packer's scheme became clear. As well as signing to comment on the

1977 series for the Channel 9 television network, Lillee was an early
signatory to the media baron's private army of international cricketers.

News of the enterprise leaked early in May, and it soon became
public knowledge that Packer, intent on grasping exclusive television
rights for Test cricket, had set about cornering the market by placing
the world's top players under contract to him for matches which he
chose to describe as "Super Tests". Negotiations between Packer,
JP Sports (John Cornell and Austin Robertson's sports promotion
company), and leading players had been in progress for some weeks,
and it was said that by May 11 a total of 35 players had been engaged
for a series of "Super Tests", one-day matches, and round-robin
tournaments in the 1977-78 Australian season. Recruitment had been
in the hands of Ian Chappell and Tony Greig. For a time it seemed that
there would be a flat refusal by official governing bodies to discuss
Packer's plans with him.

When eventually both sides did sit down, at Lord's on June 23, the
International Cricket Conference, to the surprised gratification of
many, indicated its willingness to accommodate the Packer matches,
but naturally not at the expense of scheduled tours by India of
Australia, Australia of West Indies, and England of Pakistan and New
Zealand, or of other officially arranged first-class matches. Talks broke
down when Packer revealed his motivating ambition: to have exclusive
television rights in Australia from 1978-79 onwards, when the
Australian Broadcasting Commission's agreement runs out. The ICC
would not be party to such a blind sell-out, and Packer stormed away,
saying, "After this, I will take no steps at all to help anyone. It is
every man for himself and the devil take the hindmost." The words
jangled discordantly in the ears of cricket-lovers around the world, and
as further names and numbers were issued — of those joining the
original 35 players — and plans were announced concerning Packer's
acquisition of ground rights and "mobile" wickets, the cold, damp
spring turned to warm, dry summer, and cricket tottered onwards,
wondering about its fate.

Almost every Australian player had been signed up, including Ian
Chappell, Dennis Lillee, Ross Edwards, Gary Gilmour, and Ian Redpath,
but excluding four of the touring side: Gary Cosier, Geoff Dymock,
Kim Hughes, and Craig Serjeant. Greig, Knott, Snow and Underwood
from England — soon to be joined by Amiss — were English
signatories, and Asif Iqbal, Imran Khan, Majid Khan, and Mushtaq
Mohammad from Pakistan were also part of the "circus". From South

Africa came Eddie Barlow, Denys Hobson, Graeme Pollock, Mike Procter, and Barry Richards. From West Indies came Michael Holding, Clive Lloyd, Viv Richards, and Andy Roberts, soon to be joined by "the whole West Indies team". Of all the players approached, only Geoff Boycott had refused to progress from an oral agreement to one that was written. He would not countenance any interference with his commitments to Yorkshire. Richie Benaud and his sports consultancy company were engaged to assist in the management of the series.

The first retaliation by England's controlling body had come on May 13, when an emergency meeting of the Cricket Council issued the instruction to the panel of selectors that Tony Greig was not to be considered for the England captaincy in the forthcoming series against Australia. "His action," read the Council's statement in part, "has inevitably impaired the trust which existed between the cricket authorities and the captain of the England side."

The chairman, former England captain Freddie Brown, added: "The captaincy of the England team involves close liaison with the selectors in the management, selection and development of England players for the future and clearly Tony Greig is unlikely to be able to do this as his stated intention is to be contracted elsewhere during the next three winters."

Thus, England's willowy, blond leader, who had taken dynamic command in the hour of need in 1975, who had survived the bruising 1976 series against West Indies and manipulated a famous victory in India and a gallant fight at Melbourne, fell from the peak and found himself on the slippery slopes where, for the foreseeable weeks, only the constant scoring of runs would save him from total Test match oblivion — that is, if the selectors chose to pick him at all.

It was felt by all except those who demanded complete banishment that while the "rebel" Australians remained to compete in the 1977 series, England ought not to handicap themselves by omitting Greig or the world-class Knott and Underwood. The selectors — or at least the majority of them — felt likewise. On June 6 Mike Brearley, Greig's vice-captain in India, was appointed captain of England for the first two Tests, having led MCC against the tourists and England successfully in the three-match Prudential Trophy series.

Had an England-Australia series ever begun midst such distraction? Not since 1912, when six major players refused to tour England after a bitter disagreement with the Australian Board.

To add to the general feeling of discomfort, the early-season weather remained obstinately wet, rendering the memories of the sweltering 1975 and 1976 seasons tantalising in the extreme. With ten newcomers (to Test tours of England) in the side, Australia desperately needed warmth and hard pitches, or, as a minimum, constant matchplay. Instead, they sat out eight washed-out days and further interruptions during the first 16 scheduled days' play. Perhaps "sat out" is inaccurate, for much touch football and soccer was played, and the cricketers maintained a fitness and a corporate reality, and kept on top of such things as letter-writing.

The British public, therefore, were hard put to familiarise themselves thoroughly with the party, which contained so many new faces. Chosen by Messrs Harvey, Ridings, and Loxton on the final day of the Centenary Test, the 1977 Australian touring team, the 27th to play a Test series in England, comprised:

	State	Birthdate	Tests
Gregory Stephen CHAPPELL (captain)	Queensland	7 August 1948	46
Rodney William MARSH (vice-captain)	W. Australia	4 November 1947	47
Raymond John BRIGHT	Victoria	13 July 1954	0
Gary John COSIER	S. Australia	25 April 1953	9
Ian Charles DAVIS	N.S.W.	25 June 1953	12
Geoffrey DYMOCK	Queensland	21 July 1945	4
David William HOOKES	S. Australia	3 May 1955	1
Kimberley John HUGHES	W. Australia	26 January 1954	0
Michael Francis MALONE	W. Australia	9 October 1950	0
Richard Bede McCOSKER	N.S.W.	11 December 1946	17
Kerry James O'KEEFFE	N.S.W.	25 November 1949	21
Leonard Stephen PASCOE	N.S.W.	13 February 1950	0
Richard Daryl ROBINSON	Victoria	8 June 1946	0
Craig Stanton SERJEANT	W. Australia	1 November 1951	0
Jeffrey Robert THOMSON	Queensland	16 August 1950	17
Maxwell Henry Norman WALKER	Victoria	12 September 1948	29
Kevin Douglas WALTERS	N.S.W.	21 December 1945	63

Manager: L. V. Maddocks (Victoria)
Treasurer: N. T. McMahon (Queensland)
Baggageman/scorer: D. K. Sherwood (N.S.W.)
Physiotherapist: S. P. McRae (Victoria)

The third column reveals a comparatively young crew: averaging just 26 years of age at the start of the tour. And the fourth column shows how little Test experience half the team had known: eight players totalled five Tests between them.

There were only two opening batsmen chosen, and one of them, McCosker, had suffered a sickening injury in the Centenary Test, playing a short ball from fast bowler Willis onto his jaw, which was broken. He batted in the second innings, drawing criticism from some who saw his courage as misguided, placing England's fast bowlers in an awkward moral position. The grotesquely wired and bandaged batsman received the occasional bouncer, but made 25, saw Marsh to the first hundred by an Australian regular wicketkeeper in a Test against England, and shared a ninth-wicket stand of 54 which was to have unexpected significance. His selection for the tour was assured, and if there was an element of risk about it, he was the most experienced opener available, and the expectation of his fitness must have been much greater than in the case of Jeff Thomson, whose terrible shoulder injury, sustained in the Christmas Test match against Pakistan, was far from healed as he underwent tests to satisfy the selectors only days before take-off.

Rick McCosker's medical file, too, was a long time closing. Fed on liquids for several weeks ("I'm glad my wife had a liquidiser. I could have almost any food I wanted reduced to liquid.") he lost half a stone, but knew it could have been worse. The jawbone refused to knit at first, and had to be rewired. Some splintered teeth had to be repaired. Then, to cap it all, a strike by air traffic controllers in Australia delayed his departure for England. In the (rainy) event, he missed little cricket.

His opening partner in the Centenary Test had been Ian Davis, a dapper cricketer, who had been launched into Test cricket in 1973-74, his first season in first-class cricket. He moved north to try his luck with Queensland in 1975-76, but returned to Sydney after a season, and regained his Test place upon Ian Redpath's retirement. A century against Pakistan at Adelaide came as a relief to those who had believed from the start that the young bank officer possessed rare natural gifts.

Greg Chappell was universally regarded as one of the three or four finest batsmen in the world. The situation changes fast these days, with such an abundance of talent in most departments of the game, but Barry Richards, Hampshire's South African who is so seldom able to stretch himself against the best, Viv Richards, the mercurial West Indian who seemed to borrow Bradman's 1930 bat during the 1976 series in England, and Geoff Boycott, who isolated himself from the sternness of Test cricket in 1974, all have vied for the unofficial and immeasurable accolade of World's Best Batsman. I suppose Gordon Greenidge, Clive Lloyd, Zaheer Abbas or Dennis Amiss have also had claims during the middle 'seventies. But Australia's captain, having succeeded brother Ian after the 1975 England tour (which incidentally brought him only 33 runs in six Test innings apart from a 73 not out at Lord's), soon took firm hold of the biggest job in Australian cricket by scoring two centuries in his first Test as captain, and leading his side to a crushing 5-1 victory over West Indies.

My co-author, straightbacked and undemonstrative, was faced before long with a similar task to that of brother Ian when he took over a team in its shaky rebuilding stage after the Lawry era. Great interest surrounded the matter of how Greg Chappell would react to the challenge. His determination and dedication would never be in doubt, but there were fears that his batting might be affected by the cares of leading an untried team. It was quite unlike being the classiest batsman in a world-beating side, balanced, resourceful, and overflowing with confidence. He had made a wonderful century in his first Test innings, against England at Perth in 1970-71, and four more centuries since against the number one "enemy". A special record held by this non-seeker of records was that of most runs in a Test match: 380 (247 not out and 133 against New Zealand at Wellington in 1973-74). Then there was the match when the ball followed him around everywhere and he held seven catches (Australia v England, Perth, 1974-75) — a world Test record for a non-wicketkeeper, shared two years afterwards with India's Yajuvendra Singh, whose seven catches, by all reports, may not all have touched the bat.

Chappell, then, arrived in England in the spring of 1977 with rows of cricket medals on his modest breast, but a lean previous tour of England for which to make up, and, more ominously, the threat that he was indeed in charge of the weakest Australian side in memory to visit England.

Trevor Bailey aired this view — or rather assertion — during one of the early broadcasts, and Alan McGilvray, Australia's veteran commentator, renowned for his forbearance and impartiality, replied that if England did not win the Ashes this year, it could be a long time before the chance arose again, because there was so much promise in this Australian side.

The same hopes and prayers accompanied Woodfull's boyish team in 1930. Whether there was a Don Bradman, Stan McCabe, or Archie Jackson among the 1977 tourists remained to be seen. It was a firm opinion that Hookes, Hughes and Serjeant formed as promising a trio of batsmen as had ever come out of one summer. Craig Serjeant, the West Australian pharmacist, had played in only ten first-class matches (average 66.36) before the tour, making two centuries, one of them for his State against MCC in their preliminary match before the Centenary Test. Kim Hughes, also from the great western State, scored 119 and 60 in his first-class debut match, against New South Wales in 1975-76, and was twelfth man for Australia in a Test against Pakistan. He toured New Zealand that season as well, and since he had spent a prolific summer in Scotland, it could be said that he was ready for greater things. His technique was pleasing most observers, though he tended to play back sometimes rather too often. The ''pop'' papers seemed to think that with his curly fair hair this schoolteacher would be the idol of cricket's younger followers. Yet of the three from whom so much was expected, one — David Hookes, the youngest member of the side — had already achieved something at the highest level. His Test debut came in the Centenary Test, and his exciting second innings of 56 included five consecutive fours off Tony Greig, each one cheered almost hysterically as the crowd saw a new young champion establishing himself.

Hookes's selection had been made almost a certainty when in successive innings, all at Adelaide, he scored 163 and 9 against Victoria, 185 and 105 against Queensland, and 135 and 156 against New South Wales, thus equalling Tom Hayward's record of two hundreds in a match twice running. Hayward performed the feat for Surrey during Whitsun week in 1906, when he was 35. Hookes was 21, with only a handful of matches behind him and a season of club cricket in, with a pleasant curiosity, the county of Surrey, in 1975. One evening during the Old Trafford Test I was to find him playing the hotel jukebox — Roy Orbison, Neil Sedaka, and contemporaries. ''A bit old-fashioned?'' I said, feeling that these were mine own favourites and not of any appeal to a chap a generation younger. ''I was born in 1955!'' he retorted with mock indignation and a disarming grin.

The vice-captain, Rod Marsh, knew from the start that much rested on his thick shoulders. ''Bacchus'' had injected a formidable spirit into the Western Australian XI, and for 47 Tests his fierce aggression, whether batting or taking more punishment as he kept wicket to Lillee and Thomson than any other wicketkeeper can have known, had been an important component in Australia's winning formula. Among his statistical glories were a record bag for an Australian season (67 victims in 1975-76) and most Test wicketkeeping wickets for Australia (189), a record he set in the Melbourne Centenary Test, where he carried a picture of Australia's first wicketkeeper, Jack Blackham, in his pocket. He would miss the likes of Lillee and Ian Chappell in 1977, but his forthright manner and refusal to accept repression by any adversary were expected to be as evident as ever.

The two other seniors, Walters and Walker, had yet to show consistent reflections of their great talents in England, Max Walker having toured in 1975 and performed well without tearing England apart as expected with the swing and cut that were always seen as tailor-made for English conditions. Doug Walters was an enigma apart. Three times before had he toured, and his innings of 81 and 86 in his earliest Test in England — at Old Trafford in 1968 — had still to be matched. In almost every other Test-playing country he had ripped the bowling to shreds at one time or another, and just as Underwood was kept in the England side in order to obliterate the opposition whenever conditions suited him, so Walters, the card-playing, chain-smoking, laconic little fellow from Dungog, was usually considered a vital if inconsistent part of the Australian cricket war machine. Nonetheless, on what must surely be his final England tour he had something to prove to an English public sceptical about miracles it has only read about.

Another problem player, of more recent vintage, was Gary Cosier, the huge, auburn-haired batsman and sometime bowler, who scored 109 in his first Test innings, against West Indies at Melbourne in 1975-76, and a powerful 168 against Pakistan at Adelaide a year later.

He failed twice, though, in the Centenary Test, hooking awkwardly both times, and it was decided by certain pundits that he was too leaden-footed to prosper in international cricket. This seemed a particularly gloomy view considering that the easy-going youngster had already shown his worth, and that not all successful batsmen — especially some of the heavyweights — have been Nureyevs.

The second wicketkeeper, Richie Robinson, Victoria's captain, was actually 17 months older than the first choice. Yet in Robinson's selection there was wisdom in that he had made heaps of runs in the Australian season, and he was enthusiastic and an inspiration to all who played alongside him — qualities which would be in greater demand now than for some time. Never having made a first-class century before, he suddenly reeled off four during the 1976-77 summer, finishing with the forceful argument of 828 runs for ten times out. The selectors could hardly look beyond him, especially as he knew English conditions from the 1975 tour.

So to the bowling, which, apart from Walker and Thomson, was new to English pitches, except that O'Keeffe had had two seasons for Somerset, and Dymock and Bright some experience in Lancashire league cricket. Geoff Dymock, the only Queensland-born player in the side, was the oldest member at 31, and owed his selection to Gary Gilmour's omission, an unthinkable thing only a few months before the team was chosen. Gilmour, potentially one of the world's great all-rounders, had gone into decline mainly because of ankle trouble. He soldiered on with it when two weeks out would have been all that was necessary. By the time he had the minor operation the touring side was chosen without him. How he must have cursed when no sooner had the surgeon's knife slit the heel than the fragment of floating bone popped eagerly and untroublesomely out. Ironically, Dymock, his left-arm fast-medium replacement, was on the verge of retiring from first-class cricket because he could not afford the time away from his job as schoolteacher.

Ray Bright's beard did much to conceal his youthfulness, which perhaps ought best be disguised in a spin bowler. He exuded confidence, in contrast to the other spinner, O'Keeffe, and possessed the crucial ability to bowl accurately and vary his left-arm flight. Kerry O'Keeffe also arrived with a reputation for accuracy, less easily cultivated by a right-arm leg-spin/googly bowler. His career had vacillated, as perhaps it was bound to. A boy prodigy, he had known sensational success and setback, but he now represented the last of a precious breed in

England-Australia cricket, and many were the prayers offered up for his success and for the revival of the wrist-spin culture, with its delicate varieties, its guile, and not least the faster over rate that goes with it.

There is art, of course, in medium-pace bowling, and Mick Malone, though not yet a master of that art, was showing signs of passing entry examinations. He had taught himself to bowl the outswinger in addition to a natural inswinger, and during the season leading up to the tour he had taken 49 wickets in ten matches for his State — an aggregate second only to Lillee's. The other new fast bowler was Len Pascoe, an interesting cricketer firstly in that he was Yugoslavian-born and secondly in that he had demanded inclusion when Lillee became unavailable by sheer force of results, taking 35 wickets in seven matches for his State. Born in the Macedonian village of Bitola, to the son of a migrant, who had gone back to the homeland during the war, he was taken by his parents when they returned to Australia when he was only six months old. Later in life he changed his name from Durtanovich, and became as Australian as they come, growing up in Bankstown, just outside Sydney, with his close pal Jeff Thomson. He is now a community arts officer in the town.

As for Thomson, the tough, uncomplicated, extremely highly-paid radio station public relations officer — it was upon his hefty and damaged shoulders that the 1977 series seemed to rest as much as anywhere else. He was expected to feel the strain of his savage injury, which occurred when he collided with Alan Turner in trying for a caught-and-bowled in the Adelaide Test of 1976-77. He was expected to miss the fire and brimstone of his ''other half'', Dennis Lillee. And he was expected to miss the bouncè and pace of Australian wickets, as had been the case during much of the 1975 tour of England. All the same, if by some chance he should recover his former pace, and link up with an able replacement for his missing fellow-assassin — whether it be Pascoe, bowling with Lillee-like ferocity, or Malone, wobbling the ball as Bob Massie did five years earlier — then ''Thommo'' could win for Australia, adding appreciably to his 80 Test wickets in 17 matches.

There was much to be discovered about this new combination. There always is as a tour unfolds, and it is part of the excitement, even if there is inevitably the sad spectacle of the one or two who do not find the success wished them as the final hometown glasses are raised in their honour.

Greg Chappell writes:

Another tour, another set of preparations. We gathered as usual for the pre-tour distribution of Australian blazers and sweaters for those who had not toured before, and to receive tour details. This time we gathered a day earlier, to fit in some promotion work on behalf of Benson & Hedges, who have taken such a wide interest in cricket recently. They had agreed to sponsor the 1977 tour of England, and to start things off we made a lunchtime appearance at Martin Place, Sydney, with a public reception from the Lord Mayor. We were introduced to the people by Frank Tyson before moving up to Hyde Park, where we did a net session for the sponsors.

The following day we had a team meeting and then flew out of Kingsford-Smith Airport that afternoon with Qantas. It is a long flight, twenty-odd hours, and with the players trying to get some sleep and watching movies, it was, I'm glad to report, quite uneventful. We travelled via Singapore, Beirut and Amsterdam, arriving in London early on the Friday morning, and after checking through baggage collection and customs we made our weary way to the Waldorf, "home" for the past several Australian touring teams.

At 2 pm we held a Press conference, where Len Maddocks, the manager, and I answered journalists' questions and introduced the players. From there I went off to an arranged television interview, and I lost contact with the boys. It had been my intention to combat the dreaded jet-lag by going to bed at a normal hour and sleeping — with luck — through till morning. When I got back from the TV studio there was no sign of any of the team, and I assumed they had gone out for meals or to the Sportsman's Club, a favourite haunt in London.

Okay, I thought, I'll join them. I had a bath and a shave, and sat on the bed to watch the evening news before venturing out into the cool spring evening. I lay down for a moment's rest . . . and didn't wake till one in the morning! By then it seemed pointless to go out, so I got my pyjamas on and made a formal entry into bed. This time I slept until four. At that hour there was little else to do but to telephone home, in Queensland, to let everyone know that I'd arrived safely.

My wife Judy had given birth to our second child only weeks before my departure, and it was good to hear that everything was all right. It was not the easiest thing to do, leaving them when duty called.

I stared at the walls until half-past-six, but by then I was dying for someone to talk to. I was sick of the room. I went downstairs, expecting to be the only person up and about at that time of the morning. I wanted to get a paper or two to read, but when I entered the lounge downstairs practically the entire team was sitting there, wide-eyed. They also had turned in about five in the afternoon and awoken at three in the morning. They too had been trying to fill in time until breakfast. We had some coffee, and I considered starting our programme of exercises there and then, running through the empty streets of London. That began the following day.

Meanwhile, we began practice at the Lord's nets on the Saturday, and on the Sunday we went for a run and did some exercises, sprinting and suchlike, in Regents Park. In the afternoon some of us played golf at Beaconsfield with the Golf Fanatics International, a group of golfing charity-workers who raise sums to purchase mechanical wheelchairs for the handicapped. Val Doonican has succeeded Bobby Charlton as captain of the Fanatics.

On a cold, windy day Rod Marsh, Doug Walters, David Hookes, Richie Robinson, Kerry O'Keeffe and I had a delightful afternoon. Most of us played fairly well, and I won with 43 individual Stableford points, my best performance ever on the course. Having had a lay-off of a couple of weeks from cricket and golf, I was quite surprised to have played so well.

It was a worthwhile afternoon. Val Doonican presented a wheelchair to a girl from one of the nearby homes, and at this point I reflected on what a humbling experience it had been. It made us feel so fortunate to be able to get out there and play golf and cricket and do the things we wanted to do, while these unfortunate kids were so needy. We felt we had perhaps done something worthwhile, to help them on their way.

Back to practice at Lord's, where we had some luck. On the Monday and Tuesday we were in the nets in the morning for full sessions, and each time it rained in the afternoon.

Now came the opening match of the tour, a one-day game against Lavinia, Duchess of Norfolk's XI, at Arundel, which we won. On a sunny day without warmth several of our new young players got going. We fitted as many of them in as possible, and notable performances came from Craig Serjeant (65), Gary Cosier (four wickets), and Len Pascoe, who was pretty sharp on a slow wicket.

More net practice, more training — long distance, sprints, loosening exercises, such as we devised in the New Zealand tour. Rod Marsh organised fielding exercises, including soccer fielding, where flexibility and fitness are related to cricket skills. Rain again plagued us towards the end of the week.

Our first official function was the Lord's Taverners' luncheon, where the president, comedian Eric Morecambe, made a very amusing speech.

The first major match was against Surrey, at The Oval, and with no play on the first or last days, we simply fielded, Surrey making 327 for 8, with Graham Roope hitting a century and that solid veteran John Edrich, who has haunted many an Australian touring side, making 70.

The next match, against Kent at Canterbury, was marred by rain, half-a-day's play only being possible to start with, and none at all on the second. Rod Marsh led the side in my absence, and it was at least satisfying to see Craig Serjeant again make runs, and Kim Hughes score 80 in a match that was drawn with Kent 33 for 2 in reply to our 240 for 7 declared.

After that wet event we became even more waterlogged at Hove, where the match against Sussex was reduced by rain to a mere 34 overs in the first and second days and a complete washout on the third. Serjeant didn't let the water worry him again though, making another half-century — the only bright spot on a bleak, frustrating scene.

On the Saturday night the whole team, plus Pressmen, were invited to a party at the home of Sussex and then England captain Tony Greig. It was a very happy affair, set in a huge marquee on the lawn. It became really significant, however, when the Kerry Packer professional cricket plans leaked during the evening and became a public reality. A number of cricket-writers had heard rumours, and when snatches of conversation were overheard, matters were pursued further the following morning, and on the Monday morning the story broke. Still it was disjointed. It was gradually pieced together, but what a pity it was that the news was not announced in its entirety at the outset. It might have made for less misunderstanding, though I suppose the reactions of the various Boards of Control were fairly predictable however the story came out.

I firmly believe that, were the Boards disposed to talk with Packer, to sit down and try to compromise in the early stages, there was a likelihood that the scheme would have been fitted within the present framework of fixtures with very little interruption to it. But it has always been the administration's feeling that it organises the game of cricket, raises profits, feeds the money back into the game, and therefore has a divine right to have the players do as it wants. No-one from outside, doing it for commercial reasons, apparently ought to be let near the game.

The general feeling of the players who signed for Packer is that it will be a good thing for top players now and in the future. I doubt if the average player will benefit. The rewards will go to men who have made names for themselves in Test cricket and are then able to go on to the "Super-Tests".

Cricket, by its nature and from the fact that it is played in relatively few countries, is always going to be on one of the lower financial levels of world sport, but I don't think it has to remain right at the bottom. It can certainly raise itself a few degrees. Whether Kerry Packer is the man to do it and whether this is the right kind of operation only time will tell. The aim is to present cricket in a new style, to try to appeal to a much wider audience.

Redirecting our concentration to the tour once more, we were in for further disappointment at Southampton, where the match with Hampshire was totally washed out. Again we played some soccer, and it began to dawn on us that if the rain never let up, instead of playing cricket against England we might consider challenging Manchester United to a soccer series!

Into Wales, and a match against Glamorgan. But — the same deadly story: no rain on the first day, and some tension on the last day only after Doug Walters, leading our side, and Alan Jones had made declarations. Gary Cosier made a half-century here.

At Bath, in the match against my old county, Somerset, we had some lasting sunshine at last. Rick McCosker had joined us at last after having prolonged treatment to his jaw injury — a fracture from a ball from Bob Willis in the Centenary Test. Rick was delayed by the Australian air traffic controllers' strike.

I won the toss from Brian Close (who, incidentally, was playing Test cricket before I was one year old), and decided to bat because it was a sunny day and the wicket looked spongy and slow. It was too good an opportunity to miss after our starvation of previous weeks. So here we were, confronted by 6 ft 8 ins West Indian Joel Garner ("Big Bird"). He got the ball to bounce, and soon had McCosker caught, hanging his bat outside off stump. I had hardly touched a bat for seemingly ages, but a six off the meat to a shortish leg boundary off Garner served as a confidence-booster, and from there I went from strength to strength. I found myself stroking the ball as well as at any time in my career. It was a great satisfaction to make a hundred at Bath, where I had had few successes during my seasons with Somerset. The ground and the pitch have improved considerably since 1968 and 1969.

We still managed no more than 232, and Somerset went past us, with good innings from Rose, Denning, and Botham. This young all-rounder really went after Kerry O'Keeffe quite severely. Our leg-spinner, of course, also used to play for the county.

I batted at seven in the second innings, hoping that the younger players would be able to take advantage of batting opportunities. This was certainly so with David Hookes, who reached a century off 81 balls. Serjeant also succeeded with a round fifty. Even so, Somerset needed only 182 to win, and they got them, thanks mainly to Viv Richards, who raced to 53 to help the county to its first-ever win over the Australians.

At Bristol conditions were diabolical, with a cutting wind making a mockery of the sunshine. The wicket was grassy and uneven, and it played several heights. One ball might be ankle-height and the next flying past the nose. Brian Brain fixed us up very swiftly, taking 7 for 51 with his fast-medium variations. It was the Saturday of the FA Cup final, and I think both sides were rather keen to see the football. Efforts had been made to arrange playing hours around the big match on television, but the Board and the TCCB were not prepared to set a precedent. Whether this inspired Brain I don't know, but we were all out about five minutes before the kick-off!

Now it was Max Walker's turn to bowl with devastating effect. Bowling downhill, with the wind, "Tangles" was well-nigh unplayable, swinging the ball about and utilising the uneven bounce conditions. In about an hour and a half Gloucestershire were routed for 63, Walker taking 7 for 19.

The pitch seemed to have settled down when we batted a second time, and I decided to go forward to the ball. The policy paid off and I was able to reach my second century in successive matches. We bowled Gloucestershire out, and won in two days. Then, with the need to make up for lost time very much in mind, we agreed to play a limited-overs match on the third day, and it was here that Lenny Pascoe showed his pace. Several of the boys got runs too, and we moved on to Lord's for the MCC match in good spirits.

Here we found a dry, dusty wicket — the legacy of two very dry summers before. Mike Brearley led the MCC side, a team with many young England hopefuls and recently-capped players. Our great boon, though, was the form of Jeff Thomson, who bowled fast, with bounce, and showed stamina in a couple of long spells. He troubled all the batsmen, and might easily have taken a lot more than five wickets.

There was some anxiety after he strained his bowling arm in throwing Graham Barlow's stumps down in an attempted run-out, but the discomfort was to disappear by the first Test match. As for the batting, Kim Hughes easily top-scored in the first innings with a well-made 60 and Rick McCosker ran into fair form with 73 in the second. Derek Randall made two half-centuries for MCC and Barlow also passed 50, but once they were gone a collapse took place and we won by 79 runs.

At Worcester the pitch was dry and dusty also, and when I called correctly I felt we had to use the wicket first as it could very well break up later. On the contrary, as it became even drier it was better for batting. Ian Davis played his first long innings of the tour, grafting for 4¾ hours for 83 and trying to get more side-on. He had been playing too chest-on, and this was the straightest I'd seen him play for a long time.

I managed to make my third century here, and was very pleased with the way I was seeing and striking the ball. I had to come off upon reaching three-figures, for my left knee was painful from slight damage incurred during a training session at Lord's. When I felt I couldn't trust it with my full weight I knew it was time to come off and play safe. In the second innings we delayed our declaration in order to get as much batting as reasonably possible, for the one-day internationals were almost upon us and we were still conscious of how much cricket we had missed because of the terrible spring weather.

On the Tuesday prior to the first Prudential match a dozen of us had a golf day at Whitefields, just out of Manchester, an event arranged by Ken Grieves, the Australian who played for years for Lancashire, captaining the county. We played in three teams of four and had an Ambrose tournament, where all four play the best ball each time. This results in some pretty good scores, as can be imagined. Playing without handicaps and splitting the teams up as evenly as possible, we had groups of Mick Malone, Craig Serjeant, and Rick McCosker in my side; Geoff Dymock, Kim Hughes, and David Hookes in Rod Marsh's team; and Jeff Thomson, Richie Robinson, and Kerry O'Keeffe in Doug Walters' team. At £5 per head in side-stakes there was a reasonable incentive all-round, and we ended up having a very enjoyable day, with some excellent golf at times. Rod Marsh's team won, five under par, and the other two teams managed four under. It was a pleasant experience to be playing always for pars or birdies!

The following day we practised on the fine Old Trafford net wickets in the morning, and after lunch six of us again played golf. On the Thursday we began the series of three one-day international matches against England for the Prudential Trophy.

I won the toss and decided to bat on a good-looking wicket, hoping that our fellows would settle down on it. I felt that having runs on the board would be the best thing. England's bowlers, it seemed to me, would bowl better than ours in this competition since they have far more limited-overs cricket, playing at least once a week, and having already played several this season. Our blokes get only about three one-day matches a season.

With so little cricket behind us we decided to give everybody at least one game during the Prudential series. But here at Old Trafford we got away to a bad start. Craig Serjeant (46) and I began to find our feet, but just as I was getting comfortable I got one from Derek Underwood which turned appreciably and I was given out lbw for 30. Runs were hard to come by in the face of tight bowling and skilful field-placing, and we could muster no more than 169 for 9 in our 55 overs, Rod Marsh contributing a valuable 42.

When England got away to a good start our score looked nowhere near enough, but we kept plugging away and eventually we reached a position where we felt we had a chance of winning. Graham Barlow made 42, but the vital innings came from Chris Old and Alan Knott after England were 125 for 6. This pair put paid to any chance we had, and my tactics in using key bowlers through the first two-thirds of the innings left me having to bowl in the latter stages, when the batsmen decided I "had to go". I took some stick. All the same, England's winning margin was a mere two wickets, and there was a good deal of excitement towards the end.

We moved down to Birmingham next day, and had a workout in the morning and a non-compulsory net after lunch. On the Saturday I won the toss — my eighth success, I think, in as many tosses — and with an eye on the overcast conditions and the moisture in the pitch I asked England to bat first. I felt we had a chance to get them out quite cheaply. Unfortunately the opening bowlers were often astray, and Jeff Thomson, who was still a long way from his peak, had to be rested after three erratic overs, my plan being to use him in short spells rather than in a six and a five. The total reached 19, at which point I had Mike Brearley lbw with a ball that nipped back, and then surprised Derek Randall with a bouncer first ball. I felt it was the last thing he'd be expecting. He likes to get on the front foot. Luckily for me the ball lifted over the off stump, Randall aimed a hook, and only nicked it to Rod Marsh behind the stumps.

With this quick double-success, I brought back Thomson, but, well as he bowled, it wasn't a day for the regular bowlers, and he and Mick Malone, who moved the ball about in the air, gave way to others. Max Walker was not in his best form, and it came back to Gary Cosier and myself. We both, at our lower pace, made the ball bend in the air and seam off the pitch, and with the help of some undistinguished batting by the England batsmen, whose footwork often left a lot to be desired, we finished off the innings for 171, ''Cose'' and I taking five apiece. Things would have been much worse for the home side if Old and John Lever had not put on 55 for the eighth wicket.

We felt England's bowlers would know how to use the conditions, and sure enough they did. Ian Davis was out in the first over, fending off a Willis bouncer, and wickets fell steadily from then on. Our application was astray at times. It was not the situation for playing shots. We only had to bat sensibly to reach the target, but we succumbed quite meekly to some good swing and seam bowling. All out 70 was a humiliating scoreline, and I regretted bitterly that England's bowlers had had this ego boost so early in the summer.

Before the third and final Prudential Trophy match, at The Oval on the Bank Holiday Monday, I called a special team meeting and let the players know that I was far from pleased with the general application many of them were showing. Another disturbing point was that we had been outfielded by England.

So to The Oval, two-down. Again I won the toss, and to the surprise of some critics I put England in. Geoff Dymock, coming in for his first game of the series, bowled well, as did Kerry O'Keeffe, but I thought Ray Bright's concentration wavered midway through his spell after a promising start. Our fielding this time was slightly improved, but a record-breaking opening partnership by Brearley and Amiss seemed to have taken the match away from us. They put on 161. O'Keeffe had Brearley stumped with the final ball of his permitted 11 overs, and then we really did break through. After Amiss's century no-one else apart from Old (20) reached double-figures. They all tried to play shots too early, anxious to capitalise on the sound start given them by the openers.

All the same, 243 was a tall target. We decided to use Richie Robinson, an attacking player, to open with McCosker, and after they had put on 33 for the first wicket, I joined Robinson and we added 148 for the next wicket before Richie was caught trying to hook Willis. The Victorian captain had played and missed in the early stages, but his bold methods deserved some luck, and his contribution was just what was wanted. A hooked six off Lever will long be remembered by those who saw it.

At 88 for one, around five o'clock, bad light and drizzle had sent us off the field, and it seemed unlikely we'd be returning that day. But an hour later conditions improved, and the Prudential officials, knowing that the next day was the Queen's Silver Jubilee holiday, were understandably anxious to have the match finished. There would be no television coverage of the cricket on the following day.

So out we went, and soon the light grew very poor. The conditions were not dangerous, particularly as Richie and I had grown accustomed to the gloom, but it was hardly fit for new batsmen. When my partner got out we were needing around five runs an over, and when a couple of wickets fell quickly we were starting to lose ground. To add to our problems we could see a storm approaching and light rain began to fall again. It was a difficult situation. I felt our best chance of winning was to get off and start again the next day. But we played on for the sponsors' sake.

A couple of further wickets fell, but we ploughed on. Then came the rain, steady at first, and then driving hard into the face. I was trying to get as much strike as possible and to steer Australia into the position where we didn't have to slog. Towards the end the conditions were worse than I have ever known them on a baseball field let alone a cricket field. But by now, absolutely saturated, all of us, we saw the tide turning for Australia. The ball was very slippery, as were the crease areas. I certainly didn't want to go off now that the bowlers were suffering even greater inconveniences than the batsmen. Having gone this far, to give the sponsors their finish, we were now on the verge of grasping victory. With four overs left the umpires were leaving it to the captains, and I think Mike Brearley acknowledged that having stayed out through the dark we were morally entitled to see it through. Bright had been beautifully caught by Randall at cover and O'Keeffe and Thomson (caught napping with his rubber-soled shoes on) were run out; but with Geoff Dymock as my partner I eventually drove Old through the on side for the winning runs, and with ten balls to spare we had won. I finished 125 not out, and hope never again to have to bat through such terrible conditions. At one stage the sun was beaming through the torrents of rain, and it was like looking into a dirty mirror.

Come rain or shine, it was a confidence-booster to the side just before the first Test match.

I missed the remaining two matches before the Test — against Ireland in Dublin and against Essex — because my knee was not yet 100 per cent. It meant that an extra batting place could be allocated, of course, with several members of the side still short of batting in the middle. As it happened, the wicket in Ireland was not all that good, by all accounts, and the Essex game was spoilt by rain and wind. The team were not all that appreciative, either, of industrial action at Dublin Airport that delayed their flight so that they reached their Essex hotel at half-past-three in the morning. Meanwhile, I was taking a couple of days' welcome break with friends on the Isle of Man, playing golf and watching the TT races. I had planned to have this relaxation and then two days in the practice nets — ideal preparation for the Test. Unfortunately wet weather interfered with the net practice, heavy overnight rain day after day reducing us to only running, fielding and football — hardly ideal preparation for a Test match, especially as we were still unsettled as to the composition of our team. Eventually Rod, Doug and I named 13 for the Test, leaving our options open.

On the day before the match, with the covers off, we were able to examine the pitch, and it was surprising to see it looking so good. I imagined that with some sun on it it would become better and better for batting, and at that point I began to entertain thoughts of putting England in if I won the toss. There was a good, even coverage of grass, and it was as flat a Lord's wicket as I have ever seen, though I still believe there is a ridge on it. It is at the Nursery end, but it was reasonably wide on this Test strip, and the uneven bounce from it during the game was far enough away — outside off — not to worry a right-hander. We decided to leave Mick Malone and Ray Bright out of our side, the choice between Malone and Len Pascoe being a close one. Malone is essentially a swing bowler, but we opted for the extra pace of the Sydney man.

On the morning of the match we found the nets unusable again, so we were reduced to having a hit-up on the grass. For some it had been a long time since they had seriously held a bat in their hands.

I was still inclined to put England in, but looming in my mind was the thought that doubtful weather lay ahead, and the pitch is open to the elements once play has started and until such time as stumps are drawn — a system with which I totally disagree. I believe that if the captain wins the toss he should be able to make a decision which will help his team at some stage during the match. If it is a greentop and he puts the other side in he is entitled to expect this to be a lasting advantage, assuming his fast bowlers do their stuff. If it is a sound wicket that later becomes a spinner's track, he is entitled to reap the rewards of batting first.

Be that as it may, I was somewhat relieved when Mike Brearley won the toss at Lord's and batted. When rain came on the second day my decision to insert England, if I had made it, would have looked to have backfired.

2. FIRST TEST MATCH

THE JUBILEE TEST MATCH, LORD'S, JUNE 16, 17, 18, 20, 21

David Frith writes:

FIRST DAY

It was a chill morning, with the remote sun being let through the cloudbanks only occasionally; yet the Press box was a convivial place after the Jubilee and the new Test series had been toasted in champagne sent up by the Victoria Sporting Club. When someone observed that it was Tom Graveney's fiftieth birthday I came to terms with the passage of time, saw no more the ghosts of old favourites out on the field, and became riveted to the prospect of the rebuilt Australian side coming out of its corner against the expectant English challengers (who had left Geoff Miller out of their twelve). Len Pascoe soon put us straight with a bouncer that fizzed over the stumps, proclaiming ''Lillee may not be here, but I AM!'' The Hundred Years War was resumed.

Thomson, in shortsleeved shirt, was the centre of attraction, and the way he padded in and slung himself into his rubbery delivery to start the match gave no hint that less than six months ago opinion in some areas was that his torn shoulder would never again propel a cricket ball at high speed. The last ball of his fifth over was a yorker, and Amiss, still numb from the recent death of his father, nudged it into his stumps. One down for 12. With the next ball, the first of his sixth over, Thomson forced Brearley, England's crash-helmeted new leader, into playing to short leg. Two down for 13. Randall saved the hat-trick by leaving a ball that meant no ill to his stumps. He too had had recent family news, though of a completely felicitous kind — his wife had produced a son, Simon, their firstborn. Father was his usual grinning, jittery self.

Walker had replaced Pascoe at the pavilion end for the eighth over, and Pascoe had relieved Thomson at the Nursery end for the 13th. After 65 minutes England laboured at 20 for two off 15 overs, Woolmer having played a few times without contact and Randall having top-edged a late hook against Pascoe. The bowler may have been aggrieved, but the batsman used it merely as a tryout, and swatted him square for four when he dropped another short. Pascoe

*Australian arms are flung high as England's newly-elected captain,
Mike Brearley, is caught by Richie Robinson off Jeff Thomson for 9*

continued to hurtle in with a Lillee-type cradling action until he
reached the crease, where resemblance ended: he turned side-on and
flung the ball on its way while hardly leaving the ground. Woolmer's
bat described an S on the downswing, and Marsh took the ball, looking
to the heavens and saying something monosyllabic.

Capless Randall scored four with an easy pull off Walker to the
Tavern, and when the bighearted bowler was rested in favour of
O'Keeffe he had conceded only seven runs from as many overs. The
spinner dropped onto a length, the ball dipping and curving from off.
Pascoe was pulled by Woolmer for three, and at one o'clock gave way
to Thomson, whom Randall put away consistently to the midwicket
area. Such a stroke, straighter, gave him three and brought up the 50
in the 25th over. It had taken 99 minutes, but the pressure was easing
visibly. The occasional Thomson no-ball helped.

A hit by Randall through Serjeant's upstretched hands at mid-on
resulted in an all-run five: Walker managed to stop the ball short of
the line but went full-tilt on into the crowd, who, all round the

ground, loved such an oddity. Thomson, bowling with three slips and a gully, beat Randall outside the off, and the onlookers this time drew breath sharply. The lad from Retford represented by far their best bet for some afternoon entertainment, and they didn't want anything to happen to him. His bellowed No! in refusing Woolmer's call drowned out the typewriters in the Press box, and lunch was taken after 30 overs, England 63 for 2, Woolmer 13, Randall 33.

The tensions eased after the break, with both batsmen — Randall still, as he probably always will be, the centre of attraction — stood firm against everything that came at them. Just as thoughts began to extend to realms of dogmatism concerning England's reborn batting — Hutton and Compton, May and Cowdrey, now Woolmer and Randall — the Notts man, having reached his half-century with a smooth clip through mid-on off Pascoe, slashed at a widish one from Walker and the stand was broken at 98 by a grand catch at first slip by Chappell, who probably saved himself a gratuitous vasectomy, even though he was wearing a box. He hurt his finger in the process, the digit still not having recovered from a chip inflicted by a catch off Thomson during the Australian season.

Derek Randall's uninhibited enthusiasm on the field made him a firm favourite with the crowds throughout the series. Here he pulls Kerry O'Keeffe to midwicket during his first-innings 53

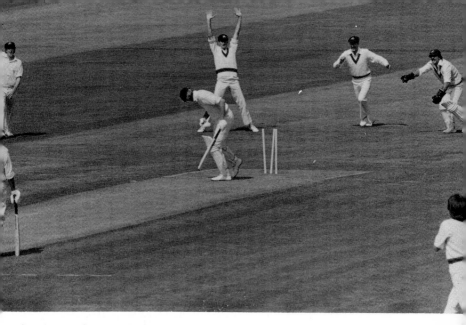

A prize wicket — Tony Greig bowled by Len Pascoe for 5, and the pressure is on Greig to put together good scores in his next few innings

Greig entered ahead of Barlow, and received something less than the roar of acclamation accorded him two years before, when he first led England against Australia and might have been St George himself. He drove Walker through cover for four second ball, was hit on the shoulder by Pascoe, and bowled by him two balls later, beaten between bat and pad, giving Pascoe his first Test wicket. He celebrated by bouncing one at Barlow first ball.

The Middlesex left-hander, golden hair bright in the sunlight that now bathed his home ground, faced the acid test. Since his England debut in India he had scores of 0, 4 and 7 not out, and fears were growing that the early visions of an exciting new regular England batsman might be made to vanish, and that he might join Frank Hayes, Graham Gooch, John Jameson, and Jackie Hampshire in the Shattered Hopes department.

Barlow made his first run with a push to cover off Pascoe, Woolmer reached 52 with a three to third man off the same bowler (172 minutes, four fours), and then Barlow was scooped up by McCosker at slip off Walker, an eerie interval elapsing while umpire Dicky Bird consulted with umpire Lloyd Budd. So, in the 56th over England were 134 for 5, and owing almost everything to the calm, pink-faced Woolmer, who continued to push Thomson away profitably to the midwicket area. The 150 came up in four hours as Woolmer pulled and square-drove O'Keeffe for boundaries. In the last over before tea he put Walker, via the pad, just wide of Robinson at short leg, and England, having lost three wickets for 92 during the afternoon, were conceivably uncertain how well or badly they had done.

There was no question about whose final session it was, for Australia struck straightaway — or rather Knott played gently into their hands — Walters' hands at cover — the first ball upon resumption giving Thomson his third wicket. Old fanned the air first ball, and was in agony against Walker's devious bowling. He edged him to the Nursery end, and finally touched one to Marsh. Lever entered at 171 for 7, and a dozen runs later Woolmer's admirable innings ended on a frenzied note. He had stroked Walker beautifully to the cover boundary by the grandstand, and sustained a painful blow on the hand next ball. At 78 he was missed by Serjeant at third slip off Pascoe, a hard, high chance; then, in the 77th over, he tapped Pascoe to cover, ran, stopped, and carried on as Lever accepted the call; Walters meanwhile had gathered the ball and run for the bowler's wicket; when he saw he would lose the race with Woolmer he underarmed the ball and scored a direct hit.

The question now was whether Australia would have to face an awkward over or two that evening. But the last two wickets lingered on, Lever lumping Chappell over cover for four before Pascoe got him, Underwood raising 200 with a scoop for three past a diving Thomson at extra cover and then driving Pascoe for four past a sprawling Walters, the oldest Australian on the field, who had saved the previous ball, goalkeeper-style. The new ball was taken, and with eight minutes of the day remaining Thomson bowled Willis middle stump for a useful 17. Australia had no need to bat that evening, but England's bowlers needed to bring their side back into the match tomorrow. Two hundred and sixteen was less than could ˙reasonably have been expected of England, and it began to look like the old, old story: Australia, weaker than ever before, were still good enough to hold England in submission. *England* 216 (R. A. Woolmer 79, D. W. Randall 53, J. R. Thomson 4 for 41, M. H. N. Walker 3 for 66).

SECOND DAY

Long, patient queues curled around Lord's some time before play was due to start, but the weather scored one of its nasty little triumphs by delaying the start. At a quarter past twelve it was announced that it was hoped that play would begin at a quarter to one. And so it did.

Irregular things were going on outside the ground, with ticket touts offering MCC members' guests' tickets worth £2 for "twelve nicker". The club set up an investigation, since the numbers of the tickets were traceable. Anyone who paid £12 for a ticket, had he but known it, was paying about 8p per ball, for fewer than 25 overs, plus some no-balls, were bowled during this uncharitable day.

Richie Robinson, who could hardly have seen himself as Australia's opening batsman at Lord's, even during his purple batting patch in the recent home season, lashed at the first ball of the innings without getting a touch, and was soon off the mark with a single past short leg. McCosker then faced Willis, the man who had smashed his jaw three months before. His second ball was a vicious bouncer which moved in from the off. The tall, slightly-stooped Australian opener turned the next to leg to erase his nought, and, after being beaten by a special leg-to-off ball from Lever, showed that he hoped to return to form by playing strokes. Some came off handsomely, others were aborted, the ball screwing off the thinner parts of the bat.

Robinson took three through square leg off Willis, and Brearley brought Lever up from third man to make a fourth slip. Robinson responded with a boundary to midwicket. With 25 up, Australia were on their way; but Lever then stopped them in their tracks by bowling Robinson, who played outside a straight one. Chappell square-cut his first ball from Lever for a single.

After eight overs Underwood replaced Willis at the Nursery end with the score 34 for one. With Greig very close at silly point and Woolmer whispering distance away at short leg, a testing over was negotiated. Old took over from Lever from the pavilion end, and after ten overs it was time for lunch, Australia 36 for one, McCosker 19, Chappell 4.

Underwood began the afternoon with a menacing field that perhaps suggested an evil in the pitch hoped-for rather than real. The Australians were vigilant, adding only eight in ten overs. At ten-to-three, after Chappell had failed to see a quick one from Willis, the umpires met to consider the conditions. Two balls later Willis pounded a short one in the general direction of McCosker, and the umpires talked again, offered the light to Chappell, and off the players trekked. It was a ruse, suggested a hardhead, to break the batsmen's concentration. Had England wanted to stay out there surely Willis would not have let any bouncers go?

They were off for 22 minutes, and Old got things under way again with a maiden. McCosker, whose last run was fast fading from memory, managed a two from a lofted cut, and the fifty came up from a no-ball by Old. It was attritional cricket.

Greg Chappell, shirt buttoned at the throat, sleeves down, was playing with his usual expressionless calm and an immaculately vertical bat, though as half-past-three approached, and the gloom and cold grew more rather than less uncomfortable, he began to show signs of annoyance, tapping the pitch, adjusting his clothing, and doing the odd bit of glaring. The drizzle intensified, the umpires had another of their get-togethers, and no-one was surprised — and only the un-reasonable were peeved — when everyone trooped off again. The spiky umbrellas popped up like bubbles in a bucket, and although it was six o'clock before the day's play was abandoned and the covers put on the pitch, few held any hope that there would be further action.

"Are you coming tomorrow?" I heard a spectator mumble to a friend through upturned raincoat collars. I admired his courage. On the way out I heard that a streaker had performed on the balcony of the Tavern Stand, evidently feeling it his duty to provide entertainment

Greg Chappell's leading role in the Australian batting line-up was underlined with his first-innings 66. Here Tony Greig acknowledges Chappell's determination not to be tied down by Derek Underwood's bowling

after the playing area had emptied. "Trying to get in on the Packer deal?" one of the Australian writers wondered. It was, of course, conceivable that the entrepreneur had overlooked this aspect of the cricket entertainment business.

When I reached the car it had a flat tyre. Not the most memorable day's Test cricket.

England 216; *Australia* 51 for one.

THIRD DAY

The first news of the day was that Randall would not be fielding. An X-ray had shown no fracture to a troublesome arm, and the mystery was some time in being uncovered. Anxiety was eventually allayed when it was revealed that the pounding given his joints when he fielded had caused inflammation above the elbow, and rest was expected to cure it. The well-rounded Kent player Alan Ealham — probably the finest of English outfielders — substituted for him.

In spite of a few spots of rain in the cool air, play began on time on the Saturday. Willis completed his over to Chappell, and Old, with his fourth ball, knocked McCosker's middle stump out with an inswinger that held its course. Before a run had been scored, Serjeant was on his way to the crease for his first Test innings, having played in only 15 first-class matches. This was the Australian way.

His team-mates called him "Bilko" — it hadn't taken long to dream up something appealingly corny; it usually didn't — and he wore a good-luck neckchain given him just before his departure for the tour. His bat was bandaged, and suggested a mutual fondness for its owner. His first ball was a no-ball wide of off. He allowed the second to hit his hip. He was going to need all his pharmacist's patience, for it was to be 40 minutes before he made his first run.

Underwood took over from Willis at the Nursery end, with a menacing field. Halfway through the over Willis was brought in to gully, building the close field to four. The question on all lips concerned the degree of moisture in the pitch after Friday's drizzle. Chappell inside-edged Underwood and, next over, when 13, gave him a sharp right-handed caught-and-bowled chance. The pitch must be difficult, concluded certain salivating sections of the crowd.

Serjeant, his bat-face turned in towards his pads at stance, in the fashion of Peter May, continued on his scoreless way, leaving a high proportion of balls alone, and once taking a hard throw on the back of the thigh when Chappell refused a run in the direction of Ealham, whom he knew but whom Serjeant may not have known. Chappell, in off-white pads reminiscent of those worn by the mightily successful Greenidge during the previous summer, lived dangerously with a swift single to Barlow at cover, the underarm throw just missing the bowler's stumps, and English hearts thumped again when Serjeant, playing across the crease, was surely lbw to an off-cutter from Old . . . except that it was a no-ball. The batsman fished at the next, and when Chappell desperately tried to break Underwood's stranglehold with a wild swish to leg life at the crease seemed almost as much a struggle as life under Healey's Pay Code.

With 35 overs bowled Australia had mustered 67 runs, and Craig Serjeant was still in peril of his second duck in first-class cricket, having just sampled the experience at last in the Essex match. A single to midwicket off Old got him moving, to ironic cheers.

A two past frantically gyrating Greig at silly point took Chappell to 30 after two hours at the crease, and his young partner aimed a haymaker at Underwood and missed, compensating soon afterwards with a four wide of Ealham at long-on.

Lever replaced Old, and was wayward down the leg side to start. Then Serjeant French-cut him for two, though by now it was dawning on all and sundry that the pitch was no more awkward than on the opening day. Chappell played Lever patiently, quietly, defiantly.

Pulses raced as Greig took a rebound at silly point from Serjeant, claiming a bat-pad catch; the umpire was unmoved, and Serjeant responded with a swept four off Underwood, whom Willis replaced from the Nursery end. At lunch, with 50 overs gone, Australia survived at 97 for 2, Chappell 39, Serjeant 17. England had hoped for better.

Old began the afternoon, charging in like a centre three-quarter. Chappell began to drive confidently, taking a two and a four, but after 15 minutes they were off for bad light. Half an hour was lost.

Chappell reached his fifty with a single to cover, having been in for 212 minutes, with only one four. Soon he added another with a classical standing-up square-cut off Old, and another with a front-foot drive through cover off Willis. There followed a hook for four off the same bowler, and the match was taking a new, positive shape. Serjeant, having missed with several attempted hooks, remained unemotional.

Then the big breakthrough came — for such is Chappell's downfall always seen to be. He edged the last ball of an over by Willis throat-high straight to Old at gully, and the Yorkshireman held it under penalty of expulsion: 135 for 3.

Serjeant, favouring the hook and pull, smacked the next ball, from Old, to the Mound Stand boundary, and Walters, with so much to prove, opened his score with a single to fine leg, where Ealham made an athletic pick-up and throw at the stumps. Serjeant survived narrowly soon afterwards when he slipped in turning for a second run and would have been out comfortably if the ball had hit the wicket. Walters was not enjoying Old's outswingers, and Brearley called up a more menacing cordon of five to Knott's right. Walters obliged by edging, but wide of Old at third slip, for four. Unflappably, with whippy wrists, the batsman then off-drove Old for three.

England thought they had another wicket when Serjeant played outside Old and Knott went up, but the appeal was rejected. Woolmer came on for Old, who switched to the Nursery end, and Walters took four off the new bowler through midwicket, followed shortly with another boundary off him from a lightning square-cut. Woolmer came in again and compelled a dab by Walters, the ball going nicely to Brearley at slip. But the England captain, unsighted, moved the wrong way initially, and muffed the catch, bent-kneed. Walters was 21, and groaning Anglophiles recognised this as just the sort of let-off that allows a batsman of Walters' calibre to go on to extraordinarily destructive things.

Old now came in for some punishment: Serjeant pulled him huskily through mid-on for three and Walters cover-drove the next for three. Serjeant took a lungful of air and hooked the next for two, and the next for one. At the end of the over Australia, 175 for 3, were only 41 behind, Serjeant 38, Walters 26.

The assembly had a fright when umpire Bird walked towards the pavilion, but he signalled good-humouredly that his mission had nothing to do with the light. He merely wanted some members to stay still while the bowling was from that end.

Ealham broke the wicket with a throw and a single became two — an incident that usually generates remarks that this is unfair to the fielding side. Serjeant was into his stride now, and seemed to be enjoying Test cricket. A two to long leg and three to third man off Underwood took him to 45. A four wide of mid-on took him to the brink of his fifty, which he clinched with a hooked single off Woolmer. At tea Australia were 190 for 3 off 77 overs, Serjeant 50, Walters 29.

Walters passed his previous highest score of the tour (38 not out) with a crisp square-cut four off Lever, and Serjeant seemed to have driven a sweet four when Amiss dived full-length and turned it into a single. At 213 for 3 the new ball was taken.

Gripping the handle high, Serjeant cover-drove Willis for four to take Australia to 220 and put their nose in front. He missed a hook and took the ball in the stomach, then pulled to long-on for three. At the other end he picked Lever off his front foot for four to the Tavern and off-drove the next to the pavilion gate. When he heaved the next to square leg for four to reach 80 one or two reference books were dragged out to check on the list of those who have made a hundred in their first Test match. The century stand had been posted, and the Australian wattle was blooming. Brearley saw fit to drop the legside field deeper for Willis. But it was an offside delivery that brought Serjeant's downfall. He aimed a square-cut and Knott did the rest, giving Willis his second wicket. David Hookes, without cap and with bandaged bat, came in at 238 for 4.

He watched Walters slash Lever over slips for four to reach 48, then broke his duck with a single past Woolmer in the gully. The spotlight was on Walters now. This small, laconic man was the greatest of enigmas. In 21 Test innings in England he had only four times passed fifty, twice in his first match, nine years ago. In this time he had torn apart one Test attack after another in his homeland and in West Indies and New Zealand. Long since had all chance been lost that he would rank with Bradman, though he continued to believe that a good English wicket was the best there was. Be that as it may, he had never come to terms with the deviating ball in England. His technique, fallible and too long established, had seen to that, and probably would go on doing so, even though I had a side-bet on that he would make a century during this series.

He reached his half-century, but ingloriously, top-edging fine over slip to the pavilion for his seventh four. Then he ducked a short ball that rose only chest-high. Without addition, he attempted to glance Willis and the ball flew from the back of his bat to Brearley at slip, who held the catch neatly low to his left: 256 for 5.

Hookes was making no impression at all. He pushed his right leg well forward and often withheld his bat inside the pad. Lever brought one back sharply that had him between wind and water, but he hung on, and received little comfort from Marsh, who was soon hit cripplingly on the left thigh by a Willis no-ball and wriggled round and round like a freshly-hooked fish.

Craig Serjeant's 81 in his first Test match was generally acknowledged to be the innings of an emerging Test star. His later exclusion from the Australian side for the third Test was a puzzle

Old came on in place of Lever and forced Hookes to play and miss, and play and miss, and play and miss . . . They ran a leg-bye after a close lbw call, and substitute fielder Ealham hit the middle stump from midwicket. The first-innings lead, it seemed, was not going to be appreciable.

Soon after driving Old attractively to the point boundary, Hookes fell, caught waist-high by Brearley at slip off the persevering Old.

O'Keeffe, bravely shunning a sweater, came in, having opened the batting in an emergency in the Centenary Test, and Willis, varying the evening animation, bowled a wide to Marsh, who was then leg-before, Willis's fourth victim. He had been bowling the same kind of horrible breakbacks that Tom Richardson specialised in during the 'nineties, and though English fingers were crossed that the Willis break*downs* were a thing of the past, it seemed now that the side had a sharp spearhead, and that all the quests for fast bowlers that had been launched across Britain were unnecessarily panicky.

Walker saw the remaining overs through with O'Keeffe, who was nearly lbw twice, and though Underwood closed in his "box" formation of close fieldsmen, and Old bowled his final ball off a few paces in an effort to get in an extra over, the eighth wicket survived till Monday, when Australia would be looking for the hundred-plus lead.

A talking point had been Brearley's sparing use of Lever (19-5-61-1), though the figures of Willis (24-4-74-4), Old (29-9-58-2), and Underwood (25-6-42-0) lent justification. More interesting was the case of Greig, who had been denied any chance of bowling himself into — or out of — the second Test.

England 216; *Australia* 278 for 7 (C. S. Serjeant 81, G. S. Chappell 66, K. D. Walters 53, R. G. D. Willis 4 for 74).

FOURTH DAY

The fourth morning brought incident aplenty. Old made a splendid left-hand diving stop in the gully. Then O'Keeffe was given not-out when Knott appealed, with a loud backing chorus, for a catch off Willis. Walker was then out, waving his bat at Willis, and Thomson defiantly clubbed Old through mid-on to the rope. Soon O'Keeffe perished, top-edging a hook against Willis to the ever-reliable Ealham, and the lifelong friends Thomson and Pascoe found themselves batting together in a Test match at Lord's.

A statistical note now crept into the scenario as it was realised that Chris Old needed one wicket for his 100 in Tests and Bob Willis wanted another to make it seven for the innings. He had known six before. Indeed, his best Test figures of 6 for 53 had been achieved only four-and-a-half months previously, against India at Bangalore.

Willis was the one to reach his target, uprooting Thomson's middle stump and making sure that it had been England's morning. In 54 minutes Australia's last three wickets had fallen for only 18 runs, and

Dennis Amiss's nightmare against Australian pacemen continued. Here he is bowled behind his legs for 0 by tormentor Thomson, who celebrates Nureyev-style

the lead was restricted to 80 overall. The match was almost, if not quite, open, and it seemed that the best chance of a result was for England to be bowled out a second time by lunch on the final day. No declaration was likely to offer much chance of a finish.

Australia struck rudely early. To Thomson's fourth ball Amiss moved right across his stumps, as he had been doing for the past year, and yet somehow the ball burst through to crack the off stump. One down for nought — or minus eighty, as the ghouls would have it.

Woolmer was called upon to dig out a yorker immediately, and when he got down the other end, after Brearley had trotted a single to point first ball, he had to play Pascoe's bouncer from in front of his nose, and was then beaten by a classical outswinger. Nerves were twitching. Bushrangers were about.

Soon after driving Thomson nicely to the Tavern for four and then backward of point for one Brearley was beaten by Walker, who had come on for Pascoe, and the appeal was loud and hoarse — but, to the Australians' astonishment, unsuccessful.

Pascoe took over from Thomson from the Nursery end, and found the edge of Brearley's bat. When Hookes threw himself full-length to save at cover, and Marsh barked an insistent appeal for a legside catch by Woolmer off Pascoe, England were patently on the rack. The ball was seaming, Aussie confidence was high (and it can reach peerless heights), and some of the pre-tour talk, if recalled, would have seemed nonsensical.

But the second wicket, which seemed so imminent, did not come yet awhile. Brearley ran Pascoe down to third man for four, and Woolmer was unmoved by Chappell intimidatingly close at silly point for Walker as the lunch interval approached. Thomson had a last fling before the break and came close to having Brearley lbw, but England made it to the watershed, 29 for one off 13 overs in the 56 minutes, Brearley 14, Woolmer 15. Godfrey Evans announced that Ladbrokes were offering 11-1 England and 5-4 Australia. No-one queried those odds.

Chappell pressed hard upon resumption, and the batsmen found runs into unguarded areas. Brearley had a fright at 18 when Robinson at short leg picked him up on the half-volley, and a run later he played to him on the full, but the fieldsman, diving, lost the ball upon impact with the ground. Yet another important piece of luck followed. Woolmer on 20 cut Walker hard to gully, where Serjeant failed to secure the catch.

Walker was a handful. Lumbering up to the crease and whipping his huge right arm over, left hanging almost uselessly by his side, he got the ball to swerve and to change direction after pitching. Brearley was rapped on the pads, drove him square for four, and was beaten again next ball, only to play the next square off the back foot for three. The fifty came up in the 21st over.

Thomson, too, had his disappointments. When Dicky Bird disallowed an lbw appeal against Woolmer he stood transfixed, head hung on chest, arms folded. The same batsman tried to pull Walker but the ball kept low, and he was hit on the thigh. A fine glance off Thomson to the Warner Stand boundary restored his morale.

Chappell decided to bowl, Marsh standing well back, as modern ''percentage'' cricket demands, and Woolmer flicked him elegantly away for two, then edged for two. Now Pascoe replaced Walker from the pavilion end, and bowled very fast indeed. One bouncer flew over Brearley's shoulder and was taken by Marsh with arms upstretched. When the England captain edged wide of third slip O'Keeffe flung himself and got a touch, but it could only be considered a technical chance. Pascoe responded with another bouncer, taken again by Marsh at the risk of a rupture. Brearley next edged a short one over slips for two, and with more orthodoxy and formality straight-drove a full-toss for three, an event climaxed in ribaldry as Marsh dived all over the stumps in a fractionally-late attempt at a run-out.

Brearley was beaten outside off by his opposing captain, but by now there was almost universal resignation that it was one of those days when the ball will just go on beating the bat, and the fielding side's number will come up when it is ready.

After leaving the field for an over Pascoe put so much into one of his deliveries that he almost threw himself off his feet. With two through square leg and three to third man Woolmer took England to 80, from which point their lead could be calculated. At 3.17 pm Brearley put his side ahead with a glanced single.

Chappell continued beating Brearley, and Woolmer daringly padded up, evoking loud shouts, but when Chappell pitched short he made a sweet-sounding pull for four to reach 49, and then turned him to leg for a single. It was the 33rd over, and his patience served as a reminder of his Oval epic two years earlier. He let Pascoe expend his energy with thunderbolts outside off stump, then turned him past square leg for four, a stroke of authority. When a Brearley cover-drive bisected the gap between Hookes and Walters to reach the Mound Stand boundary, it seemed that the balance of power was shifting again.

When Thomson returned to the attack Woolmer allowed his first ball to slide across the face of his bat for a perfect four backward of point. This brought up 103, the extent of the partnership, and Woolmer was looking larger each over. When he glanced Thomson for another precision boundary it seemed about time that O'Keeffe was tried.

Walker returned, and Brearley padded away a ball of dangerously close proximity. Again the appeal was turned down, the umpire obviously not utterly convinced. Seldom could there have been a match when so many questions have been addressed to the judges for so few positive responses.

O'Keeffe came on in place of Thomson, who had kept the ball well up and had failed to look special. Woolmer played late at the spinner and four byes resulted. After 40 overs England were 121 for one, Brearley 43, Woolmer 71.

Again O'Keeffe troubled Woolmer, who almost played on. Soon he was throwing his bat at a widish ball and securing four through point. For Brearley, Chappell placed himself close to the bat, and saw the batsman hit on the boot. Five minutes from tea Brearley's vigil ended as he played for an O'Keeffe leg-break that turned out to be the straight one and took the inside edge for Robinson to catch it two-handed at short leg. Greig came in, and there was no further score before the interval, though Woolmer was beaten by Walker's last two balls — an apt form of summary for a day of frustrations for some.

Resuming at 132 for 2, with Woolmer 76, England ought to have been hoping for 90 or so runs in the last session, but bad light was to upset plans, even if there might have existed a mutual fear between the two sides that made capitulation to the weather no sorely regrettable thing.

Woolmer cover-drove Pascoe for four then square-drove for the same result to reach 92 and raise 150 in the 55th over. He pulled an O'Keeffe long-hop to the happy Tavern spectators to reach 97. The cheers perched in the throats ready for release.

But Pascoe firstly had to have a say. He hurtled in over 15 paces and pounded in four bouncers in one over, a proportion that might have drawn a warning from an umpire less liberal than Lloyd Budd. Woolmer missed his chance with a full-toss, and nearly edged another to Marsh. A single took him to face O'Keeffe, and a tense maiden ensued, during which he was beaten once. Pascoe operated with two slips and a gully for Greig and two gullies and a slip for Woolmer, and it was through this area that the Kent man chopped him for three to raise his century (out of 161). Two boys ran on from either side of the ground, and the Victoria Sporting Club wrote Woolmer's name on the 100 bottles of champagne awarded to the first England centurymaker of the summer. He raised his cap and bat, then settled down to the continuing job of putting England in command.

The light was gradually worsening as Greig drove a four, misread O'Keeffe, and got four off Thomson between the two slips. For the sacked England captain this was a crucial innings. He needed to make runs now even more than a year earlier, when his century against West Indies at Leeds restored justification for his inclusion on playing ability. It was no secret that, having stripped him of the captaincy after his involvement in the Packer affair, the authorities — or certain of them — would welcome the chance to omit him altogether should he fail as a player.

He was 18, and Woolmer 114, when the players came off for bad light at ten-to-six. It was no surprise when they did not return that evening.

The latest distraction had been the assertion over the weekend by Ted Dexter in his newspaper column that Len Pascoe, Australia's new

Bob Woolmer followed his first-innings 79 with a fine century in the second, establishing himself as England's number 3 for the series, and collecting £1 for his efforts from grateful fans

fast bowler, threw the occasional ball. The suggestion seemed to find scant sympathy, but Dexter, who was on the BBC TV panel of commentators for this match, examined a number of playbacks this morning, both at slow and normal speed, without producing any truly convincing material. "Unless you have camera evidence it is very difficult to see," he said. When an expert cameraman arrived at the ground on the final day of the match, Pascoe did not bowl again, so the idea of photographing Pascoe's action at very high speed was thwarted.

His bowling action is unusual in that he barely leaves the ground in the act of delivery. He runs in fast and smoothly, quite like Dennis Lillee, but the resemblance ends at the point of delivery, where Lillee leaps high. As for any bend in the arm, few bowlers pass the slow-motion videotape test, which is blurred and distorted. If a bowler, in the flesh and at normal speed, raises no suspicion, there seems little point in putting him through the electronic third degree.

England 216 and 189 for 2 (R. A. Woolmer 114 not out, J. M. Brearley 49); *Australia* 296 (C. S. Serjeant 81, G. S. Chappell 66, K. D. Walters 53, R. G. D. Willis 7 for 78).

FIFTH DAY

A draw was clearly the most likely outcome as the last day's play began at 11 o'clock, and as lunch approached, two-and-a-half hours later, the situation had hardly changed. Events either side of the interval, however, revived the contest, and ensured that transistor sets remained switched on all over the country — and around the world.

Thomson and Walker took up the attack to Greig and Woolmer, and the 200 came up at the end of the 75th over. Chappell tried himself in place of Thomson, and Pascoe for Walker, who, as ever, had seemed incapable of bowling any ball in an honest straight line.

Greig batted with care and occasional belligerence. He took a four to midwicket off Pascoe, then partook of a quick leg-bye off Woolmer's pad, receiving a shove in the back from bowler Chappell as he cut in front of him and hared for home.

With the new ball imminent, and Woolmer's expertise against it likely to prove of value, he fell to the lively Pascoe, caught thigh-high by Chappell at first slip. He had added only six of the morning's 35 runs, and England, at 224 for 3, were 164 ahead. With three centuries made recently for Kent, Woolmer's stocks were high indeed, and for once the selectors could rejoice in an asset well and truly confirmed. He had faced 248 balls — 449 altogether in the match — and had come through as the epitome of cool judgment and serenity. A giant plus for England.

Walker relieved Pascoe from the pavilion end and tested Barlow, who once risked a pulled muscle as he thrust his bat skywards with the briskness of a guardsman. When the new ball was taken Walker swung it right across Barlow, who was relieved to take his first run with an on-drive. Greig, having edged Thomson just short of slip, had reached his fifty with a thrashing offside stroke off the same bowler — virtually the last bruise suffered by that ball before it was replaced.

While Greig swung violently every so often, Barlow stewed.

Thomson found the shoulder of his bat and the ball flew wide of Serjeant at leg slip. Greig brought up the 250 by turning Thomson for two, and the bowler removed his sleeveless sweater threateningly. Greig slashed through slip for four to reach 70, and called for a replacement bat, choosing from a selection taken out by Ealham. The new blade hacked Pascoe's first ball three bounces over the cover boundary. Two balls later he cracked him through gully for four. It was time to start calculating a declaration, without getting carried away by the prospect.

Then poor Barlow went, lbw to Pascoe for five, made in just on an hour, and England were 263 for 4. The Middlesex lefthander made his disconsolate way back, and Knott appeared. Where was Randall? What was his injury? It seemed he had a lump above the elbow the size of a duck's egg; he appeared to be suffering from bursitis. Knott would probably be able to push things along almost as well.

Greig drove Pascoe sumptuously for four to reach 84, but with only 210 minutes' play possible after lunch the last drops of tension seemed to be drying up, even when Walker narrowly missed a caught-and-bowled from Knott. He then beat Greig, who pretended he had played no stroke and was soon refusing a single even though Knott, head down, was charging to his end. England's 'keeper dived headlong back to safety as Australia's wicketkeeper threw from silly point: both 'keepers finished prostrate.

Greig cover-drove past Walters for four to enter the nineties, a score which had signalled his downfall two years before, when he first captained England. Now he struck out at a half-volley from Pascoe — straight to O'Keeffe at point, where the catch was safely held. The batsman was vexed (as must have been Randall), who walked to the crease with only four minutes left before lunch), but a glance at the newspapers revealed what might have been a predestiny, for Tony Greig's brother Ian had scored 96 the day before for Cambridge University against Kent.

Those who had left for an early lunch missed more excitement now when Knott lobbed the next ball, from Walker, straight to Walters at cover, as he had done in the first innings. The new scoreline set the lunchtime gatherings achatter: 286 for 6. What if . . . ?

And the drama continued straight afterwards. Old was caught at point — Walters again — off Walker, third ball, and at the other end Randall was caught at slip off Thomson for his third duck in 11 Test innings. Four wickets had tumbled with the score stuck on 286, and while Australia saw a chance of victory, it also gave England a better prospect, a declaration now looking to be unnecessary.

Underwood and Lever held up proceedings for a time, the former once playing the ball to the base of his stumps, which remained obstinately undisturbed, but Thomson swept away the last resistance with his seventh and eighth wickets of the match, Marsh catching Lever high above his head and pouching Willis first ball — the fourth duck of the innings.

So, England were all out for 305 at 2.45 pm, and Australia had 165 minutes in which to score 226 — a rate of roughly five runs an over. This one sorted out the optimists from the cynics.

Willis roared in; Robinson, who thinks bats are for hitting balls with, hooked viciously and got four off the top edge to the pavilion. Old delivered a counter-blow by striking McCosker in the stomach, and followed up by having Robinson caught wonderfully well by Woolmer at short leg — a two-handed reflex catch off a firm hit. This gave Chris Old his 100th Test wicket, in his 32nd match, and stretched the élite list for England to 24 names.

The first ball of Willis's second over darted in to hit McCosker's off stump, and Australia were 5 for two wickets, with young Hookes joining his captain and scrambling a single to fine leg when Ealham, still fielding in Randall's place, untypically fumbled. Old bowled to Hookes with a long leg, deepish square, mid-on, three slips, two gullies, and cover — no third man. The left-hander offered a composed defensive bat, and stood up tall to Willis's short one.

Chappell steered Old to third man for three — the ball fielded conjointly by Brearley and Greig, captains present and past — hooked Old for four, and square-cut Willis to the same effect. Using his full height, he cut another two, and was quick to send a no-ball down the slope through point for another boundary. His intentions were unmistakable, and after the early breakthrough England had to withhold their anticipation.

Chappell came close to being bowled as he missed a strong drive at Willis, but when England's giant pitched short Hookes swung him for six towards the Tavern scoreboard. The batsmen scrambled a slender single as Barlow's throw missed the stumps, and in 10 overs 47 runs had been made and the shine on the ball duly taken off. Underwood came on at the Nursery end.

But it was Old who redressed the balance, even if Chappell really got himself out. He failed to middle an attempted pull to a fairly straight ball, and Lever had the easiest of skyers at midwicket: 48 for 3, Hookes 16.

Walters looked for the ball to hit, but almost paid the price at midwicket, where Barlow, sprinting, just failed to get to the lofted ball. A square-cut raced down the slope for four. Meanwhile, Hookes had missed often, and got away with some attractive strokes, cutting gamely past gully, sweeping Underwood — who had no slip for him, just a silly point and short leg. Old beat him and there was an enormous caught-behind shout, turned down. Old beat him twice again in rapid succession, and then Walters popped one back to Underwood who, diving forward, just failed to get to it; Dicky Bird tripped over as he moved for a sight of things, and everyone was glad for the restoration for the nerves that the tea interval offered. In 18 overs Australia had managed 64 for 3, Hookes 22, Walters 10.

As the final session of the Jubilee Test match unfolded, both sides were on the tightrope. Not a long one, but tense all the same, for the target was ''on'' for Australia one moment, then remote soon afterwards when Walters hoisted Underwood to Ealham, who took the catch coolly at midwicket. Serjeant made only three before he too was caught off a steepler at midwicket, this time by Amiss, who was mobbed by his team-mates. When the statutory last 20 overs began, 154 runs were still needed, and logically only one side had a chance, now that Chappell and Walters were out.

Marsh consolidated with Hookes, who picked up runs in the open spaces now that fielders crowded the inner areas. He square-drove Willis handsomely for four, and later hooked him to the boundary to reach 46, Marsh meanwhile having survived an urgent shout for a bat-pad catch to Woolmer off Lever.

Hookes's fifty came with a three through midwicket off Old, but he was out soon afterwards, trying to hook Willis and merely sending the ball high enough for the bowler to collect himself steadily to catch it. The South Australian cursed himself all the way back to the pavilion.

The overs were running out. It needed a hat-trick. Hat-tricks don't happen often in Test matches. The fieldsmen crowded round the bat, reducing the oxygen available, but Marsh prodded and judged the off-line ball, and O'Keeffe employed the forward lunge, once edging just short of Brearley. When Woolmer gathered a ball off Marsh at short leg, from Willis's bowling, the crowd — what there was of it — howled for a wicket, but ''Bacchus'' rubbed his thigh ruefully and waved ''no catch''.

After 15 overs, when Willis had tested Marsh with a bouncer, the umpires conferred, offered it to the batsmen, and Marsh, bat under arm, marched off. It was ten-past-six, Australia were 114 for 6, and the first Test was a draw, disappointing few, apart from those who subscribe to the view that a decision in the first match of a series guarantees that at least one side has to attack from then onwards. In this respect it might have been to spectators' advantage if Australia had pulled off a win, compelling England to launch an all-out assault for the rest of the series if the Ashes were to be regained. Notwithstanding, there were few complaints about the conduct of the match. There are never enough overs bowled, and never will be, until some ''incentive'' is introduced. If there was a villain it was the weather, which for most of the game was vile. Indeed, no drinks were taken, though there might have been a case for the players having hot beverages, as had been served in the New Zealand Test at Edgbaston in 1965.

In counting the gains, Australia could look to Serjeant and Hookes, among the batsmen, together with Walters, who offered the promise of old. Thomson's return to Test cricket had been smoothly successful, and Pascoe impressed with his keenness. The opening batting remained a problem, but with Davis, Hughes and Cosier in reserve this seemed a problem not beyond solution.

Just whether England were a slightly better or worse side than Australia was still unclear. They also had no cause for complacency in the matter of the opening partnership, and Barlow surely had to give way in the middle order. Willis had asserted himself, though the doubters would never be convinced of his continuing chances of full fitness even if his stamina seemed greater than before. England had used no off-spin during the match, and one question was whether this in due course would be supplied by the erratic Greig or another — probably Miller.

Somehow the match had an unreality about it. The Packer controversy hung in the air like a thin mist of which one was not always necessarily fully aware. For some, too, there was a feeling of hangover after the greatest of Anglo-Australian parties, the Centenary Test celebrations in Melbourne. In a sense, it was like reaching a hundred and then taking guard with the intention of going on for a double-hundred: there is a flat period — a kind of post-natal depression.

All the same, the complexities of the campaign would in all probability develop with fascination as the series went on, as the weather improved, and as one side put its nose in front, drawing the best from its noncomplaisant opponent.

Greg Chappell writes:

I was a very happy man when we managed to bowl England out for 216 on the opening day. Jeff Thomson's performance was excellent. He bowled quickly, he bowled an excellent line. Len Pascoe's debut was impressive too. He worried all the batsmen, and kept a superb line. His bowling to Tony Greig was very intelligent: he let him have a bouncer early, which he didn't pick up; it hit him on the left shoulder and unsettled him; he had a lash at a couple of well-pitched-up deliveries after that, one of which bowled him. This did Len's confidence a world of good so early in his Test career.

Max Walker also bowled admirably. There wasn't a great deal of movement, and the pitch was slow, which hardly helped the batsmen either. The bowlers just had to keep plugging away and we needed to hold our catches. The runs were restricted also by good fielding. At last we were saving runs and holding catches as people have come to expect from players in Australian caps.

Randall and Woolmer were easily the best of the English batsmen, and I think that the Notts player is the best of the lot. His technique is pretty good; he is a good judge of the balls to leave alone, and of the length of the ball. Woolmer was a bit scratchy early, playing and missing a lot to Max Walker. O'Keeffe also worried him early on, but once he settled down he played some good shots, including two expert hooks against short balls from Pascoe and myself. His confidence has grown immensely.

Dennis Amiss is chancy in the early stages against the fast bowlers, especially around off stump, and at this stage Brearley is really an unknown quantity. "Thommo" wrapped him up in the first innings with a short one that he fended off his ribs to short leg. Barlow had not been all that impressive in the one-day series, playing without contact numerous times, and when he came in at Lord's we tried Maxie against him to swing across his body. He props on the front door without going right forward. This time "Tangles" got one to bounce and it hit the top part of the bat; Rick McCosker made a good catch of it, diving forward.

We were glad to get rid of Knott right after tea. He has often been a thorn in our side with his thirties, fifties, and even a hundred.

Our timing was good, too, in that "Thommo" dismissed England's last man Willis at 6.20 pm, and therefore our openers didn't have to face an over or two in awkward light.

We started out fresh on the Friday morning, looking for a worthwhile lead by the end of our innings. The conditions were anything but ideal for cricket again, overcast, quite cold, and there was still a little moisture in the wicket. Richie Robinson started with a bang, but the England bowlers, as expected, used the conditions well, and after Lever had bowled Robinson, Rick McCosker and I tried to see off the fast attack, not bothering too much at this point about making runs. We needed a foundation.

There were interruptions during the day, and I had to complain once about the covering of the bowlers' run-ups when I saw some sacks over bare patches where the bowlers followed through. The regulations state that the run-ups should be covered only up to four feet in front of the crease. There is no mention of any other covering. The sacks were removed, after my request, from the cut section of the wicket.

The sighting at Lord's is not always good. The sightscreen at the Nursery end, although perhaps the best in England, is not quite high enough when a tall chap like Bob Willis is bowling, and this had a lot to do with our coming off when the light was poor. Thought really ought to be given to blocking out the trees beyond the screen at that end. One ball from Willis I didn't see at all until it whistled waist-high over the off stump. It was too close for comfort. At the pavilion end the problem is the dark windows above the screen. A slow bowler operating from that end can pose sighting problems too when he tosses the ball up.

Less time would be lost if these matters could be adjusted. I'm sure we could have returned for play earlier at times if only the batsmen could have been certain of watching the ball all the way from the bowler's hand.

On the third day Craig Serjeant and I, with some luck, made progress. We had luck. When I tried to hit Underwood down the ground when he tossed a rare one up I gave him a sharp caught-and-bowled chance which he just failed to pocket, and "Bilko" was scratchy before he got off the mark. He did at least reveal a very sound temperament during this period, and, containing his frustration, he eventually began to flow, and surely deserved a hundred on his Test debut. He waited for the balls he wanted, and hit hard when the opportunity presented itself. He had a bash at one widish ball from Underwood, after which I told him to keep on waiting for the suitable ball. When "Deadly" tossed one up it was likely to turn more on the still slightly damp pitch, and a drive lofted into the open spaces was likely to discourage him from tossing too many up. Underwood needed to take risks like this if he was to get us out, and if he wasn't going to take those risks, I didn't see much point in our taking them.

I felt we were getting on top after lunch, but the light remained grim, and when the umpires offered it I felt we had to agree. When we resumed, things were going well until I edged one from Willis that bounced, and Chris Old caught me in the gully.

Doug Walters had some luck when Brearley, probably unsighted, missed him at slip, and he then kept things moving in a very useful half-century as we chalked up a reasonable first-innings lead. It might have been larger but for the fine bowling of Old and Willis. The big Warwickshire bowler earned his Test-best figures, gaining bounce that troubled all batsmen. In the past he has often sprayed the ball all over the place in his search for extra pace.

When England batted again we aimed to break through early and get at the suspect middle batting. The first object was achieved when Dennis Amiss was bowled by a beauty from Jeff Thomson, fourth ball. He tried to work it on the leg side, but it swung back late towards slips just as Dennis had closed the face of the bat. That, though, was it for a while, for the Brearley-Woolmer stand kept us waiting a long time for another success. Woolmer's innings was the best I'd seen him play. Brearley, on the other hand, was for the most part decidedly uncomfortable, but his courage can't be denied, and he fought his way almost to a half-century. We thought we'd got him fairly early when a ball from Walker went between bat and pad, and there was a good "nick" sound. The appeal was knocked back, and Mike looked displeased that we'd even bothered to appeal. Then Richie Robinson at short leg almost pulled off a matchwinning catch when he caught Brearley left-handed at short leg only for the impact to jolt the ball from his hand as he hit the ground.

Craig Serjeant was very disappointed when he couldn't quite hold a hard chance off Woolmer in the gully. We had to hang on to this kind of opportunity if we were to break through. It was just the way the game goes. Rod Marsh almost brought off a sensational catch when Brearley edged Pascoe low down. So near and yet . . .

Len Pascoe tended to get a little frustrated during the big stand, and dropped several short. They merely stood up, posing no real problem to the batsmen. Len is a willing workhorse. His stock answer to enquiries after his fitness has been: ''I came over here to bowl, didn't I?''

On the last day we were again looking for the quick breakthrough. It didn't come, but after Woolmer's dismissal wickets tumbled as England possibly relaxed in the knowledge that defeat was quite improbable. Suddenly we saw a chance to go for a win. We had worked hard for it, holding the whiphand most of the time, and I felt we had to seize the opportunity. With an inexperienced side such as ours it seemed to me that a defensive draw, with ourselves losing a number of wickets in the process, would be damaging to morale, whereas a win would do us untold good.

Sadly, we lost both openers quickly, and David Hookes, after Rod Marsh's suggestion, went in at number four to join me. He is a stroke-maker, and the situation could well have been ideal for him. His confidence was not high, but the requirements of the moment could well be all that was needed to bring out the talent that we all knew is there. He fought his way to 50, which did his confidence no harm, and we had Craig Serjeant to steady things up — or so we thought. But the late flurry of wickets forced us to shut up shop.

I got out when I went for a ball too close to the body and hit it high on the bat. Had it been to leg or off it might have been four runs; but it was dead straight. As I walked out, Doug Walters looked enquiringly at me as we crossed, and I told him to play it by ear from then on. When he and Serjeant fell to aggressive shots after tea we had to forget any hopes of victory. It was, as they say, an honourable draw, with Serjeant and Pascoe having made fine debuts, and Thomson having come through his comeback to Test cricket with much credit and little soreness.

ERRATUM

Australian bowling figures omitted from page 57 are as follow:

Bowling: Thomson 20.5-5-41, Pascoe 23-7-53-2, Walker 30-6-66-3, O'Keeffe 10-3-32-0, Chappell 3-0-12-0.

Thomson 24.4-3-86-4, Pascoe 26-2-96-3, Walker 35-13-56-2, Chappell 12-2-24-0, O'Keeffe 15-7-26-1.

FIRST TEST MATCH

Lord's, June 16, 17, 18, 20, 21

Paying attendance 86,790; takings £220,384

ENGLAND

ENGLAND		min	6	4		min	6	4
D. L. Amiss	b Thomson	4	37	—	—	b Thomson	0	2	—	—
*J. M. Brearley	c Robinson b Thomson	9	43	—	—	c Robinson b O'Keeffe	49	175	—	4
R. A. Woolmer	run out	79	270	—	7	c Chappell b Pascoe	120	305	—	13
D. W. Randall	c Chappell b Walker	53	125	—	4	+(7)c McCosker b Thomson	0	8	—	—
A. W. Greig	b Pascoe	5	20	—	1	(4)c O'Keeffe b Pascoe	91	167	—	11
G. D. Barlow	c McCosker b Walker	1	25	—	—	(5)lbw b Pascoe	5	56	—	—
+A. P. E. Knott	c Walters b Thomson	8	26	—	—	(6)c Walters b Walker	8	36	—	—
C. M. Old	c Marsh b Walker	9	32	—	1	c Walters b Walker	0	2	—	—
J. K. Lever	b Pascoe	8	35	—	1	c Marsh b Thomson	3	28	—	—
D. L. Underwood	not out	11	41	—	1	not out	12	25	—	—
R. G. D. Willis	b Thomson	17	32	—	2	c Marsh b Thomson	0	1	—	—
Extras (b1, lb3, nb7, w1)	12				(b5, lb9, nb2, w1)	17			
		216			+ and one 5	**305**			

Fall: 12, 13, 111, 121, 134, 155, 171, 183, 189

0, 132, 224, 263, 286, 286, 286, 286, 305

AUSTRALIA

AUSTRALIA		min	6	4		min	6	4
R. D. Robinson	b Lever	11	26	—	1	c Woolmer b Old	4	7	—	1
R. B. McCosker	b Old	23	109	—	1	b Willis	1	10	—	—
*G. S. Chappell	c Old b Willis	66	263	—	4	c Lever b Old	24	45	—	3
C. S. Serjeant	c Knott b Willis	81	288	—	10	(6)c Amiss b Underwood	3	16	—	—
K. D. Walters	c Brearley b Willis	53	124	—	7	c sub (A. G. E. Ealham) b Underwood	10	29	—	1
D. W. Hookes	c Brearley b Old	11	35	—	2	(4)c & b Willis	50	138	1	3
+R. W. Marsh	lbw b Willis	1	20	—	—	not out	6	72	—	—
K. J. O'Keeffe	c sub (A. G. E. Ealham) b Willis	12	64	—	1	not out	8	23	—	—
M. H. N. Walker	c Knott b Willis	4	52	—	—					
J. R. Thomson	b Willis	6	25	—	1					
L. S. Pascoe	not out	3	16	—	—					
Extras (lb7, nb17, w1)	25				(nb8)	8			
		296			6 wkts	**114**			

Fall: 25, 51, 135, 238, 256, 264, 265, 284, 290

5, 5, 48, 64, 69, 102

Bowling: Willis 30.1-7-78-7, Lever 19-5-61-1, Underwood 25-6-42-0, Old 35-10-70-2, Woolmer 5-1-20-0.

Willis 10-1-40-2, Old 14-0-46-2, Underwood 10-3-16-2, Lever 5-2-4-0.

Umpires: H. D. Bird and W. L. Budd

Toss won by England

(*captain; + wicketkeeper; figures in brackets indicate second-innings batting order)

MATCH DRAWN

3. THE LOW POINT

Greg Chappell writes:

On the rest day following the Lord's Test many of the team went to Wimbledon, where they were guests of the All-England Club, and watched some of the first-round singles matches. Then we went on to Oxford for the two-day game against Oxford and Cambridge Universities. Rod Marsh, Rick McCosker and I spent the rest day at Moor Park, where we followed Rod's brother Graham around in the Uniroyal Golf Tournament as he shot a 67, five under the card, to be right up with the leaders at the end of the first round.

The Universities match never looked likely to provide a finish, despite a couple of declarations, and from our point of view the only real joys were half-centuries from Ian Davis and Kim Hughes and a 74 containing a few shots by David Hookes. The match was fairly light-hearted. The pick of the comments came from Max Walker, who turned to one of the Universities batsmen and asked: ''What's batting here, a six-year course?''

Rod Marsh captained the side in the match against Nottinghamshire, although I played. It made a change, and I quite enjoyed standing at slip without tactical worries, and even running around in the outfield for a break. I think the captaincy helped Rod to concentrate, so the switch served two purposes. We lost the toss, but dismissed Notts for only 210 and then made over 500 ourselves. After Rick McCosker was lbw padding up to Hacker without playing a shot, I went in and scored 48 in just over half an hour, and was quite happy with the way I was hitting them, until I was bowled playing a poor shot to the Indian left-arm spinner Doshi.

We then saw Craig Serjeant play some good shots in the remaining 60-odd minutes of the day. He came in with 83 not out and Ian Davis, having played some lovely strokes, was 64. He added only eight runs next day, but Craig Serjeant carried on, and might have had a chance of making the fastest century of the summer only he became bogged down in the nineties, losing a lot of the strike. He reached his hundred, his first of the tour, although he had notched six half-centuries in all matches, and then really opened his shoulders. His 159 was an excellent innings, marking a continuing improvement with almost every innings. Kim Hughes and Gary Cosier then got together, both struggling for form after relatively few opportunities, and Hughes worked through his innings, improving his footwork as he went, and finished by butchering a certain hundred by trying for a six when he was on 95. He was caught in the outfield. It was still a very useful outing for him on a good, fast wicket and swift outfield. Gary Cosier, despite a sore foot, made a good hundred, which was also his first in England. The foot was hit by a full-toss from Len Pascoe in the nets that morning, and the pain grew worse as the innings went on. Gary went for a precautionary X-ray, and in fact with Rick McCosker's right wrist injury and Craig Serjeant's finger injury we were using up a bit of hospital film around this time!

We bowled Notts out a second time to win by an innings, Mick Malone again bowling well in a long unbroken spell and Ray Bright putting in a good performance. They took three wickets each. "Thommo" had a long bowl, as he was having the next game off, and his form was also satisfactory. The performances all round were pleasing, perhaps with the exception of some of the fielding, and the team now seemed to be falling into shape, with a healthy competition among the players for places in the Test side.

As it happened, Jeff Thomson had some after-effects from his long stint at Trent Bridge, and the London specialist advised him to rest. Consequently he missed the Derbyshire and Yorkshire matches.

A great disappointment awaited us at Chesterfield, for the hotel into which we were booked was below the standard that I believe is required by any touring team. It was antiquated and the facilities were poor, but though we investigated the possibility of transferring, there was no alternative. We had to stay. Unfortunately this happened round about the halfway point of the tour, which historically tends to be a bit of a low period. The accommodation here was depressing, and some of us tried to overcome it by going on a shopping spree. Rod Marsh, Richie Robinson and I bought a lot of cassettes, and during the three days in Chesterfield, when we were not at the cricket ground, we had something of a "music festival". There was very little else for us to do.

I was 13th man for the Derbyshire match, but I soon became 12th man when Geoff Dymock fell as he delivered his first ball, damaging ligaments in his right ankle. After bowling five overs he had to pull out of the match, and Craig Serjeant fielded for him, making me drinks waiter for the duration.

Len Pascoe used the pitch well, getting pace and bounce. He troubled young England hopeful Geoff Miller in both innings and dismissed him twice, and picked up the Man of the Match award. Kim Hughes unluckily missed out narrowly on a century once again, but showed signs of settling down and gaining in confidence. Richie Robinson made 77, and another encouraging feature was Kerry O'Keeffe's bowling, which was right on the spot.

For the last match before the second Test we moved on to Scarborough, where once again the accommodation was sub-standard. It was a very old hotel this time, run-down generally, and without radio or television in the rooms. There was no point in trying to move to other premises, for Scarborough, being a popular holiday resort, was fully booked. We just had to put up with it, though a complaint was registered on behalf of the players with manager Len Maddocks and treasurer Norm McMahon. I hope there is no repetition on future tours, for it is damaging to morale. Our morale up to this point had been terrific, but six days of poor accommodation can quickly change players' attitudes.

Had I won the toss at Scarborough I would have put Yorkshire in. Rain preceding the game had left conditions in favour of the bowlers. When Geoff Boycott won the toss he delayed his decision about ten minutes, and consulted Chris Old before asking us to bat. Rick McCosker was given out caught behind off Old's second ball, though he thought his bat had hit his pad rather than the ball. He was very disappointed. Craig Serjeant, who opened, and I then batted together for some time, not making a lot of runs but holding firm against bowling which didn't seam around as much as I had thought it might.

Wickets then started to topple, and at lunch we were something like 70 for seven wickets, a situation that was retrieved by Richie Robinson and Kerry O'Keeffe with a stand of 55. The instructions at lunch to these batsmen were to bat through until tea so that we could watch the Wimbledon final between Borg and Connors. We were eventually bowled out soon after tea for 186, the final wicket going during the last service game of the men's final. Perfect timing. We had missed out on the FA Cup final earlier in the season by being bowled out cheaply by Gloucestershire so this was some compensation!

As we took the field Max Walker said he would give Boycott the leg-cutter first ball and the inswinger next — the reverse of what the batsman was probably expecting. The leg-cutter was duly sent down, and hit straight to Doug Walters at cover. The inswinger then ducked in and hit his pad, and he was out lbw for nought, a decision with which he didn't seem to agree all that readily but which was supported by just about everyone else as well as the TV playback. By the end of the day we had Yorkshire four down for 29.

Next day Mick Malone bowled very well into the breeze, swinging the ball both ways, and eventually we had Yorkshire all out for 75, their lowest against an Australian touring side since 1948, the year I was born, when Don Bradman's team bowled the great county out for 71 and 89 (and still won only by four wickets).

Rick McCosker and Craig Serjeant got us away to a good start in the second innings, aided by a little luck, but then came a mid-innings slump, and it was left to David Hookes to retrieve the situation with a very fine knock of 67 which contained some powerful and attractive strokes. He was experimenting at this stage with his footwork. He had been lunging onto the front foot rather too often, and we had talked about certain variations that he might employ. The first results, here at Scarborough, were very promising.

We declared about half an hour into the final day, leaving Yorkshire to make 327 in roughly even time. The sun had come out and the wicket had improved and was now playing easily, which suited Geoff Boycott, who really seemed intent on only one thing: making sure of a big score for himself. His hundred took 80 overs! At the start he took very little of Max Walker with the new ball — perhaps four or five balls in the first nine overs.

I had my first bowl for a while, just eight overs, and then had to leave the field as I felt dizzy. The cause undoubtedly was the blow on the head the evening before, when I had stood up on a bench in the dressing-room to pull my trousers up and hit my head on a beam above the lockers. I had a throbbing headache that night and next morning, and running in to bowl I felt wonky. I saw a doctor at lunchtime and he suggested that though there was no serious injury I would be wise to take a rest. Rod Marsh, acting 12th man, took over the captaincy.

Yorkshire finished up almost 100 runs short, with five wickets down, and I felt they had missed a good chance to go for the target. They needed 108 off the final 20 overs, but the game was halted with 12 still left, no result seeming likely.

The second Test match followed, to be played at Old Trafford, where the pitch had been taking spin recently. Geoff Miller had taken

6 for 64 for Derbyshire against Lancashire, and we prepared to play two spinners by giving both Kerry O'Keeffe and Ray Bright some work in the Yorkshire match. When we saw the Test wicket on the Wednesday it looked as if it would respond to spin. It was dry, though fairly well grassed, and there were a few cracks in it. Time alone would tell when it would start turning and how much, but a spinner's wicket it had to be, and accordingly we made room for Ray Bright by omitting one of the pace men, Len Pascoe. I felt I could use myself and Doug Walters as medium-pace back-up bowlers, and this was much preferable to dropping a batsman to include the second spinner. We didn't want to take any risks with the two fast men, Max Walker and Jeff Thomson, and in view of the doubts surrounding Jeff's shoulder I put it to him that only he could say if he was up to it for a five-day match. He threw himself into it at a net session, and I can honestly say that one ball he bowled to me at the Old Trafford nets — which clean bowled me — was one of the fastest balls I have ever faced anywhere. It was about two yards faster than anything else he had bowled that day, and afterwards he said he felt all right. So it was a question of whether he felt any after-effects on the morning of the Test match. He reported fully fit.

Richie Robinson was left out of the side from the first Test, since Ian Davis had fought back strongly to earn his place. Richie was probably not best suited to the role he was asked to play at Lord's, and fits better into the middle order, yet if he was asked to open the bowling for Australia he would jump at the chance! He was unlucky to miss out at Manchester.

4. SECOND TEST MATCH

OLD TRAFFORD, MANCHESTER, JULY 7, 8, 9, 11, 12

David Frith writes:

FIRST DAY

The second phase of the '77 campaign began on the seventh day of the seventh month, and it was the 77th day of the tour, a coincidence remarked upon by even some usually phlegmatic persons. The numerical symmetry apparently happens only 13 times this century, so it augured well for a special day's play. In the event, it was exceptionally and noticably average, even if Walters reached 77 in the 77th over, when his partner was Marsh, Australia's number seven.

England retained the same twelve who had served at Lord's, though bringing in Geoff Miller, the 24-year-old Derbyshire batsman-off-spinner, for his second Test, and his first against Australia, in place of Graham Barlow.

Australia brought in Ian Davis for Robinson as opening batsman, and, heeding the warnings of the Press and the evidence of their own eyes, exchanged fast bowler Pascoe for left-arm spinner Ray Bright, who had never played in a Test match.

Anxiety over the lasting qualities of the pitch stemmed from the resignation some weeks earlier of the new head groundsman Gordon Prosser, who had had such success over the years at Worcester. In his absence the Test wicket had been prepared by deputy John Taylor, under the guidance of Bernard Flack, of Edgbaston, TCCB's inspector of pitches. Some observers were quick to seize upon thin cracks at the Warwick Road end. They were sealed with grass clippings, which would not stay for long, and widespread was the supposition that the cracks would soon widen. Thus, two spinners in each team, something which had once been standard practice.

Tony Greig had well and truly ignited the matter with a tirade in the *Sun* newspaper on the first morning, promising that the pitch would be sub-standard and claiming that groundsmen on the whole were a lazy lot. For this he was later reprimanded by the TCCB and Sussex were fined £500 for allowing the article to appear. As always in these circumstances, it was a relief to get the contest under way.

Australia were not entirely without support, for a caravan of

Dormobiles, each with a handful of (ticketless) young fellows from Down Under, took root off Greystone Road the night before. There is no more ''fair dinkum'' supporter than the one 12,000 miles from home.

Greg Chappell won the toss this time, and batted, with his players not immediately engaged in the action sitting on the balcony stripped to shorts on this hot morning. Willis, from the Warwick Road end, got several balls to fly.

Davis edged him just short of Brearley, and missed another outside off, but after 20 minutes, with only four on the board, it was McCosker who went, caught by Old at third slip. Chappell, sleeves down, opened his score with a boundary glanced off Willis, and followed with another through cover, where only Randall patrolled. Davis waved his bat again to a short ball from Willis, and when Old replaced Lever after nine overs one reflected on what an asset England's fast-bowling trio now was, following the years of want. Even when John Snow ruled, he seldom had steady, convincing support.

Willis was rested after Chappell had taken a four through point and a three to third man, his figures 6-3-17-1, and Underwood came on for the 13th over. Chappell had brazenly hooked Old for two, and so free was his strokeplay that it might have been thought that he was going for the runs while the pitch was wholesome. However, there was nothing in Underwood's bowling to raise alarm.

With a beautiful square-cut off Old followed by a clip through midwicket for three, and a sweep off Underwood high over Miller's head for four followed by a firm punch for three towards the pavilion, and a smooth four off his toecap off Old, Chappell raced to 37 of the first 48 scored, batting as well as he could ever have done. It was almost like a single-wicket match, for Davis played the wax model at the opposite end. When the young Sydney man swept Underwood for four he went to seven in 78 minutes. Heartened by this acceleration, he pulled Old dramatically through mid-on for another boundary.

Greig came on for Underwood (4-2-11-0) for his first bowl of the series, to a mixture of boos, cheers and whistles. Many agitated spectators had too much to cope with — with Greig's association with the Packer enterprise followed by the newspaper article — to be able to express their disdain adequately. If Davis had holed out to mid-on as he pulled a long-hop it would have been too much to take. Davis maintained his calmness and was soon stylishly late-cutting Lever to the rope to go to 19 out of 68, and while Greig bowled a width,

Underwood tried the other end, letting Davis have a no-ball which he hit over Randall for four, and taking two through gully, with Randall, grabbing for the racing ball like a long-armed gibbon, for once misfielding. Lunch loomed, and all was now well with Australia, Chappell allowing ball after ball from Greig to sail by wide of off stump. One that was straighter he hit down the ground for four; but there followed a fateful delivery. Pitched well up, it tempted the Australian captain to drive, and he edged to Knott, who took the catch right-handed: 80 for 2, Davis 27, Serjeant, in a white sunhat, coming in but not needing to take guard as the final over of the morning — a maiden — was bowled.

A breeze ensured a slight relief as the afternoon's play got under way, but it was not long before Australia were counting another important loss. Davis, having added only seven, including a boundary, steered *over* slips off Willis, was caught behind off the inside edge off Old.

Walters, whose highest scores in Tests in England were 81 and 86 in his first match here at Old Trafford nine years earlier, took two to square leg from his first ball, from Old, and then had one from Willis whistle straight through his defences. A bouncer followed, a no-ball, and this brought up the hundred, in the 37th over. When Greig returned, Walters drove him straight for four, and it was clear that Brearley, by his sparing use of Underwood and non-use of Miller, felt there was nothing of interest in the pitch just yet.

Randall was the best thing on show about this time, playing a ''dare-you'' cat-and-mouse game at cover, and once knocking over the one stump visible from 20 yards. At drinks, after 44 overs, Australia were 118 for 3, Serjeant 12, Walters 15. Soon the senior man was cutting Lever with a fine flourish, and Serjeant's white hat blew away with the breeze, and he handed it to umpire Alley.

Enough liquor had been put into the human jukeboxes now for the beer-can band to start up, a grating, monotonous noise that made television with the sound down seem preferable. Serjeant, with hat back on, then gave pleasure to the hordes by missing one from John Lever and being adjudged leg-before. He had batted for 80 minutes for his 14, and had managed only one four. Hookes arrived with a new bat, the bandaged favourite used at Lord's apparently having given in at last. He opened his score with a glanced single, then hooked Greig to the stand where an outsize Union Jack flapped opposite a smallish Australian flag.

Hookes missed connection as he tried to drive Greig, but Walters was more successful, getting four from a flashing cut. At the other end Hookes managed to touch Lever, but only with the finest of edges, and Knott made his third catch of the day to place Australia in the ailing position of 140 for 5.

Doug Walters' first-innings 88 gave English crowds — now almost resigned to hearing about rather than seeing his great ability — a glimpse of just how exciting a batsman he can be

Vice-captain Marsh strode belligerently to the crease, dark eyes peering from under a squashed cap-peak, nostrils pointing forward over the bushiest of moustaches. He began cautiously while Walters spent the time before tea edging Greig, cutting him fiercely, cover-driving him, and half-volleying Lever — all for fours. He was 47 as the players came off, and his side were 162 for 5.

Runs came fairly fast after tea. Marsh cut strongly, sending Greig away from silly point, and was, as always, prepared to loft his drives. Walters drove Willis square to reach 53, with nine fours, equalling his highest of the tour so far, then leg-glanced another four and twice cracked Underwood through mid-on in one over. Marsh yanked Underwood over midwicket for another four, and was then shouted against for lbw when he squatted and missed a vicious pull-shot.

The 200 came up when Marsh smashed Old through gully, where Woolmer's wrist got in the way — it was put down as a technical chance mainly by those who had never fielded in the gully themselves — and Brearley spoke with Underwood in mid-over before bringing Amiss in from long-off to mid-off, setting an obvious trap which still could have been effective.

Australia's indomitable wicketkeeper, always looking for the hittable ball, clubbed Old for two boundaries, through mid-on then mid-off, and a quiet period followed, broken when Walters stepped forward to Underwood and adapted his stroke to a splendid cut for four. At drinks he was 73, Marsh 31, and Australia were on the way back into the game at 218 for 5.

When Barlow (fielding for Woolmer) and Miller got in each other's way on the boundary four leg-byes were recorded, and soon Walters scored four from a big drive that only edged the ball through the slips/gully gap. He was now 77, and had a good chance to reach his century before the end. At five-to-six Miller was called up at the Stretford end, having bowled one over earlier in the day. Marsh stroked his first ball, short, to the cover boundary. The fifth ball beat him.

The field was now lit by brilliant sunlight, but the crowd were restless. They had had it mostly their own way for two sessions, but their hunger for further wickets was unappeased. Some of them began an "Eng-lernd" chant, urged on by conductor Randall, and perhaps stung by this, Marsh tried an almighty hit at Miller's flighted delivery and topped it high to point, where Amiss held it. The stand was worth 98, but needed to be even larger. Yet even as the Australians were still lamenting its end, with only a further eight added, and five minutes left to the day's play, Walters, having earlier thick-edged Miller for four, hit a full-toss low on the bat straight to Greig at cover. It was just what England needed, and it sent the locals away happy and the tourists back to their Dormobiles in ruminative mood.

Australia 247 for 7 (K. D. Walters 88, G. S. Chappell 44, R. W. Marsh 36, I. C. Davis 34).

SECOND DAY

It took almost an hour and a half to dismiss Australia's last three batsmen, but only 50 runs were scored. The new ball was taken after eight overs (96 in all) and Bright was not spared the bouncer by either Willis or Lever. He had thumped a four off Underwood and now off-drove Lever to the boundary past Willis's outstretched boot; but life seemed temporary, even though O'Keeffe was the first to go. He tried to hook a short one from Willis and gloved it to Knott, who took his fourth catch. Then Bright went, aiming at Lever and snicking head-high to the right of Greig at second slip. It was a magnificent catch.

Lever conceded three boundaries to the last pair, Walker and Thomson, who expectedly missed once in a while, and the Essex left-hander was replaced by Underwood, who hit Walker's off stump third ball. Australia were three short of 300, and their performance was about to be judged against England's reply. Brearley ordered the light roller, and there was time for just six overs before lunch.

Amiss and Brearley weathered them, letting a number of wider balls past, Brearley nudging Thomson for four and Amiss getting one ball from Walker from around the wicket which was suitable for a juicy hook.

The dozen runs had been enlarged only to 19 after the break when Brearley was out. Thomson was too fast for him, and though McCosker at second slip couldn't hold the flying missile, Chappell coolly took the rebound. Four runs later Amiss was out as well, trying to hook Walker but somehow steering the ball fairly softly to first slip, where the captain took another catch, the other fielders giving him room like a well-trained team of acrobats. England 23 for 2, prompting half-a-dozen in the Press box to guess at a final score: the offers ranged from 153 to 250.

The long, drawn-out Australian nightmare of Dennis Amiss was therefore continuing. This man who had batted himself into a near-stupor in West Indies in 1974 and had fought his way back as an accredited England batsman in 1976 with a double-century against Holding and Roberts at The Oval, was unable to wriggle out from under the huge figurative Australian studded boot. In 1968, in his first Test against Australia, he bagged a pair; next, in the 1974-75 series, he had Test scores of 7, 25, 4, 90, 12, 37; another pair, and 0; at home in 1975 he made 4, 5, 0 and 10 in his two Tests; in the Centenary Test, batting down the order, as in the previous Test, he made 4 and 64. In the first Test of this 1977 series he had made 4 and 0, so that his figures against Australia after his first innings at Old Trafford were 277 runs from 20 innings (seven ducks), average 13.85. Viewed against his overall Test figures at this point — 3584 runs in 87 innings, average 45.95, with 11 centuries — the contrast is staggering, and quite without parallel. His technique against pace may often have been discussed, but his unabashed courage in continuing to try to overcome the seemingly unanswerable can never be doubted.

There was nothing surprising about England's being two down for few. What did surprise, though, was the way in which the crisis was remedied. No hour-after-hour grind, with only the rare bad ball scored off, but a thrilling, strokesome stand between the boyish bulwarks of the Lord's Test, Woolmer and Randall. They made 96 before tea, and kept the match on an even keel besides giving English followers a genuine pride in their play.

Derek Randall, sleeves buttoned and without a cap, got straight down to the job, square-cutting Walker for four, then two. Then he decided he wanted some gum, so he embarked on a lengthy pantomime in the direction of the pavilion balcony, watched in silent amusement by Bill Alley, who finally produced a stick of the necessary from his pocket.

After coming close to being caught by Serjeant in the gully off Thomson, Randall collected himself with a loose-limbed cut for four. Bright came on for his first bowl in Test cricket, and Randall dabbed his third ball away for a single before turning his sparrowlike alertness to Walker, whom he placed all along the ground through third man for four, then for two square, then four backward of square past O'Keeffe's desperate boot. Enjoying himself immensely, Randall was 22 out of 52 at drinks.

As the sun peeped through, Woolmer reminded everyone of his

presence by sweeping Bright very fine with the kind of paddle stroke often used by Cowdrey. Randall went after Bright now, taking four to cover with a glorious back-foot shot and three to midwicket. Woolmer glanced him to the boundary, and when Walker dropped just short, he hooked him surely for four, only to see Davis bring off a wonderful diving save. He then greeted O'Keeffe with a cover-drive for four.

Three more boundaries to Randall took him to the verge of his fifty and England to the hundred, and after O'Keeffe (two overs for 14 runs) had given way to Thomson, Woolmer took one to square leg to bring up 100 in the 33rd over. O'Keeffe took over from Bright (seven overs for 22) at the Stretford end, and Randall swept a no-ball for four to reach 52 in 86 minutes, with nine attractive fours. He then edged Thomson for four, and with Woolmer tickling O'Keeffe's last ball before tea for three, England had had, after all, a satisfactory afternoon, losing two wickets but adding 107 runs off 32 overs.

Thomson got a good head of steam up after tea, and I found myself studying Marsh's method of taking the fast stuff. Often, knees bent, he took the ball in front of his face, baseball-fashion. It contrasted with the way Godfrey Evans used to take Frank Tyson, jumping and jack-knifing as the ball buried itself in his gloves in his midriff.

Woolmer brought up the century stand with a fine cut, but was then dropped by McCosker at slip, a low and fairly comfortable catch off Thomson. The hapless fieldsman could not have looked more crestfallen, and Thomson himself was not exactly a picture of hilarity. Australia were at their worst about now, giving away a needless single as Chappell hurled the ball through Marsh's gloves from mid-off when no run was being attempted. Soon Woolmer had his fifty, playing O'Keeffe sweetly off the back foot for four and then turning Thomson for three. His half-century came in 135 minutes, with seven fours.

Runs continued to come freely and pleasantly. Woolmer found his way through thin gaps in the covers and Randall let the ball come as he rocked back and stroked it square, watching the ball race to the line, needing to make no effort to run, and grinning as if he'd just made the winning hit in a beer match.

Walker returned, and conceded a five as Marsh's throw broke the bowler's wicket and ran away for two more runs after Randall had taken three when McCosker, feeling even more wretched, had failed to cut off the original stroke.

"Candles" Bright came on for O'Keeffe (10 overs for 44), looking like a Caucasian Bedi: rotund, sleeves down, bearded. Randall late-cut

Bob Woolmer stroked his way to an excellent 137 in England's first innings, and further underlined his rise to world-class status

him prettily for four, and drinks were taken at 5.30. A quieter period followed, with the attack in the hands of Bright and Walker, but when a drive by Woolmer ended in the hands of Walters, Australia's frustration blew up again as the ball bounced out as the fieldsman hit the ground. The Kent batsman took his luck expressionlessly, but Australian faces lit up soon afterwards, when a full-toss from Bright

After making a typically action-packed 79, Derek Randall got a ball on the toe (''Me bloomin' size elevens!'') from Ray Bright and was lbw

hit Randall on the foot (''Me bloomin' size elevens!'') and Bill Alley, having taken his time, gave him out. It was a good first Test wicket for Bright.

Greig was booed as he strode out, but was quickly off the mark with two to leg off Walker, and when Woolmer steered Bright away for a couple he reached 62 — and a total of 500 runs against Australia in only his ninth Test innings, and fifth Test, against them.

He then picked up a short one from Walker and hooked it with great certainty for four, and performed a perfect cover-drive to the boundary in the same over, taking him to 71. He was a model of patience blended with timely flashes of aggression.

Greig gathered a gratuitous four when O'Keeffe hurled at the bowler's end when he saw Woolmer bolting off, and Hookes dived but failed to cut off the overthrow. Unruffled, Woolmer unwrapped a wristy square-drive off Walker, something that Greig was soon emulating in his own way.

As the batsmen played for stumps, Chappell positioned himself at silly point, but Woolmer's forward defence was White-Cliffs-of-Dover stuff. A late-cut for four off Bright brought up 202 in the 70th over. The threatened spinners' paradise had still not come to pass.
Australia 297; *England* 206 for 3 (D. W. Randall 79, R. A. Woolmer 82 not out).

THIRD DAY

Manchester did not respond to the promising English position on the Saturday. Only 16,000 were in attendance on a cooler, cloudy day, and the empty rows of seats were conspicuous. The batsmen played themselves in, Greig making the first gesture of offence with a driven four off Walker. Woolmer responded with a cute delayed drive backward of point off Bright, who then nearly yorked him, four byes resulting.

Chappell came on for Walker, and Woolmer took four more with a fine glance. As the sun peeped through, he played Bright late to third man for two to reach 97, and Greig took a swift single to give his partner the strike. As Walker at mid-on stumbled, Woolmer took a single to make him 98, and when he turned Bright for what seemed a quickly-run two, the crowd had to hold itself as Walker this time fielded adeptly and restricted the stroke to a single. With a touch of drama the new ball was now taken, after 86 overs.

Thomson to Woolmer, who tried for a single to cover, thwarted by Bright. Then he steered Thomson through the slip area for four to record his third century in four home Test innings against Australia. It beat Maurice Leyland's record for England in England (three hundreds in five successive innings against Australia in 1934), and equalled Don Bradman's three in four twice: in 1930 and 1938. Only Charlie Macartney had pulled off a hat-trick of Test hundreds for Australia in England. Rare company for the 29-year-old who had been kept in the lower depths of the Kent batting order until a couple of years ago.

Walker took the new ball from the Stretford end, with Hookes at slip and McCosker now out at mid-off. Greig hit the first ball violently through cover for four. A single was then turned into two as McCosker's poor throw went under Marsh's gloves, and a bye as Greig tried to hook brought up the 250.

A short one from Thomson had Greig erect to his full 6 ft 7 ins and banging the ball backward of point for four, but the bowler came back with a loud appeal, with Marsh, for a leg-side flick, and then forced Greig to French-cut. An off-driven four followed in this all-action sequence, and then the controversy of the day, a flyer from Thomson from which Greig tried to remove his bat as it came at him from the off side. Contact with the high part of the bat was undoubtedly made, but umpire Spencer can have seen nothing, since by then Greig's body and left arm had swung round towards point. Rod Marsh was apoplectic when Greig was given — and took — his reprieve.

A boundary through cover off Chappell took Greig to 45 and posted the hundred partnership, and when Davis let the ball through at square leg to give Woolmer a single, bowler Thomson was a picture of dejection. Brisbane 1974, with infallible catchers everywhere, Lillee at the other end, and a responsive pitch, were light-years away.

Woolmer turned Chappell strongly and then drove square for fours, the second let through on the line by Pascoe, substituting for Hookes, and with a pull and a cover-drive for further boundaries he went to 123 at lunch, with Greig 49 and England 288 for 3, only nine runs in arrears. The highest fourth-wicket stand in 21 Tests at Old Trafford by England against Australia had long since been overtaken: a mere 77 by Sutcliffe and Hendren in 1934.

O'Keeffe resumed, handicapped by fluid on his spinning finger, and Woolmer got moving again with a late-cut for four. Now Greig, after nearly half an hour on 49, hit rather desperately at Walker and got four over slips. His half-century came in just over three hours, and he marked it with a lofted drive to raise 300 and put England ahead. From the other end, with his own king-size brand of confidence, the former

England captain struck O'Keeffe for six. A fierce off-drive followed — four only this time.

Umpire Tom Spencer seemed concerned about Walker's follow-through, and spoke to him about it. The big man toiled away, finding the edge of Woolmer's bat twice, both thick edges going for four, the first raising the 150 stand.

Bob Woolmer by now was feeling utterly exhausted. He had a severe headache, which must have had a lot to do with almost six-and-a-half hours of concentration, and claimed he "could hardly see". O'Keeffe was troubling him, though there was no reason why he shouldn't play himself through the difficulties, as he had so often done. But the spinner found the edge and a bat-pad catch went dolly-like to Davis and Woolmer's epic was over. He had stroked 22 fours and the stand with Greig amounted to 160 in 217 minutes.

Wickets henceforth were to come at regular intervals while England's lead mounted. Knott got into the swing of things with an off-side four off O'Keeffe, and then in one over struck him to the midwicket, long-leg and long-on boundaries. The valiant, toiling Max Walker applied the next brake. Seeing Greig alter his off-drive only to pop the ball uppishly towards short cover, "Tangles" unravelled his limbs in time to clutch the catch with his left hand before collapsing in a heap, rather as he had done in finishing Mike Denness's 188 at Melbourne in 1975. Greig's 76 had taken just over four hours, and the danger of England tearing away to an astronomical lead receded with his dismissal.

Geoff Miller had batted only twice before in a Test match, making a competent 36 and 24 at The Oval against West Indies. Now, frankly, he seemed out of his depth. With Walker having earned a rest after 100 minutes of bowling since lunch for figures of 14-6-30-1, Thomson came back, and after four from a Knott swipe to third man, Miller was late in an attempted hook and Marsh took a simple skyer.

At tea England were 367 for 6, Knott 30, Old yet to score.

The temperature slipped a little in the evening session, and Pascoe had to take some sweaters out to the fieldsmen. Knott, though, was bent on keeping himself warm, sweeping O'Keeffe from wide outside off to the midwicket boundary. For 35 minutes runs had come only from one end of the batting partnership — until Old at last opened his score with a single through gully. No sooner had the ironic cheers died than Knott was out — in an extraordinary way. Slashing at Thomson,

As ever, Max Walker bowled many excellent overs without getting the wickets he deserved. But he made no mistake about this caught-and-bowled chance from Tony Greig on 76

he was caught by an alert O'Keeffe diving in from third man, fully 45 yards from the wicket.

More boundaries followed, Lever with a square-cut, Old with three lusty hits off O'Keeffe, the last taking England's lead to three figures, a milestone not unnoticed by the perceptive crowd.

Bright, who hadn't bowled for five hours, took over from O'Keeffe, who had managed 24 overs straight, and the 400 came up in 567 minutes, off 151.3 overs, hardly a tearaway rate in spite of the spasms of aggression. When Lever was bowled by a ball from Bright which dipped and straightened there was a good chance that England's innings would be finalised that evening, but Marsh missed Old off the left-arm spinner and after a couple of fours owing much to Underwood's strong forearms and a couple more from Old's powerful shoulder movement, Old was missed by Thomson at mid-on, again off Bright, who himself fluffed a catch from that batsman which Marsh clasped on the rebound. The Yorkshireman had been in for almost two hours for his 37. Willis saw it through with Underwood in a day which had produced diminishing productivity to the extent of 82 runs off 32 overs in the first session, 79 off 35 in the second, and 69 off 30 in the last. Nevertheless, an England victory was firmly expected as everyone took a day off.

Australia 297; *England* 436 for 9 (R. A. Woolmer 137, D. W. Randall 79, A. W. Greig 76, A. P. E. Knott 39, C. M. Old 37, J. R. Thomson 3 for 73, M. H. N. Walker 3 for 131).

FOURTH DAY

Sunday served the purpose, for me, of examining the dense under-growth of Delamere Forest golf course, losing four balls, developing sore feet, and enlarging the cash reserves of John Thicknesse of the *Evening Standard* and Peter Lush of the TCCB. It was good to climb up to the sanctuary of the Press enclosure on Monday morning and watch the cricketers wear themselves out before a surprisingly large gathering. Bright bowled Underwood with the seventh ball of the day, with only a bye added, and Australia set about erasing a deficit of 140.

The first over brought disaster. McCosker, as sad a sight as Amiss had been in his encounters against Australia, tried to pull Willis's third ball and was caught at mid-on. With Test scores of 23, 1, 2 and 0 since the painful Centenary Test, McCosker was going to need a remarkable return to form in the matches before the third Test if he was to hold his place.

This let in Greg Chappell, who was about to play one of the most delightful innings seen in England-Australia Test cricket. Beginning with a single off Lever, and a bowed-head evasion of a Willis bouncer, he played through Amiss at gully for four and pulled Lever noisily for two, then hooked Willis way over the long-leg rope for six in front of the Ladies' Stand.

Ian Davis had moved smoothly into second gear meanwhile, with one nice boundary off Lever to midwicket, until, hooking at one of Willis's many short ones, he failed to strike it as well as his captain had done, and Lever held the catch a yard or two in from the line: 30 for 2.

Someone had done steady business with sunhats: six Englishmen wore them, and Serjeant emerged wearing one as drinks were taken.

Chappell, with an elegance all his own, off-drove Willis for four and took two straight boundaries off Underwood, who had replaced Lever. The captain now had 31 of the 49 runs posted.

Old came on for Willis and beat Serjeant twice, but an on-driven four off the last ball opened his account and brought up the fifty. Chappell continued on his royal journey, stroking Underwood between a sprawling Randall at midwicket and a diving Lever at mid-on, and following it with a three in the same direction. When Serjeant tickled four more it meant 11 off the over plus a no-ball. Chappell then moved to 46 with an erectly-struck off-drive and a square-cut, both for four, off Old. Was ever Hammond or Headley or Hutton pre-eminent among his contemporaries to a greater degree?

Serjeant was next to go, caught by Woolmer at short leg off a firm stroke to Underwood in the 18th over: 74 for 3. After an over from the energetic Old, Walters squirted Underwood for a single to point, and Greig was removed from the close position in deference to Chappell's sureness of touch, which he showed again with a short-arm pull against Old which took him to 52 in 91 minutes. It had been England's morning all right, but conclusively so when Brearley called up Greig to bowl the last before lunch, and Walters, having struck Underwood confidently through midwicket, played across Greig's second ball and was adjudged leg-before. At 92 for 4 it was beginning to look like a four-day decision.

Hookes, with his old bat, settled down with his captain to bail Australia out. He began with four across the fast outfield backward of point off Greig and off-drove Willis for three, Randall provoking a huge roar as he cut off the boundary. The tall left-hander square-cut Willis for four, and as Greig continued at the opposite end there was cause to wonder if Underwood or Miller ought not to have been in action. Willis asserted himself with a nasty lifter to Chappell which had the batsman toppling over and rolling backwards to avoid his stumps. He sprang to his feet and stood sphinx-like as the crowd expressed their excitement. Soon he was dropping Willis onto the crease and gaily reverse-kicking the ball away to square leg. Willis plunged another in short and he hooked him for four. The next reared lethally at his face and he stunned it with the splice. A rare contest.

Underwood unmistakably was causing concern to the batsmen. Hookes played him just wide of Old at leg slip and Chappell was beaten while playing across his crease and then edged a no-ball onto his off stump. Playing him to leg, he sent the ball to point off the back of the

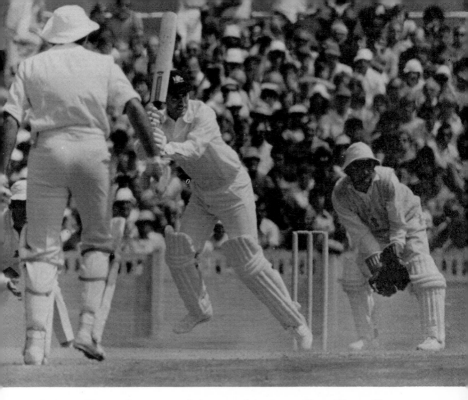

With Australia on the rack in their second innings, Greg Chappell put together an innings of 112, one of the best seen in Anglo-Australian Test cricket. The title ''world's best batsman'' belonged to him in this innings

bat. Yet with it all Chappell seemed relaxed, sanguine. When Randall shaped to throw from cover, he adopted the stance of a baseball batter, and spectators wondered whether to laugh out loud, since Greg Chappell had never been associated with slapstick.

After three overs from Old, Miller took the end opposite Underwood, and Hookes swept him for two and cut him for two and four to take Australia to 138, two runs behind on aggregate. It was a good time for drinks.

When Hookes tucked Underwood away for a single, the scores were level, and there was to be no innings defeat. Chappell drove Miller to the rope almost as a reminder that Australia were not even out of the hunt while he prospered. But a further setback followed. Hookes, with feet aggressively apart, as is his style, sparred at the young off-spinner and Brearley at slip took the catch as it brushed past Knott: 146 for 5, Chappell 76.

Marsh walked in, to a chorus of booing inspired by causes best known to the creators of the noise, and took a single. Then, from a shot off Underwood that was hardly the most responsible of the innings, he whacked him to mid-on, where Randall made a three-course meal of the catch, finishing flat on his back, arms outstretched, in relief. When Bright was caught-and-bowled third ball, giving Underwood his third wicket, Australia were 147 for 7 and fading away fast. It was a quarter-to-four, and O'Keeffe, a determined straight-batter, came in.

There now developed a not-too-intent battle of tactics as Chappell was offered a single wherever he wanted it. He took one, showing confidence in his partner, and from the other end saw an Underwood short ball early and hit it through the covers. He was now 81 out of 152.

Another shortish ball from Underwood invited a sweep-drive, but the captain for once missed, and took it in the ribs. He recovered his poise with four off the back foot when a no-ball was offered up. When they tried to keep him away from the bowling he dropped the ball to the off and made a speedy single, but for the moment O'Keeffe was able to look after himself, glancing Underwood coolly for four. Chappell's final salvo for the afternoon — a square-cut off Miller — saw Australia to tea with the sad score of 171 for 7.

Underwood started the last session with a no-ball, which O'Keeffe smacked back over his head as the five close fielders watched in relief. Willis, too, overstepped the mark, and Chappell hooked for four. A cover-driven two took him to 98, and a straight-drive to the Warwick Road boundary off the fast bowler brought up his century, his sixth against England (only Bradman, 19, Morris, 8, and Lawry, 7, had made more, and Harvey, Trumper and Woodfull as many), and his 14th in all Tests. It had taken him 245 minutes and included a six and 15 beautifully-struck fours. All that was needed now was for him to convert it into a McCabe-like 232!

Chappell and O'Keeffe raised their stand to 51 in 80 minutes, but the captain's innings was about to end. The 200 had just been raised when, moving back to make room to cut Underwood, bowling over the wicket, Chappell touched the ball into his stumps. When O'Keeffe was missed at slip by Willis off Greig straight afterwards it hardly seemed to matter.

Walker's innings was animated. There was a loud, disallowed appeal for caught at slip; he square-drove Greig for four; Greig bowled him a bouncer; Greig then lost the ball from his grasp as he bounded in to bowl, just as Walker had done when bowling to him the day before; he

Derek Underwood's Test tally climbed inexorably with his 6 for 66 in Australia's second innings, once again putting England into a match-winning position

called for a sunhat, which Pascoe took out; then he was caught via his pad at silly point.

Thomson, last man, took strike, shaded his eyes, surely unable to see much against the low sun, and after watching O'Keeffe hook Greig for four, hit out, and Randall took the high ball at midwicket to seal Underwood's sixth wicket of the innings. Australia had disappointed — with the sole, sparkling exception of their leader — with only 218, leaving England to make 79 for victory, of which Amiss and Brearley made eight that evening.

They were not easily made, however, for Jeff Thomson seemed to have got it into his head that this match could be won. He was hostile, and the two skulls, one protected, the other not, seemed in some danger as the short ones hurtled through.

"Come on, Englernd!" came the patriotic cries, many fuelled by Norwegian lager. It seemed to spur "Thommo" on. Brearley withdrew his head from the line with a hundredth of a second to spare. That evening Thomson pointed out to me that in *The Fast Men* I'd written that his speed had been measured at 90 mph. (I'd gone on to say that in Perth he was measured at 99.688, but by then he must have tossed the book aside in disgust.) "Anyway, in the morning I'll be bowling at a bloody hundred and twenty!" he said, grinning.

Australia 297 and 218 (G. S. Chappell 112, D. L. Underwood 6 for 66); *England* 437 and 8 for 0.

FIFTH DAY

Running 25 paces, four more than usual, Thomson was very fast on the final morning, when the term "obsequies" took on a potentially macabre double meaning as the England batsmen had to put their heads in a safe place as the ball flew. Admission prices were dropped to 40p and 20p in the certain knowledge that hardly more than 25 overs would be bowled, and as the opening partnership asserted itself the record books were pulled out to see how often England had achieved the comparative rarity of a ten-wicket win over Australia.

Amiss broke his duck third ball from Walker, and Brearley had to evade three very short deliveries from Thomson, who was racing in like a Derby-winner. Having hooked Walker for three, the England captain saw his side nearer to the great prize with a deliberate uppercut for four off Thomson, the ball sailing high over the crowded slips cordon. The next he steered also to the boundary, there being no third man covering.

Walker switched ends and O'Keeffe came on at 30 for 0, and Amiss cut Walker fine for four. Brearley then took three boundaries in quick succession off O'Keeffe with a cut, a good-sounding drive, and a thick edge past a diving McCosker. When Thomson came on for Walker Amiss punched him square for three to raise the half-century. O'Keeffe, perhaps thinking of the legendary Benaud coup here in 1961, went to around the wicket, with two slips.

Thomson, all guns blazing as Australia slipped under, had Brearley swaying out of harm's way again and then jabbing to the third-man

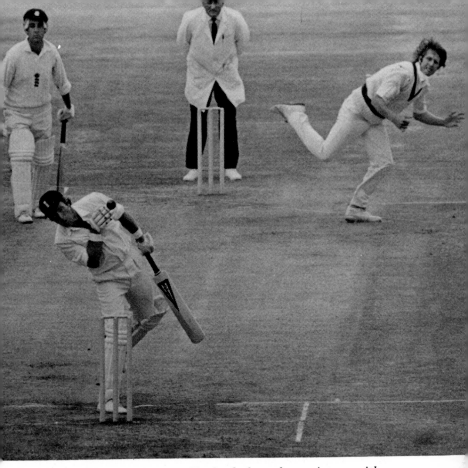

Although Dennis Amiss saw England through to victory with an undefeated 28, this picture sums up his torrid, confidence-sapping experiences against Australian pace bowlers over the years

boundary. Bright came on, and the action swung to the other end as Amiss pulled a short one from O'Keeffe for four, then edged a cut high over McCosker for another. Brearley got four to long leg off Bright, and two runs later, only four runs from victory, his innings was snuffed out as he drove a half-volley from O'Keeffe straight to Walters.

It was left to Dennis Amiss to enjoy the satisfaction, in his 50th Test, of making the winning runs, a solid off-drive to the extra-cover boundary that helped to erase the memory of so much personal suffering. The stroke had a poignancy 11 days later when his name was missing from the list of those called up for the third Test.

For the moment, all was celebration in the England dressing-room, for this was England's first Test victory at home since the innings defeat of India at Edgbaston three years ago. In that time there had been nine draws and four defeats; never before had England had to wait so long for a home success. As for the ratio against Australia, this was only the second victory in the last 14 contests between the two countries. No wonder the corks popped, and no wonder Mike Brearley, having just been appointed captain for the remaining three Tests, seemed just a little distracted at the after-match Press conference.

He said that the difference between the sides had been in the matter of catching. The constant wind had compelled use of the spinners throughout chiefly from the Stretford end, and the Warwick Road end thus became more worn from the spinning.

He paid tribute to the team spirit built up under Tony Greig's leadership, saying that Greig, manager Ken Barrington and he himself had encouraged the players to have their say in India and to think for themselves. Miller, he thought, could become a fine England all-rounder. He was nervous when called upon to bowl, but luckily was allowed to get away with a few bad overs early.

Certainly the young man could be pleased at having bagged the wickets of Walters, Marsh and Hookes in his first Australian Test.

When Greg Chappell faced the Press he was analytical and direct. The most refreshing of his statements — though it was no attempt to conceal certain serious considerations — was that it was not the end of the world.

A couple of hours later and a couple of hundred miles south of Manchester a veteran warrior of England-Australia cricket, John Edrich, was uncorking champagne of his own, having scored his hundredth first-class hundred. July 12 1977 was a bit of a day for English cricket.

Greg Chappell writes:

When I won the toss I had no hesitation in batting. The English players must have been rather disappointed, for any advantage that was going stemmed from batting first, with the pitch expected to take more spin as time passed.

After the early setback of Rick McCosker's dismissal to Chris Old's juggling catch Ian Davis and I pushed things along, and the ball from Tony Greig that got me was one of perhaps only two all day that did anything. I had been feeling as good as at any stage of the tour, seeing the ball well from the start, when I glanced Bob Willis's first ball to me for four. One from John Lever pitched leg stump and moved away towards slip, and I missed it by some distance, but otherwise I felt well in control, and the pitch gave no cause whatsoever for anxiety. I was especially sorry to get out just before lunch since we had worked ourselves back into a sound position.

Ian Davis and Craig Serjeant were out after lunch, and David Hookes, trying to force the pace, went to an inside edge, and we were five down before the great recovery partnership between Doug Walters and Rod Marsh. Rod invariably gets runs when we need them, and Doug applied himself well. It seemed to be his day at last. He has not been all that successful in England, and many critics seem to think he has a lot of faults in technique. He didn't show much emotion when he was caught — off a full-toss of all deliveries — just twelve short of his first hundred in a Test in England, but he was bitterly disappointed.

The loss of Doug and, just before, of Rod, when he tried to hit a flighted ball from Miller over mid-on but skyed the ball, which pitched in the bowler's footmarks, was a severe double blow to us. From 238 for five wickets we were suddenly 246 for 7, with a new ball due. We had lost a lot of ground, and England probably finished the first day slightly ahead in the honours. We hoped to get up around the 300 mark on the second day.

I had arrived at the ground about ten o'clock on this opening day, and as soon as I'd put my gear down in the dressing-room Tony Greig came in and said, ''Have you heard the news?'' I hadn't heard any news, and didn't know what he was talking about.

He said he had just had a phone call from someone at the Sydney *Sun* newspaper to say that Kerry Packer had just been killed with three others in a car accident. My initial reaction was to ask Tony whether he knew the fellow who had rung him. He didn't, and my impression was that it had to be a hoax. Apparently the man had said that he would ring back later, and I suggested that we oughtn't to pay too much attention to it until we heard further. I tried to get in contact with my brother Ian or Richie Benaud, and went off to the nets. When Ian eventually saw me he said that he had been talking with Austin Robertson only an hour previously, and no mention of any accident had been made. Meanwhile, Tony Greig had made a telephone call and established that it was a hoax call.

The second day of the Test saw England into the box seat. Mike Brearley's spin bowlers did not break through at the start, so he took the new ball, and we lost Kerry O'Keeffe and Ray Bright before Jeff

Thomson and Max Walker put on 25 for the last wicket that lifted us to 297, which was just respectable. But I was far from happy with that total, because the wicket was getting easier.

We got rid of the openers after lunch, Brearley falling to a catch which rebounded to me from Rick McCosker next door at slip, and Amiss getting out in an unusual way. He tried to swing a ball down to fine leg but only succeeded in taking it on the thigh-pad, from where it brushed the back of his bat and flew over his head to me at first slip, where I was able to take a fairly simple catch.

We needed a further breakthrough now, and I kept Walker and Thomson going as long as possible. "Thommo" was unlucky when Randall cut him hard and low to Craig Serjeant at gully. He got both hands to the ball but wasn't able to hold on to it. It was off the meat of the bat and would have been a very good catch. This was the kind of half-chance we missed from time to time at Lord's, and they need to be held if Test matches are to be won.

From half-chances we later got into difficulties from straightforward chances when Rick McCosker missed Woolmer off Thomson at slip, and later in the afternoon, when we really were looking for wickets in the last session, Doug Walters misjudged an attempt at a catch in the covers. I had gone up to Max Walker when we were having drinks and asked him if he had any thoughts, and he said he could either bowl round the wicket, to change the angle, or keep bowling a straight line, with the occasional slower one wider, hoping for a catch in the cover area. I suggested the latter approach, and lo and behold Bob Woolmer went after the first slower one served up by Max, and Doug, moving perhaps too quickly, got too close to the ball, left-handed, and it was knocked out. It was the kind of catch I've seen Doug make quick work of so many times.

It was left to Ray Bright shortly afterwards to pick up the very important wicket of Derek Randall with a faster arm ball, which the batsman played over, to be leg-before when it hit his foot.

Another wicket that evening would have made the game pretty even, but Bob Woolmer batted on steadily and took the score, with Tony Greig at the other end, to 206 for 3 by the close. We lived in hope: a couple of quick wickets in the morning, and we would be in contention. We needed to restrict England to around 300, though an English lead of fifty would not have troubled us all that much, with England having to bat last on a worn pitch (even if there was still no sign of it breaking up).

We had been under a cloud in the final session, for Jeff Thomson's legs had cramped up after a longish spell of bowling, and he was unable to stretch out in delivery, and Kerry O'Keeffe's finger had fluid on it. I was forced to use Max Walker and Ray Bright in long spells, and missed the third fast bowler. Cricket is always producing the unforeseen.

I was disappointed with our ground fielding during the middle session of this second day, and gave the boys quite a rocket during the tea interval. Everybody seemed to have their bums dragging along the ground, and the fielding was so sloppy that I simply had to demand an immediate and marked improvement.

The third day started with a shock when Ian Davis accidentally trod on a cable connected to the television set in the dressing-room. His spike caused a minor explosion, which blackened the sole of his boot and gave him a fright, but fortunately, apart from melting half the spike, the only damage was that the TV set was put out of action in the middle of a Bugs Bunny cartoon being watched intently by Mick Malone and Kim Hughes.

The early inroads into England's first innings were not made, and the new ball made little difference either. I changed the bowling around several times before taking the new ball, and Max Walker got only slight movement from it into the wind. I replaced him, lining him up behind Jeff Thomson downwind. Jeff was bowling particularly well, beating the bat often and forcing streaky shots through the slips. I felt we were unlucky not to get a decision when Tony Greig touched one that flew head-high from "Thommo". Rod Marsh took the ball with both hands high above his head, but Tom Spencer was apparently unsighted, and shook his head. I am not against batsmen not walking. The game is best left to the umpires. But I was somewhat disappointed to see Tony indicating that the ball had touched his shoulder.

After lunch, not having picked up wickets, we had to try to contain the England batsmen and wait for the mistakes. But the edges didn't come. They continued to play and miss from time to time, and Rod Marsh was going absolutely berserk. His despair was so great that I signalled to Len Pascoe and Gary Cosier in the dressing-room to have a straitjacket ready for our wicketkeeper at the tea interval! It was just one of those days. Max Walker put in a tremendous effort between lunch and tea, and Kerry O'Keeffe's marathon was worth much admiration. He thoroughly deserved the prize wicket of Woolmer when he found the inside edge with a wrong'un.

Greig was tied down on 49 for a long time, and tried to keep the score moving, but Max Walker was bowling so well that there wasn't much he could do about it. Max's off-balance left-hand catch to end "Greigy's" innings was a superb effort.

The time spent occupying the crease while runs came slowly, of course, was in our favour in one way, but we failed to capitalise later in the day when Jeff Thomson spilled a catch and Rod Marsh missed a difficult one from Ray Bright's bowling, out of the rough patch outside the left-hander's off stump, Chris Old being the lucky batsman each time. Again our fielding left a lot to be desired, but I was proud of our lion-hearted bowlers.

I must pay tribute to Bob Woolmer. He has improved greatly since I first saw him. He plays very well off his legs, though, like most batsmen, he is slightly suspect outside the off stump early in his innings. Given anything short or overpitched he is swiftly into his stroke. After lunch he was obviously under instructions to see the new ball off, allowing later batsmen to tear us apart and get the total up around 500, when batting last would be less of a worry to England. Also, the longer we were kept in the field the more tired and demoralised we would be likely to became.

It might have seemed like a dull day's cricket, but there was much tactical thought given to it by both sides.

On the rest day most of us treated it as just that — a day for rest and relaxation. Max Walker spent it with his wife and young son at a local friend's place, and Jeff Thomson had a quiet day at the hotel. Some of the lads took part in another Golf Fanatics day, this time at Dunham Forest, with Bobby Charlton and Eric Sykes among the celebrities, and Rod Marsh won the trophy, making it two victories out of two for us cricketers. We presented five autographed cricket bats and the pads I'd worn in the Jubilee Test in the hope that raffles would raise further money for the purchase of more motorised wheelchairs.

Foot trouble — tendonitis in the arches of both feet — was beginning to bother me again. It had first flared up during the Centenary Test, and had been aggravated during the Brisbane club final a week later. I had felt it on and off during the tour, and after running on hard ground at Chesterfield it troubled me once more. Spending Saturday in the field didn't help, so I decided to take it easy on the rest day. If I'd gone to the golf I would have spent the day standing and talking, so it was better that I should have my feet up.

When we finished the England innings off on the fourth morning we then had to keep their bowlers at bay while we established a foundation to our second innings. There was a possibility that we could throw the pressure back on their batsmen when they batted last.

But Rick McCosker was out almost immediately and I found myself facing the fourth ball of the innings. I think that technically this was my best innings against England. The hundred I made in my first Test, at Perth in 1970-71, had a fairy-tale touch about it. I never dreamed that a century would result in my debut. The 131 I made at Lord's in 1972 was, to my mind, the best from a defensive technique point of view. Probably the only mistake I made then got me out.

Today, occupying the crease was not going to be enough. I had to look for runs. If we were only 100 or 150 in front by lunch on the last day that wouldn't be much good. Honestly, I felt that we could still turn this match, and put England under pressure on the final day. So I played it naturally, looking to play shots when the ball was there. I knew Bob Willis was going to let a few go at me, and if I picked the right ones to hit I was in with a chance. The hooked six was meant to go squarer than it did. Derek Randall had been put back three-quarters of the way to the fence, so I knew a few bouncers were on the schedule. Hitting with the wind, I aimed to carry any leg-side delivery on its way.

I think I concentrated as well as I've concentrated for a long time. I could not let the disasters going on at the other end affect me; I could not afford to get out; I had to apply my mind to making runs. There is a limit to how long you can concentrate, and you have to spread this out as long as possible. I "switch on" as the bowler nears delivery, and try not to waste mental energy between times. This is a time to relax. I glance around the ground and try to free the mind.

The by-play with Derek Randall helped me keep my spirits up. He's always playing around, so he's as good a target as anyone. We've had a few little bits and pieces in the past, when the ball has been hit in his direction and the batsman calls "No!", and Randall hisses "Come on, take one, take one!"

David Frith writes:

Greg Chappell stood out like a lighthouse on the rocks during Australia's second innings, and I asked him at the end of the match just how it felt, carrying the side through this dark hour.

DF: Sometimes a cricket team depends a lot on one chap, and

sometimes he happens to be the captain. This is the position you're stuck with right now, and it's a new experience for you. I know you had a similar situation with Queensland, but this is Australia. A lot of people are interested to see how you react. At Lord's you weren't in this position. Here the downhill slide began as England crept up towards 400 and the fielding became ragged, all this after a dismal Australian first innings. You're aware of it. You're more aware of it than anyone. It was an interesting study to see how you would take it. And it has produced one of your finest innings.

GC: I decided before the tour got under way that we were possibly going to have problems. We are a young and inexperienced side, and the worst thing I could do was to let it affect the way I played. I think I let it affect me in New Zealand. I tried to play the sheet-anchor role, to graft, to make sure I didn't get out. I was scared to play shots in case I got out to a shot that really wasn't on. Even during the innings here at Old Trafford I had to fight against that feeling. I tried playing the sheet-anchor in the Centenary Test, and in the first innings it was probably what was required. But I did it in New Zealand, and made a forty in Christchurch and a fifty run-out in Auckland, only I was occupying the crease for a long time without getting full benefit from it. So I decided before this tour that the best thing I can do for the team is to play naturally. Doing that in the early games I got three hundreds, and I thought that this has got to be the way to play.

DF: Will you open the innings in the next Test?

GC: I think it's preferable that I don't at this stage. The thought entered by mind yesterday. When you do open, at least the field's up and you can sometimes get to 20 or 30 quickly — as I did yesterday. Wherever I bat I've got to get runs. Going in later, you usually find the field set back, and runs are more difficult to get.

DF: There are three matches before the third Test. Perhaps a few things will sort themselves out in that time. There is one subject I want to broach, because it means so much to a great number of people, and that is the question of the Ugly Australians — the image that has grown over the past few tours. A considerable recovery was needed on this tour, as I saw it, to restore Australia's proud name. Manners on the field, behaviour off it

— you know what I mean, don't you? I'm not speaking as a puritan.

GC: I think we were conscious of this when we went to New Zealand. We had much the same sort of inexperienced make-up as on this tour. Australian cricketers had had a good deal of criticism in recent years, some of it perhaps deserved, some of it not deserved. These things snowball. In New Zealand we were practising on one of the grounds where no nets were available. Gary Gilmour needed some special bowling practice, and we had him bowling to Rick McCosker, standing back with a baseball glove to take the deliveries. A couple took off and Rick couldn't get a glove to them. They hit the sightscreen, which was pretty ancient, and a few bits of it fell off. So the papers said that the Ugly Australians were at it again!

As a young side, it seemed to me important that we shouldn't receive too much criticism off the field that would affect us on the field. We really did put in a lot of hard work on that tour, and we're trying to carry it through on this tour, but it's a lot harder, because we stayed together as a group in New Zealand. Here, there are always three or four players not involved in a match, and it is a long tour.

When you're winning a lot of matches it's easier to shrug off criticism, but right now we need to be careful about our image. We used to be able to say to Hell with it, as long as we're winning matches on the field.

On this tour, with all the wet weather around in the early stages, I thought it was marvellous the way the blokes maintained morale. We were all frustrated at the small amount of cricket we were able to play, but we kept together, we played football, we kept on training, varying it. It could very easily have been a rough period.

Every tour I've been on has a mid-tour slump, when morale dips a little, and I think this time it coincided with this Test match. Perhaps we went into it not quite as determined to get our heads down as at Lord's, where we'd had so much interruption to our preparation.

DF: It's been suggested that the Packer business has had a disturbing effect on some of the players, particularly the younger ones?

GC: I don't accept that. I think it's an easy target to choose. It reminds me of 1972, when we lost the first Test match here after a slow start to the tour because of the weather. You could feel the atmosphere go dead. We're in trouble now, we thought. We're a young side, inexperienced, just lost the first Test. What hope have we got? Well, everybody picked up and fought back. We had a terrific win at Lord's. Everybody got out there and applied themselves. That's the only thing we didn't do here at Manchester during the past five days. I would hope — and expect — that we'll do the same as we did five years ago — come back fighting.

DF: Has the presence of some of the players' wives had any effect, do you think? What do you think of the principle of allowing wives on tour?

GC: It's a pretty contentious issue and I'm not quite sure whether it's a good or bad thing. My wife realises that while I'd love her to be here in one way, the cricket is the most important thing. I'm here to play cricket, and particularly as captain I have so many commitments that I would see very little of her. You'd have the worry on your mind of thinking "I should be there, but I'm not there." It would affect me, I know.

No, whatever's missing at the moment I can't pinpoint it. It's not the Packer business. Perhaps team spirit does need lifting. As I said, my hope is that we'll come back fighting at Trent Bridge.

SECOND TEST MATCH *Old Trafford, July 7, 8, 9, 11, 12*

Paying attendance 44,918; takings £98,611

AUSTRALIA

			min	6	4			min	6	4
R. B. McCosker	c Old b Willis	2	20	—	—	c Underwood b Willis	0	2	—	—
I. C. Davis	c Knott b Old	34	144	—	5	c Lever b Willis	12	46	—	1
*G. S. Chappell	c Knott b Greig	44	95	—	7	b Underwood	112	282	1	15
C. S. Serjeant	lbw b Lever	14	80	—	1	c Woolmer b Underwood	8	33	—	2
K. D. Walters	c Greig b Miller	88	205	—	15	lbw b Greig	10	22	—	1
D. W. Hookes	c Knott b Lever	5	24	—	1	c Brearley b Miller	28	81	—	3
+R. W. Marsh	c Amiss b Miller	36	115	—	6	c Randall b Underwood	1	6	—	—
R. J. Bright	c Greig b Lever	12	75	—	2	c & b Underwood	0	2	—	—
K. J. O'Keeffe	c Knott b Willis	12	57	—	1	not out	24	124	—	3
M. H. N. Walker	b Underwood	9	33	—	1	c Greig b Underwood	6	19	—	1
J. R. Thomson	not out	14	27	—	2	c Randall b Underwood	1	13	—	—
Extras	(lb15, nb 12)	27				(lb1, w1, nb14)	16			
		297					**218**			

Fall: 4, 80, 96, 125, 140, 238, 246, 272, 272

0, 30, 74, 92, 146, 147, 147, 202, 212

Bowling: Willis 21-8-45-2, Lever 25-8-60-3,
Old 20-3-57-1, Underwood 20.2-7-53-1,
Greig 13-4-37-1, Miller 10-3-18-2.

Willis 16-2-56-2, Lever 4-1-11-0,
Underwood 32.5-13-66-6, Old 8-1-26-0,
Greig 12-6-19-1, Miller 9-2-24-1.

ENGLAND

			min	6	4			min	6	4
D. L. Amiss	c Chappell b Walker	11	47	—	1	not out	28	107	—	4
*J. M. Brearley	c Chappell b Thomson	6	42	—	1	c Walters b O'Keeffe	44	101	—	7
R. A. Woolmer	c Davis b O'Keeffe	137	389	—	22	not out	0	5	—	—
D. W. Randall	lbw b Bright	79	166	—	12+					
A. W. Greig	c & b Walker	76	244	1	11					
+A. P. E. Knott	c O'Keeffe b Thomson	39	110	—	7					
G. Miller	c Marsh b Thomson	6	40	—	—					
C. M. Old	c Marsh b Walker	37	115	—	5					
J. K. Lever	b Bright	10	30	—	1					
D. L. Underwood	b Bright	10	53	—	2					
R. G. D. Willis	not out	1	11	—	—					
Extras	(b9, lb9, nb7)	25				(lb3, nb7)	10			
		437	+ and one 5			1 wkt	**82**			

Fall: 19, 23, 165, 325, 348, 366, 377, 404, 435

75

Bowling: Thomson 38-11-73-3, Walker 54-15-131-3,
Bright 35.1-12-69-3, O'Keeffe 36-11-114-1,
Chappell 6-1-25-0.

Thomson 8-2-24-0, Walker 7-0-17-0,
O'Keeffe 9.1-4-25-1, Bright 5-2-6-0.

Umpires: W. E. Alley and T. W. Spencer

Toss won by Australia

ENGLAND WON BY 9 WICKETS

5. DISSENSIONS IN THE CAMP

Greg Chappell writes:

We had three spare days after the second Test, and a number of the players went down to London to do some shopping and to have a break. After the Test loss, some of the Pressmen seemed to think that this was a strange thing to do, but I felt it was in the interests of the boys to have a complete break away from cricket. The players with wives accompanying them stayed around Manchester, where those who had played in the leagues had friends locally or spent some time with other Australians playing in the leagues. While some of us went over to Leeds to select suits from a clothing factory, Rod Marsh went off to do some work for a brewery firm, and others went on a coach tour of the Lake District or played golf.

The BBC cameras should have been at Delamere Forest when Doug Walters and I had a great battle against each other which had all the ferocity of the recent Tom Watson-Jack Nicklaus battle in the British Open. Playing off 20, Doug won the first; we halved the second when I chipped one in from 20 yards off the green, and, playing off 17, I levelled at the third. The lead seesawed until the 17th, where I led by one hole. Here I hooked, but recovered with the second shot, though I was in rough close to the green; Doug had hit a beauty but hooked his second, also into a difficult lie. From there I was able to win that hole, and the match. We did a double-or-nothing on the 18th, and I managed to win that too, to make quite a good day of it.

The following day Doug, Richie Robinson and Australian journalist Brian Mossop and I played tennis, just for a change. It was another enjoyable afternoon, and from there we travelled down to Northampton for the match against the 1976 Gillette Cup-winners.

Again I called "tails" and won the toss, and Rick McCosker and Ian Davis got us away to a good start. I was pleased with the way I was striking the ball in an innings of 161 not out; Kim Hughes, who had been pushing for a Test place, unfortunately failed and Gary Cosier holed out on the boundary, but David Hookes made quite a good fifty, and we declared with an hour to go. Unfortunately we didn't manage

Woes forgotten at Northampton as Ray Bright (centre) dresses up as Northants and Indian spin bowler Bishan Bedi, complete with coloured patka. The Australian players are: back — Mick Malone, David Hookes, Gary Cosier, Ian Davis, Ray Bright, Greg Chappell, Len Pascoe; front — Craig Serjeant, Rick McCosker, Geoff Dymock, Kim Hughes. (Picture by Bob Thomas)

to take a wicket that evening, and as the match ran its course to a draw, the bonuses for us were a fine display by Len Pascoe, who took 6 for 68, and useful match practice for Ian Davis, Gary Cosier, David Hookes and Rick McCosker.

We remained concerned at the general pattern of the tour, now that a Test match had been lost, and among the significant points made was one by Rod Marsh, who suggested that the younger players in the team had grown up during years when Australia reigned supreme. This may just have led to a sub-conscious belief that you only had to walk onto the field with a green cap on your head to make things happen, without needing to work too hard at it. Perhaps there was a lot of truth in this. The great days were, temporarily, behind us, and we needed to work much harder to win Test matches.

The effect of the Packer business was also brought up. A Melbourne writer had gone off the deep end, suggesting that half the signatories wanted ''out'' because they realised they were signed up with a company with only a two-dollar capital. A lot of stories circulating in Australia had been started by administrators. This was disturbing, because Len Maddocks, our manager, had asked us all to maintain silence over the matter, and we had complied. This was not going to stop newspapermen snooping about, asking questions, and the answers were not always coming from the players direct.

If our morale was being eroded by anything, it was the poor accommodation. In this, the Australian Board of Control, perhaps trying to cut costs to offset the increased payment we were receiving for the tour, have done us a disservice. Going without showers, with only old-fashioned baths available, for a long period is something we were not glad to put up with. Facilities were much better on previous tours, and we were surprised and very unhappy about some of the antiquated conditions.

For the Warwickshire match I took a game off and Rod Marsh led the side in what turned out to be a hectic three days. We were starting to show a bit of form: Richie Robinson made 70 and 137, both not-out, and Rick McCosker, given a chance to re-establish himself, made 77 in the first innings. We didn't want to alter the side unduly, and Rick's runs were timely and welcome. I had spoken to Craig Serjeant at Northampton about the prospect of opening the innings in a Test match, and he was not over-happy at the thought. He had played most of his cricket batting down the order, and said he would certainly open if we thought it was in the best interests of the team. I favoured recognised openers doing the job if it was at all possible. The side for the third Test was beginning to select itself. Richie Robinson's success in the Warwickshire match, bearing in mind his experience, attacking methods, and fielding skill in the bat-pad position in the Lord's Test, gave him a strong case, and the recent lack of success for Kim Hughes, Craig Serjeant, and Gary Cosier argued against their inclusion.

We had probably wasted the opportunities of winning a few of the matches against the counties in our efforts to give chances to all our batsmen and bowlers, but the victory over Warwickshire came as a tonic. Now that the weather had settled down, and almost all the players were getting their chances, winning became more important.

During the match at Edgbaston the need for a team meeting arose. It was about time we had such a get-together, but what made it a pressing necessity was an incident off the field. Len Maddocks took

Geoff Dymock and Mick Malone along to Rohan Kanhai's champagne breakfast, and the team also dropped in on the way to the ground. Len had given Geoff permission to skip 12th or 13th man duties that day since it was his birthday. Instead he could do PR work with Len, visiting the sponsors' tents and boxes and so on. Unfortunately Mick stayed with Len and Geoff, not one of them realising that he should have been with the team as emergency fieldsman. In due course a substitute was needed when Jeff Thomson had to leave the field, and Rod Marsh was furious when one wasn't available. With Geoff and Mick in one of the sponsors' bars with the manager, it looked bad from the team discipline point of view, even though the situation had occurred purely through innocent oversight.

That night, back at the hotel, Rod Marsh was very upset, and, with Doug Walters, we decided it was time for a reappraisal of some aspects of the tour. We put it to Len Maddocks that while we realised he meant well in having fairly lenient charge of the team, it was not in the best interests with a young and relatively inexperienced group. A firmer hand was needed. Len accepted this.

I mentioned also that we were unhappy at some of the stories that were coming out concerning the Packer affair — emanating from the management. We had agreed some time ago that this was something that ought not to be discussed while we were expected to devote all our time and energies to making a success of this tour. Len accepted this too.

It was agreed to call the team meeting at Leicester, where we were due to play our next match.

Len had a criticism to offer: that it was probably not in the best interests for Rod Marsh and me to have matches off at the same time. We saw his point, though in our attempts to give everyone as much cricket as possible we had sometimes found this, in our opinion, unavoidable. We did decide now, for one thing, that players not engaged in a match would stay with the team rather than go their own way. We would travel together and train together as we had done in New Zealand.

The meeting developed into an open forum, with all the players able to have their say. Len Pascoe said he thought it was more important that we should win matches rather than give everybody match practice. Many agreed with him, feeling that victories improved morale. Some of the younger players felt that some of the seniors were not concentrating sufficiently in the county games, though here it needs to be understood that when you know you are playing in all the Test matches you can't keep up 100-per-cent concentration all the time when you're away from the big matches.

Rod Marsh, backed by Doug Walters, made the point that it was up to the younger men to motivate themselves. The senior players were always there to give advice on technical matters, but the motivation came from within. There was competition for places in the Test side, and motivation ought not to have to be drummed up artificially.

As the healthy exchange of views went on I stressed that the only way we could answer the criticism that had been coming our way was to improve our performance. It was as simple as that. We had to find extra effort.

I think a lot of good came out of the meeting. Several players wanted to ask questions relating to the Packer series, but I felt this was not the time to go into it. It was best left till the end of the tour.

Apparently one writer was hanging around outside the room where we had the meeting, and picked up stray remarks, because a story went back to Melbourne to the effect that there had been confrontation between Rod Marsh and Len Maddocks, just as there allegedly had been earlier between the manager and Max Walker. This was absolute rubbish. Max had not even attended the earlier meeting in Birmingham, and the discussion between Rod and Len here at Leicester came after Len had said that everybody was deserving of some criticism for occasional lack of effort, to which Rod had retorted that he didn't want to hear anybody criticising my performances on the tour because he felt I'd done more than my share. He declared that he'd punch anybody on the nose who said otherwise! That's as far as it got.

After this amicable meeting a different atmosphere could be sensed. Everybody was keen to get down to the ground early. We were there at nine o'clock — 2½ hours before the start — doing loosening exercises and playing in the nets, Leicestershire being one of the few counties where we had access to really good practice wickets at the start of each day.

There was a little bit of green in the wicket, and Ray Illingworth put us in to bat. We made only 229, and I made nought, which was not entirely a bad thing, because it put some pressure on the other batsmen, and we had a couple of good stands. David Hookes, Ray Bright, and Gary Cosier all made a few, and when we had bowled Leicestershire out for only 178 we saw an opportunity to go on to win another game. But weather interfered and spoilt what could have been an interesting finish. At least we all came away with all-purpose knife gadgets presented to us by Bostik, who have sponsored the last two or three Australian matches at Leicester.

Just before the Trent Bridge Test match eight of us took part in a golf event for Ray Illingworth's benefit fund, and a very enjoyable day finished quite Australian in flavour, for Kim Hughes won the Stableford singles and team prize, Richie Robinson finished second, and I was third. There was quite a large crowd, and Ray will have done well out of it. We went to Nottingham that night, practised on the Wednesday morning, and had a fright when one ball took off from a length and struck Ian Davis over the right eye. The doctor put one stitch in it, observing that the injury could have taken more stitches but that this would have affected his vision. Rick McCosker was then hit on the lip during fielding practice! Fortunately both these injuries were minor, and our opening pair were fit to play.

Most of us went that afternoon to the Viyella factory, where we were presented with some shirts and given the opportunity to buy cloth and garments at favourable rates. Then that evening we had a very constructive team meeting, going through the whole of the England side, discussing individual tactics. We had to bounce back from here, and we planned to go for a win from the start. We simply could not afford to put in a bad game at this point.

The lighthearted touch came after dinner, when Rod Marsh and Gary Cosier rendered a medley of songs to which they had adapted words of their own concerning every member, playing and non-playing, of the touring party.

News of the International Cricket Conference ban on "Packer players" in Test cricket had been delivered to me by a BBC reporter. I had no immediate comment to make. My first reaction was that it could have been worse. The ICC had not gone so far as to threaten a *life* ban. A day later, after the team dinner, Jeff Thomson came to me and told me that Radio Station 4IP's representative had put it to him that if he played for Kerry Packer his contract with 4IP would be affected. The advisor, Frank Gardiner, and Jeff's manager, David Lord, had asked for an immediate decision, so Jeff was not so much seeking advice as keeping me abreast of developments. He had signed for 4IP some time before signing his Packer contract, and he could not afford to lose the former. Within half an hour of Jeff's leaving my room the decision had been made, Gardiner had told the Pressmen, and I was being pressed for comment. By then I was quite fed up with the phone calls that had been coming in at all hours following the ICC statement. It was just what we didn't want on the eve of a Test match. I had told the hotel desk that I wanted no phone calls after 11.30 pm, yet I got four more up to 2.30 am. Each time the mind was set working and sleep was harder to find. The following night I left strict instructions for no calls between midnight and 8 am. This time I was left in peace.

I normally take little notice of newspaper reports, but just prior to the third Test my attention was drawn to a couple of reports suggesting that Craig Serjeant had been omitted in favour of a Packer ''rebel'', Richie Robinson. I think people who know Rod, Doug and myself would know that accusations of favouritism would be false. I lost some respect for one or two writers who ought to have known better.

Meanwhile, David Lord was holding court at every opportunity, telling the world how he had looked after Jeff Thomson's interests. During the Test match we saw him on television in our dressing-room, and one of the lads turned up the volume. ''Thommo'' listened for a while before crying out: ''Turn that rubbish off'' . . . or something similar. ''Why don't you tell the truth!'' he said. Lord professed to be passing on Jeff's feelings on the matter, but Jeff, governed by his tour contract, could say nothing publicly to explain that he had simply made a choice based on financial considerations — not moral grounds.

Those who thought there was a sinister meaning in Craig Serjeant's omission now presumably expected we would drop Jeff Thomson for, say, Mick Malone for the fourth Test. I should explain that I spoke to Craig when the team was chosen, and mentioned that we had to go for current form and experience in this crucial Test. Earlier in the tour he had seemed to throw away a few innings after a couple of hours at the crease. Now his form had deserted him. It was something for this exceptionally promising young batsman to think over.

6. THIRD TEST MATCH

TRENT BRIDGE, NOTTINGHAM, JULY 28, 29, 30, AUGUST 1, 2

David Frith writes:

FIRST DAY

The Packer drama went from act to act, and we were not spared further developments even when the third Test, with all its inviting prospects, was about to get under way. On the afternoon before, Australia's side was announced, and surprisingly revealed that Serjeant had been dropped in favour of Robinson. This made it an ''all-Packer'' side — until the next day, when news broke of Jeff Thomson's intended withdrawal from the Packer series because it endangered his contract with radio station 4IP in Brisbane, worth some £45,000 per annum. And, we were led to believe, there were more changes of heart to come from among the fifty or so signatories.

Now for the inviting prospects: there was Geoff Boycott back in the England side after three years of self-imposed exile, and there was a probable Test debut for Ian Botham, the strong 21-year-old Somerset player who had been making runs and taking wickets with his medium-pacers at a greater all-round rate than anyone else in the country. Graham Roope was recalled to the twelve, having played his last Test against Australia at The Oval in 1975, making 0 and 77, and Mike Hendrick, Derbyshire's sharp medium-pacer, replaced Chris Old, who had an injured shoulder.

Boycott's selection naturally overshadowed all else. Since he declared himself unavailable for England after failures against India in 1974, for the reasons that strain had built up to an almost intolerable level and he was keen to give his all to Yorkshire, the national side had suffered grievously at the hands of Australia's fast bowlers in 1974-75 (when Boycott had allowed himself to be chosen for the tour and then withdrew) and the West Indians in 1976. Among the reactions worth listening to would have been those of some of the England batsmen who had weathered the fire and fury during this time. My own view was that if Boycott was worth a place in the England XI — and I am pretty sure that he was — then he had to be chosen, and history would take care of the rest: cricket-followers, and their successors, would never forget Boycott's Garbo act. Now, at 36, he was about to show us how much stern international cricket was left in him.

Dennis Amiss made way for him, and Hendrick replaced John Lever, who had seemed jaded after his long and arduous winter tour. It was made clear by Alec Bedser, chairman of selectors, that the Essex left-arm bowler needed to be rested, and it was implied that he would be called up by England before too many more Tests had passed. The fourth new name, Roope, was made 12th man. England, therefore, had made three changes from their winning team, one of them forced by injury. Bright was Australia's 12th man.

It was warm as England took the field, Chappell having won his second successive Test toss, and the fluffy white clouds looked better through sunglasses. After all, then, we had McCosker and Davis opening the innings again, as at Manchester, after which it had seemed certain that Australia would have to try yet another opening pair. Willis chugged in from the Radcliffe Road end, and dealt McCosker a bouncer fifth ball which was enthusiastically clapped, though surely a fairly slender proportion of today's Nottingham crowd could have seen Larwood and Voce in action — a sight to spark a lifelong relish for the hostile delivery. Willis did it again next ball, and McCosker hooked it square for four.

Hendrick bowled from the pavilion end, and soon Botham was getting his first touch in a Test match, fielding smartly at gully off Davis. Some pleasant strokes were finding fieldsmen, but, after taking a blow in the stomach from Hendrick's bowling, which caused a slight delay, Davis began to pick up Willis, driving him straight, through the bowler's hands, for two, then easily to the midwicket boundary. An off-drive off the same bowler brought him three, but Willis was almost presented with a catch at third slip when Davis edged Hendrick, who, as usual, was moving the ball about. After 10 overs 24 runs had been made.

Ian Botham was now called up in place of Willis for his first Test match bowl, the senior man having taken none for 19 off five, and McCosker edged his second ball just wide of Greig at second slip, taking two more legitimate boundaries in Botham's next over, when he twice turned him through square leg, to reach 22 out of 38.

Davis asserted his presence with a bold pull over square leg for six off Hendrick, a surprising stroke in one so slight of stature and so early in the game. When Greig came on for Hendrick, Davis pulled a long-hop for four and played the next off his body for two to put up the fifty in the 16th over, after only an hour's play. A back-foot drive for two meant eight off the over, and time for drinks, with the general opinion being that the pitch had perhaps nearer 2000 than 1000 runs to offer before the final evening.

Boycott drew applause when he ran hard around the long-leg boundary and saved a McCosker glance from going for four. But the batsman was enjoying Botham's bowling, and pulled him for a smooth four once, twice, and yet again. When the bowler was taken off after six overs all 26 runs conceded by him had been scored by McCosker, reminding some of Serjeant's peculiar domination of John Birch on this ground, when he took all 55 runs off his bowling in the Notts match.

Underwood came on for the 23rd over of the innings and bowled a maiden — nothing unusual for him — and McCosker took three from a stroke to square leg, where Botham saved a run, off Greig. Davis then played an attractive shot off him: a pull, with plenty of right shoulder, but hit later, so that the ball sped off to the long-on boundary. When McCosker cover-drove an Underwood no-ball for four, things were looking promising for Australia, though the reality was that Ladbrokes had already closed their books on a draw.

A rare fielding error by Randall at cover let Davis through for a single, and, fatefully, he met his end against Underwood, driving a half-volley at comfortable catching height to Botham at mid-on. It was ten-past-one, and Australia's first loss came at 79.

Underwood appealed when Greg Chappell padded away his third ball, but a square-cut sent the next to the boundary and the Australian captain was on his way again. Hendrick came back for a second spell, Greig having bowled six tidy fast-medium overs for 17.

McCosker went to his half-century — one that was indescribably welcome to him and his supporters — with an extra-cover drive off Hendrick that seemed a certain four until a sliding Randall hooked a boot around the ball a yard from the rope. They ran three, and with a single to Chappell Australia took lunch at 94 for one off 32 overs. This, of all the Tests, had every feel of being a batsman's benefit.

Yet the feel was soon transfigured. In 23 minutes after lunch McCosker added nothing to his score and was then caught at slip as Hendrick found the edge. Brearley held the ball easily low and between his spread feet. Greg Chappell had begun the afternoon with a thunderous-sounding off-drive off Hendrick for four to raise the hundred in the 34th over, but an intense period followed, one in which

The Australian selectors' faith in Rick McCosker after his fearsome injury in the Centenary Test, and subsequent nightmare run of low scores, paid handsome dividends in this Test. He top-scored in both innings with 51 and 107

Underwood and Hendrick commanded the utmost respect. The English grip was maintained even when the free-stroking Hookes joined his unflappable captain.

Chappell passed 1000 runs on the tour when he played Willis through midwicket off the front foot for four, and Hookes, aware of an extra slips fieldsman, worked the ball away for twos either side of the wicket. Willis needed watching. His pace was brisk and he managed a high bounce, especially when he gave a short one to Hookes off something less than 22 yards, the no-ball penalty meaning considerably less to England than Hookes's discomfort as he got his chin out of the way and fell over backwards towards short leg. This followed a ball which had beaten him and Knott to go for four byes, and which must have made Harold Larwood's eyes light up in the guests' enclosure.

Chappell was not getting the ball away, and resembled the Manchester batsman only in stance; but Hookes was always looking for runs, and played a lovely extra-cover drive off Willis for four, following it with a two in the same area, and later an almighty swing at a Willis bouncer that produced two runs into the vacant square-leg outfield. When drinks were taken Australia were poised on 131 for 2, Chappell 19, Hookes 17; after the refreshment the poise, such as it was, was completely shattered.

Botham replaced Hendrick at the pavilion end, and his first ball, close to a length but just wide of off stump, found its way into Chappell's stumps via the inside edge, and Australia's key wicket — perhaps better described as lock, key, and hinges too — had been flattened. Chappell had batted for almost an hour and a half for his 19, which included three boundaries.

So there it was — the gate open, an absurd situation with only three wickets down, but such was the mood. Walters shuffled to the crease and was greeted by a bouncer, not a ball one normally associates with a bowler of Ian Botham's mien. But then perhaps a remark Brian Close made to me three years ago has had, after all, an echo of some veracity: "I'm going to make this lad into a fast bowler." This after Botham had just won a sensational Benson & Hedges Cup quarter-final with his bold bat after being felled by Andy Roberts. He was 18 at the time. It was odd that on this day, as Botham performed so well on his Test debut, Close, aged 46 and in his 29th season, announced his impending retirement. For some it might have been the biggest shock on a day of shocks.

The first ball of Willis's next over was bowled across Hookes, and flew from the edge to Hendrick at third slip, where the fielder made a magnificent full-length dive to hold the catch. This brought in Robinson, who came straight to grips with the sudden crisis by running across to his first ball, from Willis, and belting it to the cover boundary. Soon he was putting Botham away to the same position at the other end, and Walters, nowhere near as frenetically, pushed Willis through point for four.

Greig replaced Willis, and gave Walters a mischievous bouncer, but a broadshouldered hit through point for two brought up 150.

Underwood, not wishing to be seen behind Randall in athletic prowess, tumbled over to save a boundary on the long-leg rope,

Robinson getting three, but Botham now chimed in with his second wicket, forcing an edge from Walters, playing away from his body, Hendrick taking the catch almost casually an inch above the turf. Australia were now half out for 153, and this became a fatal figure for some time. Robinson fell at it, swishing at Greig and being taken two-handed and high by Brearley at slip. Then Marsh, in his 50th Test match, having lived on the edge of his bat, was lbw playing crookedly to Botham, who, two runs later, added Walker's wicket when the big man gave Hendrick the easiest of his three catches in the slips cordon. Thus Ian Botham had taken 4 for 13 in this spell, and had stamped his name irrevocably upon this England-Australia Test.

Jeff Thomson came in, nonchalantly. He might almost have been whistling, like a schoolboy. The crowd gave him, it seemed, an extra welcome, probably in recognition of his decision not to play for Kerry Packer. One journalist with binoculars reckoned he was blushing. He opened his score with four off Botham to an unpatrolled third-man boundary.

Just before tea O'Keeffe pulled a Greig no-ball for four, and they all trooped off at 166 for 8, Australia having lost seven wickets while 72 runs were added in 29 overs. It was one of England's most successful sessions ever against Australia on an undamaged pitch.

The cascade of wickets slowed after tea, and Australia owed much to O'Keeffe's resolution. He waited for the loose ball and invariably scored from it, and played the rest with feet spread and bat straight. While Thomson was watchful, O'Keeffe first gained a fluky four when he tried to withdraw his bat, sending the ball scudding through slips, then square-drove nicely for four.

Thomson was not idle. He lofted a two and smashed Botham straight back for four, stinging his hand on the way through. When Hendrick had his first bowl from the Radcliffe Road end the fast bowler ran him through gully for four, then edged him just in front of Greig. A big full-toss to Thomson met with a scowl from the batsman — and the best retort of all, a thumping hit high to midwicket which landed no more than a foot from the boundary rope.

O'Keeffe got only two from a steer through point when Randall, with a flick back, and Miller, with the throw, combined to save runs, and after Underwood had come on at Hendrick's end Botham, sticking to his task, gained his fifth wicket when Thomson's cross-bat drive edged the ball to Knott. Just after five o'clock Her Majesty the Queen arrived at the ground, late because of congestion in the streets,

Coming into the England side in place of the injured Chris Old, 21-year-old Ian Botham grabbed the opportunity with 5 for 74 in Australia's first innings, some useful runs and a catch

wearing turquoise and perhaps regretting having missed out on the fun of the day's second session.

O'Keeffe raised 200 with a single to third man off Botham, the last ball of the 70th over, and soon his big drive at Underwood was flying just wide of Brearley at slip and going for four. If it had been straighter Brearley might have needed his crash-helmet.

Pascoe was now beginning to do himself proud, and was obviously not the worst number 11 to have played for Australia. Twice he sliced Botham along the ground for four to third man, and when the return of Willis failed to break the last-wicket stand it was clear that the Queen should not be kept waiting, and the players broke off at 5.27 pm, when the score stood at 220 for 9, O'Keeffe 35, Pascoe 10.

Amazingly, it was time for the old joke again: When Boycott is introduced to the Queen, who will bow to whom? Certainly Her Majesty exchanged pleasantries with the new boy, Ian Botham, who can surely have had no more memorable day in his life. He was asked if he had been working hard: his flushed face would have indicated so. At the end of the day he told reporters that this wife Kathryn was eight months pregnant, and after his performance he was hoping she remained so.

Botham was relieved at last after a spell of 14 overs, broken only by the tea interval, in which he took 5 for 48, but Greig found no success and Pascoe surprised by driving Willis straight and then just wide for successive fours. Hendrick came close to his fourth catch when O'Keeffe edged Greig for two, but attention now turned to the umpires as the worsening light impelled them to debate it. They carried on, and after Hendrick had been called back into the attack, and Greig had conceded four to O'Keeffe through the covers, leaving the fair-haired all-rounder two from his half-century, Hendrick found the edge as Pascoe aimed a drive and Greig did the rest.

Australia all out 243, a modest score on a hard pitch, but appreciably better than had seemed likely. The last two wickets put on 88 runs.

Now came the moment we had all been waiting for, as the showman with the megaphone would have put it: Geoff Boycott's return to the batting crease. It was delayed just a few moments by Brearley's taking of the strike against Thomson. The captain killed the first ball, a brutal riser, and played the next to point. Boycott's call of "No!" swept across the field. The over ended, and Pascoe purred in to Boycott. He turned him to leg and set off for a run, to the protracted and joyous cheering of the audience. The nasty bouncer that was expected went instead to Brearley, who finished on the seat of his pants.

The over was a long one, with three no-balls, three runs to Brearley, and no shortage of electric tension in the air; but there was still time for another, and though one from Thomson thudded into Marsh's upstretched gloves, there were no casualties, and the crowd dispersed with a satisfied look on its collective face.

Australia 243 (R. B. McCosker 51, K. J. O'Keeffe 48 not out, I. C. Davis 33, I. T. Botham 5 for 74); *England* 9 for 0.

SECOND DAY

The England openers had some fast and lively stuff to contend with on the Friday morning, beginning with the first ball, from Pascoe, a no-ball to Boycott which suggested that the bowler had already done his warming-up. It reminded me of the old Ted McDonald story, when a South African batsman asked Australian captain Herbie Collins if McDonald was as fast as he was made out to be, and was told, "He's quick all right, but he needs a few warm-up overs first." The Springbok had his bat splintered and his stumps shattered by "Mac's" second ball, the bowler having for once got loose with an over or two behind the pavilion.

The first hour was torrid for both batsmen, and when drinks were taken at 12.35 the score had advanced to 31, Boycott seven, Brearley 14, after 80 minutes' batting. Not that the run rate mattered. A large service to England had been performed against the hostility of Thomson, Walker and Pascoe, with frequent no-balls aiding the cause. There were three in Pascoe's opening over, which also included three bouncers. Thomson replaced him, while Walker operated from the pavilion end, Brearley working him for three to third man, and Boycott played at and missed his first ball. A period of five maidens was broken when Boycott made his first runs of the day, after half an hour, by turning Walker for two. When he played him down into his crease an involuntary, loud, agonised noise sprang from Walker's throat.

Thomson bounced one at Brearley, then removed his sweater, and Brearley took two runs square. Pascoe took over at that end, having bowled only the opening over of the morning.

There was an animated murmur as, in setting off for a hasty second run, Boycott dropped his bat; he had to walk back three-quarters of the length of the pitch to retrieve it.

Chappell now bowled from the pavilion end, and Boycott took two through gully, where a diving O'Keeffe failed to get to a near-impossible catch. Then, at a quarter to one, the first wicket fell. Pascoe bowled one off-stumpish and Brearley, off the back foot, played strongly to gully, where Hookes clung to a stinging catch to his left — natural — hand. It was an over of some sensation, for Woolmer, England's batsman of the series so far, survived only three balls. The third whacked his pads, and after some moments' thought, Dicky Bird raised his index finger, a time-honoured gesture to make batsmen shudder, and, on this occasion, to cause England to pause for nervous reflection.

We were entering up the details, England 34 for 2, Boycott now nine, Pascoe 2 for 7 off six overs — when a huge cheer caused a raising of heads: Randall, the local hero, was trotting through the gate and out across the field. Chappell, when he reached the other end, bowled him a high bouncer second ball and shouted loudly for lbw to the next.

The first boundary of the innings came at last when Randall tried to help a ball from Pascoe down the leg side, and spooned it. Marsh dived desperately after scuttling after it, but his goalkeeper dive was in vain. It was ''in the net'' for four runs fine. Hearts leapt again as Boycott was dropped by Hookes at gully, diving forward for the ball as it lobbed off the bat's shoulder. It would have been a devastating breakthrough.

Chappell bowled a curious mixture now. A slow full-toss was let off by Randall, but the next ball, a long-hop, was swung away for four to raise 50 in 25 overs. Walker replaced his captain.

There now occurred an incident which stunned Trent Bridge into shocked, sickened silence. Randall had caught Boycott on 13 with a two through point, and with Thomson, having come on for Pascoe (9-4-15-2), bowling from the Radcliffe Road end, Boycott, whose form between wickets had occasionally been erratic enough to remind everyone of his notorious reputation in this department, played a ball towards mid-on and ran, even though Thomson was swiftly on his way across to intercept. He stopped it without gathering it, and still Boycott kept on running, with Randall in no position to assume a run was there. As Thomson picked up the ball, Boycott had just about completed the run, so Randall, with an astonishing willingness in the face of certain suicide, took off for the 'keeper's end. The ball reached it long before he did, and Marsh broke the wicket with violent relish. Boycott covered his face, distraught, as Randall shrugged his shoulders and sauntered off, looking back just once as he went. The hooting from some quarters had an unearthly sound about it.

Thus, Greig, as in many a Test innings past, came into a crisis at 52 for 3, but was soon cracking Thomson square for four and smoothly through the covers for another. ''No such thing as a crisis,'' old W.G. used to say, ''only the next ball.''

At lunch England were 61 for 3 off 31 overs, Boycott 14 (in 2¼ hours) and Greig eight.

The grim tempo continued. Under high but unbroken cloud, and with a chillness in the air, Thomson and Walker took up the attack, and the latter was soon howling an lbw appeal against Greig. Umpire Constant put another stone into his pocket, fooling some into believing he was going to give Greig out, and the batsman took a two to fine leg, Pascoe's ongoing throw turning it into a three. Then Greig's number

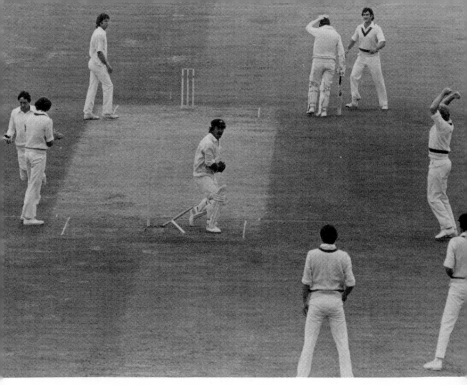

Long before Geoff Boycott settled into the groove towards his first-innings century, he ran out Trent Bridge hero Derek Randall. Hand-on-head in this picture, full realisation of what he has done hits him

did come up: Thomson brought one back to hit the top of the middle stump and remove it like a piece of bamboo in a gale: 64 for 4. Miller came in, having recently made a career-highest score of 86 not out — and taken 27 wickets in three matches. Chappell placed an extra short leg, forward.

Geoff Boycott had now been in for 2½ hours for 14, and one wondered how long it might be before the strain drove him out of Test cricket again. He moved to 15 at last with a single to fine leg, still never having shown a sign of panic or anxiety when many another might have exploded long ago. Miller, too, was very correct in his strokeplay, taking singles calmly. The next resounding cheer came when Boycott hit his first boundary, a square-cut off Thomson after 165 minutes. That, to emphasise the matter, is two hours and 45 minutes. Who is the patron saint of patience?

Pascoe struck the next blow. He dug one in, and Miller was utterly confounded. He started to play with an upright bat and then converted the shot into a pull. But he was never there, and the ball was scooped gently for Robinson to skip across and hold the catch. The young batsman had just edged Pascoe for four, but 13 became a fatal figure for him.

Knott was greeted by a bouncer and then an lbw shout as he played jumpily and missed. He opened his score with a four cut off Walker.

Some dropped catches mean more — much more — than others. To drop a Boycott is to let Napoleon off Elba, or to let Ronald Biggs over the wall. McCosker had the awful distinction of putting down a fairly straightforward chance at second slip, just to his right. The horror all round was clearly visible. Boycott, 20, put the suffering bowler, Pascoe, away to long leg for a quick two.

A memorable Walker over followed. Knott cut him violently for four, then three squarer, bringing up 102 in the 45th over; Boycott took one through a diving O'Keeffe at gully, Knott took one to midwicket, and Boycott finished off with a cover-drive that ended up among some small boys, with a policeman losing his helmet in the confusion. Thirteen off the over: Whoa, she's bolted!

Boycott now had another close shave, hooking Pascoe high towards Walker, who could not quite reach it. The bounce eluded him and they ran three, taking England to 112 for 5 as drinks were brought out, Boycott 32, sitting dejectedly alone, and Knott 17.

Chappell came on at the pavilion end and conceded three singles in exchange for a close leg-before shout. Then it was back with Len Pascoe, the day's spearhead bowler. Knott straight-drove him for three, and Boycott, with a deliberate "off glance" between slips and gullies, found the boundary, and found it again with a technically perfect square-drive to go to 44 out of 129. Thomson replaced Pascoe.

Knott's four to midwicket off Thomson's first ball, well up, brought up the fifty partnership, in 47 minutes, and the runs were starting to come, just as the sun broke through. The crowd did not bother to applaud ironically, as they often do, because the cricket was enthralling. Knott was sent back firmly by his partner when Hookes was quick to field a drive, and the same man saved four with a dive to his right immediately afterwards.

For the 55th over, spin was seen at last: O'Keeffe came on at the pavilion end, and Boycott was not seen to object: he cut the second ball to the rope to reach 52 (234 minutes, five fours) and cover-drove the last methodically also for four. In O'Keeffe's next he tickled him fine past Walker for yet another boundary, and was looking like his old self when Pascoe, having pounded down a lot of bouncers, let Boycott have one too many for umpire Bird's liking, and an official warning was issued. Bird informed his colleague, and the Australian captain. It gave the gathering yet more to discuss during the tea interval, at which point England had steadied to 163 for 5, Boycott 63, Knott 34.

The excitement continued immediately when Boycott narrowly beat a throw from Davis, but the sparks came from Knott: a superb cover-drive off Pascoe, a cut also for four to reach 53 (112 minutes), and to post the century stand, then a fast top-edge over Marsh's gloves and to the left of Chappell at slip for yet another boundary.

Boycott greeted Thomson's return with a two to midwicket off a full-toss, and Marsh was sent diving and leaping for the rest of the over, calling for a replacement pad at the end. When Knott inside-edged a four, Chappell slapped his thigh with his cap in frustration, not for the first time since lunch, and his face was a study when Mc-Cosker's throw from short third man was wide and careered through to the Hound Road stand to give Knott five for the gentlest of cuts. This brought up the 200, in the 73rd over, after 293 minutes, and a neck-and-neck race between the batsmen ensued. Boycott went to 72 with a perfect cover-drive off O'Keeffe through the off-side field of four; Knott reached 71 with an off-drive off Thomson and repeated the shot for three to pass Boycott's score. Boycott then regained the lead with a choice hook to the rope, and Thomson had conceded 11 in the over.

After two impudent cuts to the third-man boundary by Knott, O'Keeffe was rested, to spend his time instead making some brilliant saves in the gully. Thomson switched ends, Walker taking over from him at the Radcliffe Road end, and luring Boycott into a rare edged stroke: four to third man, and 81 runs to Knott's 83.

The 150 stand came as Knott played to mid-on, where Thomson at full-stretch flicked the ball across to Davis. Davis threw and hit the base of the middle stump at the 'keeper's end, but Boycott, whose departure was late, just made it. Then we saw Walters, coming on for his first bowl of the series, hoping for one of his lovely breakthroughs before the new ball became due. The only immediate trouble was caused Boycott by his contact lenses.

When Knott spooned Walker back over his head, the ball dropped between a converging Davis and Thomson, and the batsmen had 87 apiece. Just after six, the 85 overs had been bowled, England were 242 for 5, and with Pascoe peeling off his sweater, the umpires looked at the light — what there was left of it — and the batsmen agreed that they would be better off in the pavilion at this stage. They were not to come back.

Returning to Test cricket after his self-imposed exile of three years and 30 Tests, Geoff Boycott had it all to prove. His scores of 107 and 80 not out were the perfect answer

So the thrills of two men approaching centuries as the clock-hands moved down to six-thirty were aborted, but the day, all 5½ hours of it, was yet another to keep the attention riveted, to engross, to surprise, to frustrate.

Boycott said at the end of the day that he felt ''very humble'' at the amount of public support given him by way of letters, telegrams, and word of mouth. People had been ''embarrassingly nice'' to him. But the Randall run-out had distressed him greatly. He was not pretending. Poignantly he pointed out that he had not been responsible for a run-out for two or three years. He had chosen, it might be observed, an unfortunate time and place.

For the umpteenth time Alan Knott played an innings for England that pulled them out of a poor situation. His 135 was probably his best-ever Test innings and he provided Geoff Boycott with the support he needed

Australia 243; England 242 for 5 (G. Boycott 88 not out, A. P. E. Knott 87 not out, L. S. Pascoe 3 for 54).

THIRD DAY

On a beautiful morning, before another full house, Boycott and Knott headed towards their centuries. There was incident all the way. Boycott cut Pascoe's second ball juicily for four to go to 92 and put England ahead, and the new ball was taken. It was used waywardly. Thomson sprayed it: an offside wide, a legside wide, and soon another down the off side. Knott trotted along with a four guided wide of slip, and strokes in several directions for ones and twos, the most extraordinary a flick high over slip for a single, the ball bouncing no more than five yards inside the line. This took him to 96.

Now, to the acute anguish of every Australian, Boycott (92) was missed. An extra slip had been brought in, and the batsman edged Thomson between Hookes and Robinson, the deputy 'keeper seeming to get a touch with his left hand. They ran two.

Knott got into the pole position of 99 with a square-drive for two, cut off on the line, and Boycott moved to 97 with a back-foot cut for two, and 98 with a single off Thomson, who showed signs of settling down. The century race had all eyes facing the front.

Knott cut Thomson fine and raced off for the single that gave him his second century against Australia, and his fifth in Tests, and the race was over, with the winner applauded heartily. His innings had lasted 203 minutes so far, and he had found the boundary 12 times, plus a five. Denis Compton, now resplendent in braces and scratching away with his newspaper story, had made the last hundred for England against Australia at Trent Bridge, all of 29 years ago.

Pascoe bowled a maiden over, and then Boycott reached *his* century, off virtually Thomson's next ball. He cut him, made one, turned, and came back very fast to beat Walters' throw. It was his 13th Test hundred, his fourth against Australia, and the latest in the annals of great comeback innings. None, though, had ever had quite the drama of this, and Boycott was given a standing ovation as he held his bat aloft and shook his free hand towards the sky. He had been in for six hours 18 minutes, and stroked 11 fours. For English eyes the vision of 100 by each batsman's number was a gorgeous sight.

There was a delay when Marsh damaged a finger in trying to hold a high riser from Pascoe which went on for four byes, but Knott was soon putting the willow to use again, lifting Pascoe feet over slips for four and registering the 200 partnership, in 234 minutes. Drinks were taken, and then Thomson bowled from the Radcliffe Road end, the 15th over of the innings, and sent a monstrous full pitch past Marsh for four more byes. When Boycott took two through mid-off, the partnership reached 215, equalling the sixth-wicket record for England against Australia, set in 1938 at The Oval by Hutton and Hardstaff (when the score was taken from 555 to 770). This record, though, was not yet to be erased from the books, for Boycott's long innings now drew to a close. He edged Thomson to McCosker, who had not had the best of matches, or series, in the field, and might not have been wanting much to do with any further fielding activity. But this one stuck, and Geoffrey Boycott walked off after a memorable seven-hour innings, having saved England as of old, and his own vacillating reputation after the Randall run-out. At 287 for 6 England led by 44.

Botham, Thursday's hero, came in to face his first ball in Test cricket. His third was almost the last for the moment: Thomson found the edge and Chappell floored the catch. Soon someone would have to aggregate the catches spilt by Australia in the series; it was becoming noticeable.

Alan Knott now threw himself into his strokes: it might have been a limited-overs match. A square-drive brought up the 300, and after Botham had made his first Test run, Knott took 14 off a Thomson over — an off-drive for two to take him to 117, his highest in Tests, then a cut that sounded like the chopping down of a sapling. This four was followed by two others, a full-toss through square leg and an off-drive that bounced only twice before reaching the rope.

Botham mixed confident play with error, but survived, though hurt by a blow in the groin from Walker's bowling, and the last aggression of the morning came from a strong cut for four by Knott off Pascoe. At lunch, after 26 overs, England were 326 for 6, with Knott 135 and Botham three. The lead was 83.

It wasn't much of a lunch break for some, for David Lord, who had gravitated towards the centre of the Packer complications by virtue of his involvement as Jeff Thomson's manager, held a conference in the Press box to announce that he had persuaded Alvin Kallicharran to withdraw from the Packer deal. "Kalli" had been worried about the probability of a ban on his playing for West Indies, Guyana and Warwickshire, and had decided to return the advance cheque for £400 and to cancel his contract, which was to provide him with £16,000 for each of the next three years. Rumblings concerning Viv Richards had been heard, but for the moment he remained silent. Lord was also investigating the importance of UK work permits. The Dreyfus case and the Tichborne case were brief and uncomplicated by comparison.

"Knotty" did it again. Just as at Lord's in England's first innings, he hit the first ball after an interval into point's hands. This time the shot went in a gentle curve while Davis rushed in 25 yards from the boundary. Who was to argue that his chanceless 135, made in just on five hours, was not his best, as well as easily his highest Test innings?

The next ball almost made England 326 for 8, for Botham hit firmly to gully, where O'Keeffe could not accept the offer. A glanced four to Underwood and a driven three by Botham, and it was time to blush once more: Underwood edged Thomson and, with Marsh moving instinctively, Chappell missed the catch. It was the fourth to be put down off Thomson's bowling, and the sixth of the innings, three of them having benefited Boycott.

Botham began playing some rich strokes now, hoisting Thomson to the square-leg boundary then cutting deliciously, and turning his attention to Walker with a drive for two and an exquisite cover-drive for four.

Pascoe came back, perhaps just the man to finish off the innings, and Underwood's off stump was soon brutally dispatched. The end was nigh. Walker, having toiled through 38 overs with many an "Aaargh!", at last took his first wicket, Botham's, as he played cross-batted and nicked the ball into his stumps, after getting the feel of batting in a Test for just over an hour and a half. Hendrick was bowled in Walker's next over, aiming an ambitious drive and after 8¾ hours England's innings was over: 364, a lead of 121. It so happened that the match was exactly at the halfway point.

Australia now needed to muster every grain of resolution, and for a time things went reasonably well. Davis played a delightful cut followed by an off-drive, and McCosker eluded the gullies with a tuck for four. Willis then troubled Davis, hitting his glove as he swayed back from a lifter, the ball dropping short of the slips, and then finished him off altogether with an edge that Greig caught groin-high at second slip. It was only the seventh over, and first loss came at 18.

Greg Chappell came in to a familiar situation, except that two of the six pride-damaging fielding blemishes were his, albeit not costly. He was soon on his way with a head-high cover-drive wide of a leaping Randall, and a brisk hit, leaning back, brought him four more through point. Yet another boundary followed, through the gullies, and when Hendrick switched ends, Botham coming on, Chappell on-drove the Derbyshire man for four, a classical shot presaging a near squeak when Botham at cover just missed with his throw as Chappell, some distance out, got a single that, considering the danger, seemed hardly worth the try. Poise undisturbed, the captain took a couple more boundaries to reach 24 out of 49 by tea, having passed 4000 runs in Test cricket. Since he had been at the crease there was a tendency to forget who was at the other end.

The score advanced to 60, and then Australia suffered a body-blow.

Hendrick got one to dart back sharply, and it was too much for
Chappell's defensive stroke. England's glee was unconfined.

Now the calculations began. What odds the match finishing Monday?
What odds (extreme optimists/pessimists speaking) the match being
over tonight? They never said this in the days of Bradman's side . . . or
even Lawry's.

Hookes was soon off the mark, and after Botham had got one
through his defensive bat, he pushed for a few through mid-off. The
game went on in a deathly quietness, and the crowd did not overdo
their response even when McCosker pierced the covers for four and
pulled Hendrick for another to reach 30 out of 75 in the 23rd over.

Greig was called into the attack, and bowled a width, without
tempting, and Willis, back from Hendrick, beat McCosker and then
gave him a short one which he hooked quite unconvincingly, the ball
dropping between a sprinting Woolmer and Boycott. A handsome
square-drive by Hookes fetched only two after Underwood's boot
stopped it on the line, and when drinks came out on this sunlit evening
Australia were entrenched at 85 for 2. Underwood bowled from the
pavilion end, and Willis continued to pound them down from the
other. He tested Hookes with several short balls, with a man on the
square-leg boundary, and one particular ball which cut away to slips
had Knott diving to save, and would have been extremely awkward to
a right-hander.

After Hookes had swung Willis to square leg, where Woolmer
completely lost sight of it as it ran for four, it was noticed that Phil
Slocombe, the young Somerset player, was substituting in the field for
Greig. His team-mate Botham now came on at the Radcliffe Road end,
and beat McCosker with a good-length leg-cutter. He had paid tribute
to Tom Cartwright, who had coached him at Somerset, and it seemed
a good bet that he would play more than his mentor's five Test
matches by the time he was through.

Underwood went over the wicket to left-hander Hookes, and flighted
the ball teasingly, compelling some rather tentative forward pushes. A
slightly distracted crowd were forced to pay attention when Hookes
just got home for a single for McCosker as Randall's throw missed the
'keeper's stumps, another unnecessary risk ventured and salvaged. An
over in which Botham conceded seven, four of them to an elegant,
upright Hookes cut, enlivened matters, and a four by Hookes through
an obscure gap on the leg side from a shorter ball from Underwood was
pleasant to behold. The hundred came up in the 36th over, a two to

McCosker, who shortly afterwards padded up to Botham to a mighty
mass appeal. When umpire Constant rejected it, the bowler almost
grazed his forehead on the ground in his gesture of frustration. A
smooth square-drive by Hookes, right leg thrown well forward, off
Underwood for four, diverted attention, as did the obnoxious sight of a
young man in jeans and foreign legion headgear, who trotted across
the ground carrying a column of beer-cartons.

Botham finished the day with a lifter to Hookes, but further
disasters had been avoided during the 100 minutes since Chappell's
dismissal, and with the arrears now only nine, it was still a contest of a
kind. It remained the seniors' day — Boycott and Knott, with 151
Tests between them, Knott having passed 4000 runs in this his 87th
Test, and Boycott having made one of cricket's most emotional
centuries.

Australia 243 and 112 for 2 (R. B. McCosker 40 not out, D. W.
Hookes 31 not out); *England* 364 (A. P. E. Knott 135, G. Boycott
107, L. S. Pascoe 4 for 80, J. R. Thomson 3 for 103).

FOURTH DAY

There seems to be no such thing as a quiet Sunday during this series.
This time the big news was that Kerry Packer was on his way to
England again, apparently with a legal advisor, to take up the matter of
"his" players' contracts, two of which were now known to have been
broken, with several others being questioned. No peace for the weary,
especially Australian journalists, who have grown used to being awoken
by phone calls from Sydney or Melbourne at four in the morning. The
phone call this time was made to a startled Alvin Kallicharran by a
Packer lawyer.

In bright sunshine and before another large crowd, which included
some members of the Australian Olympic Paraplegic team, Willis
bowled to McCosker from the pavilion end. The tall batsman, who
seemed to be providing a strong answer to those who felt he had no
place in this third Test match, edged just short of Greig at second slip
and got four. At the other end he faced Underwood, who took up with
Saturday figures of 8-6-8-0, and the ball, well flighted, sometimes
eluded the centre of the bat. McCosker and Hookes, unshaken, kept
their heads down.

A top-edged hook off Willis brought McCosker his half-century, in

183 minutes, a stroke fraught with risk which nevertheless erased England's first-innings lead. Hookes took three with a cover-drive off Underwood, but then felt a Willis bouncer whistle past his neck. Continuing to reveal an off-stump frailty, Hookes helplessly edged a fast no-ball into the gloves of Alan Knott, who was now almost always seen in the field wearing an old-maidenish cloche sunhat.

Willis had bowled only four overs when Hendrick took over, inducing McCosker to essay a hook against one which hardly got up: one run resulted. A thick-edge glance for four had the bowler raising his arms, and the three slips (no gully) looked none too enchanted either.

Geoff Miller was at last called upon to bowl for the first time in the match and conceded a single off his first over. His Edwardian moustache giving him an appearance that belies his youth, he runs in at an angle, a loose run, and has a high arm. He was to bowl five overs for as many runs in this spell, coming close to a wicket when Hookes cut a ball very close to his stumps, the ball cannoning onto Knott's boot and running fine for a single.

Drinks were taken after the 150 had come up in the 62nd over, and, his concentration perhaps disturbed, David Hookes played at a widish one from Hendrick and missed, was hit on the pads — a fairly close call — and then provided Hendrick with a wicket he had worked for and deserved. He was plumb lbw for 42, and Australia were 154 for 3, Hookes having managed only three singles in his last 40 minutes.

Hendrick had two slips and two gullies for Walters, who, not unexpectedly, looked uneasy at the start and played with an incurably crooked bat. Hendrick forced him to inside-edge at least once before he rested with figures this morning of 9-4-12-1, a fine display of fast-medium bowling.

When Botham offered a full-length ball to McCosker he drove it to the boundary with a touch of class, head over the ball, feet balanced with a beauty that was almost Hammond-like. And when Willis bounced one at him he ducked very low to safety. Walters, on the other hand, cut Willis waist-high through gully for four, causing the bowler's face to resemble one of the traditional theatrical masks — not the happy one. In a torrid spell Walters twice took his eyes off the flying ball, shot down to the crouch position, but left gloves and bat on offer, suspended in front of him, as in the dreadful days of old, when the England and South African fast bowlers had him at their mercy. Between the two escapes — for escapes they were, no thanks to the batsman — Walters received a ball where he likes it, well up on his leg stump, and placed it through midwicket for four. Another shortish one he cut, but mistimed, and the ball bounced through to Knott. He was still looking for his touch up to lunch and afterwards. The score at the interval, with Greig coming on for the final over, was 179 for 3, McCosker 78, Walters 12, in 77 overs.

The off-field story of the morning was an offer by David Evans, a London businessman, to buy the contracts from Kerry Packer of the five England players in his squad, and to sponsor every England player to the tune of £1000 per Test match played, and each member of a pool of 50 players under consideration for the England side at £1000 per annum for three years. The estimated cost of that little deal was around half a million per annum. It served as a further reminder that the match we were watching was really, at times at any rate, only a backcloth to a serial drama of seemingly endless proportions.

Australia's need was obvious, and McCosker and Walters went on doing their best to meet it. Greig was not averse to dropping short to Walters and he in turn was willing to hook, but the power and timing weren't always right. Woolmer was given a bowl before the new ball was taken, and a Walters single raised 200, in the laborious time of 326 minutes.

Greig now, with Walters' own conspiracy, got him out. He drove a four, exquisitely, but an attempted repeat of the stroke sent the ball navel-high direct to Randall at cover: 204 for 4. Robinson came in, an X-ray having revealed a cracked right index finger after he had joined a few other Australians in having precautionary film taken. Rod Marsh was found to have two broken fingers to go with his badly bruised palm, and Pascoe had a slightly damaged hamstring.

Attention now focussed on Rick McCosker as he approached his hundred. Aptly using a Gunn & Moore bat on this Nottingham ground, he went to 90 with a four off Greig to midwicket, and took another next ball, squarer. The new ball was taken after 91 overs, with McCosker 96 and the ebullient Robinson yet to score. McCosker glanced Willis's first ball fine for two to reach 98, and the next for one only. Where, one searched, could he take that vital single? There were gaps enough in front of the wicket, but he found one backward of square — and smacked a six off Willis's short ball to reach his century in the grand manner, his second against England and fourth in all Tests. His fine restoration effort had taken 347 minutes, and included a standard ration of boundaries: 10 fours and a six. He held his bat aloft a long time as the applause rang out, and like Boycott before him he

Rick McCosker acknowledges the warm reception he received when his own storybook century was reached with a hook for six off his jaw-breaker, Bob Willis

could not conceal his pleasure at having made not just another hundred.

Robinson was still hesitant, lifting his head sharply as he played his strokes, most of them with springy heels and bristling elbows. His first runs came from a spasm of a stroke wide of third slip, and he placed Hendrick through square leg for another four just before the drinks break. Afterwards, he was almost caught by Knott, the ball going through low. It came as a surprise when the next wicket to fall was McCosker's and not Robinson's. It was an inglorious end to a sterling innings: a poke at a ball from Willis, caught comfortably by Brearley at first slip. With Australia half out and only 119 ahead, McCosker's loss was heavily important, and the joyful reactions of the England fieldsmen underlined it.

Marsh watched from the other end while Robinson edged, played and missed, and generally looked agitated, and then had the horrifying experience himself of "bagging a pair", probably becoming the first batsman ever to make nought in each innings of his 50th Test match. It took a great flying right-hand catch by Greig at second slip, the ball in all likelihood due to fall short of Brearley at first.

Australia had thus lost two wickets with the score on 240, and Willis had struck twice — wickets of consequence, with the refreshing tea interval approaching. Many a glowing pink torso (the gates had to be closed again) bore testimony to the power of the sun. At tea, with eight hours left to the match, Australia were 264 for 6, 143 ahead.

Richie Robinson, always a man for the action, had a beanfeast when the players came out. He edged the first ball just wide of Brearley at slip, and before Underwood's over was through he had played sharply to Greig at silly point, and another catch went down. Justice was done in Underwood's next over when Robinson was out, rather unusually: attempting a stroke square, he hit the ball after it had hit his pad, and umpire Constant gave him out leg-before.

Walker came in and proceeded to play cautiously well forward, as if breaking in a bat. He edged one low to the third-man rope off Hendrick, but otherwise showed no interest in acquiring runs, so intense was his concentration. Woolmer was added to Underwood's close net of fieldsmen and had a friendly argument with Greig as to who should field exactly where, but neither was in the path of an O'Keeffe square-cut for four. Underwood now bowled over the wicket.

There was a lot of space around, with five men employed in close catching positions, and Walker on-drove and swept boundaries before, at the other end, nicking another very fast one wide of Hendrick.

The 300 came up from overthrows by Randall as he tried to pin O'Keeffe as he scampered back to his crease, and then that batsman edged the last ball of the over clear of a diving Brearley, to put four more runs against Underwood's debit account. The bowler looked disconsolate as he padded his way back to third man.

The last three wickets fell in a heap, and suddenly England knew their target: 189 in 20-odd minutes and a day. Willis made sure there was no nonsense from Walker or Thomson, bowling them both, and Underwood's toils were rewarded with his second wicket when the innings ended with the ball in Hendrick's safe hands via the edge of Pascoe's bat. Hendrick's contribution in the match had been four catches and four wickets, and with Botham's success it must have left Chris Old wondering if and when he would return to the Test side.

Thomson beat Brearley with the first ball of England's second

A Breughel-like scene as the Englishmen celebrate the fall of Australia's last wicket, Len Pascoe caught by Mike Hendrick off Derek Underwood, knowing their target for victory to be 189

innings, a rocket of a delivery which Marsh, wearing the gloves in spite of his injury, just had to take, with a grimace his only reaction. At the other end Boycott took two of Pascoe and four cut off the next, and the cheering was urgent, loud, and reaffirming that all was forgiven for the Randall run-out on Friday.

Brearley glanced Thomson fine for four to open his score, but was destined to be beaten many more times than once before the end of the evening session; he stood looking quite fed-up. An energetic stop by Davis in the covers, some immaculate batsmanship by the sure, neat Boycott, and the day's play drew to a close, with conversation turning to the weather. It had become cool and the sky was murky in some quarters, and so high did English confidence seem that the prospect of rain or otherwise remained the only complication.

Australia 243 and 309 (R. B. McCosker 107, D. W. Hookes 42, R. D. Robinson 34, R. G. D. Willis 5 for 88); *England* 364 and 17 for 0.

FIFTH DAY

There was heavy rain about north of Nottingham — a cloudburst in Edinburgh — and it was thought that there could be weather disturbances here later in the day. So if the Australian bowlers weren't to make early inroads into England's batting, the best chance of tensions came perhaps from the meteorological factors. No-one seemed to doubt that England would get the runs.

The latest on the "other" business was that the Evans proposal was not all it seemed. Mr Evans wanted companies to provide a million pounds' worth of business for his office-cleaning firm each year for three years, with publicity in return, and any profits going to the Test and County Cricket Board. "I am saying to the businessmen of England: it is up to you to send Packer packing." Something else upon which to keep an eye.

The 2½-hour morning session began with a fanfare of seven runs off Pascoe's opening over, with a two and four to Boycott through the off side. Thomson took the pavilion end, and runs came slowly, very slowly. Brearley was hit on the shoulder by Pascoe, and Thomson struck Boycott, but on the whole the batsmen looked secure, Boycott quite impregnable. After conceding only 13 runs in five overs Pascoe gave way to O'Keeffe, who spun his fifth ball past Brearley's bat. Thomson's figures were even tighter: six overs for two runs. Walker came on for the 21st over, but if anyone was going to strike it seemed likely to be O'Keeffe. The spinner was hit for four by Brearley, with a rather ugly sweep, to lift the score off 40 after what seemed a very long time.

Boycott obtained two off Walker when rough ground helped the ball past Davis at cover, and when drinks were consumed England were 47, easing their way ahead like a punt along a reedy stream.

O'Keeffe, expectedly, was getting turn and some bounce, and though Brearley square-cut chunkily for four to raise the fifty, and swept uppishly for two, the spinner commanded respect. Ron Allsopp's pitch had played well throughout, even though it might be better for the game if the spinners are able to get real assistance from the fourth morning.

Pascoe came back, and there was minor chaos as Boycott ran home just in time as Walters' throw arrived. With Marsh arriving at the same time, a stump knocked askew, and the ball finishing in the palm of Boycott's left hand, it was a welcome ripple of activity.

When O'Keeffe overpitched fractionally, Boycott was right to the pitch of the ball and clipping it to the rope at extra cover. Pascoe rapped his pads, but umpire Bird was not interested, and O'Keeffe was rested after 11 overs (25 runs) in favour of Walker at the Radcliffe Road end, while Thomson tried again from the pavilion. He found the edge of Brearley's bat — which was now demonstrably more daring than Boycott's — and four runs more resulted. The Australian exasperation was this time being kept under control, though Thomson's unrequited appeal for lbw against Brearley prompted a feigned physical collapse by the bowler. When Brearley inside-edged a four matters weren't helped much. But this took the first-wicket stand to 77, the best so far in the series by England. At 80 it became the best for either side.

There were two more boundaries as the session drew to a close, a Brearley cover-drive off Walker and an open-chested swat to O'Keeffe by Boycott, and this saved the lunch score from appearing totally undernourished. At 92 without loss England had advanced 75 runs closer, at a rate of 30 an hour, or, in 40 overs, less than two an over. Even Mick Jagger, as fanatical a cricket-lover as any, must have been hard put to maintain concentration as he sat among the members' guests.

Boycott reached 49 with a four through mid-on off Thomson, this bringing up the century stand, and he reached his fifty with a single in the same direction. Brearley reached his half-century ten minutes later with two to long-leg off Thomson, and lost his cap as he reached the crease upon his return. For a second or two he stood in his plastic skull-cap, not a pleasant sight. It was his first fifty against Australia, and this time he must have had vivid hopes of being in at the finish, perhaps with his first Test century. He missed out on the victory honours at Old Trafford by only a few minutes.

The England captain now moved into top gear, playing a super square-cut off Thomson, and then getting over a short ball from Pascoe for four more. The next hit the splice. This pitch was the sort which called for a good deal of courage *by* as much as *against* fast bowlers. Boycott pulled Pascoe firmly for four, Walker beat Brearley, and Brearley on-drove O'Keeffe for four and pull-drove him almost for six. These were the highlights of a ten-minute period when the feeling of resignation deepened — resignation that the match was over though a number of formalities still had to be attended to. The Australians stood in the field as if awaiting their turn in a supermarket queue. There was nothing they could do but wait for the inevitable, and pay the bill.

Pascoe let Boycott have a bouncer, but all thoughts that the Yorkshireman couldn't handle pace were absent for the moment. He remained the epitome of organised technique and foot movement. Brearley pulled O'Keeffe to the boundary just before drinks, during which break McCosker and O'Keeffe just sat, heads bowed, thinking about goodness knows what.

Brearley brought up the 150 and a four by Boycott off an O'Keeffe full-toss took the stand to 154, at which point Walker brought to the game just the touch of excitement it had needed all day. He forced Brearley to play on, and had Knott caught in the same over. Brearley had reached 81, ten short of his highest Test score, when his luck ran out. He had batted 261 minutes and hit 13 fours, and among those who applauded him warmly all the way back was Boycott. The captain had risen in stature with this sensible innings.

Knott, coming in presumably to ensure a finish by tea, played Walker square and gained two overthrows, but in trying to steer him between slip and gully he nudged the ball low to O'Keeffe, who picked it up left-handed on his haunches.

And now a third wicket fell. In Walker's next over Greig went for a duck, bowled leg stump by Walker as the ball careered through so far below the eyes of this very tall man. Greig's stumps in disarray have been a strangely familiar sight in the past few Test series.

Walker had taken three wickets in six balls for two runs, but it needed much more than that to invoke any genuine tension. Randall was a while getting his first run, and there was a vague possibility that Boycott would still have scope for his second century in the match. Walker bowled a wide. If Boycott was to get his century he didn't want too much of that. The big man continued to press, and struck Randall's front pad. The insistent, hoarse appeal was turned down.

O'Keeffe came on as tea was being poured, and Randall swept him, a tangle of boots and gloves and black hair, to the boundary. A shorter ball asked for similar treatment, but he mistimed it and it bounced to Walker. And before the over was out Randall almost was. He hit

Captains Greg Chappell and Mike Brearley happily take a back seat for the man of the moment, Geoff Boycott

O'Keeffe firmly back, but the chance was missed as the ball bounced out of the midriff. At tea England needed 17, with Boycott on 75, Randall seven.

It was soon over. A lovely square-cut off O'Keeffe brought Randall four runs, and after Boycott had nudged Walker through the slips gap for four to reach 80, Randall took the winning runs off O'Keeffe — a fine glance to the boundary and an on-drive to a well-pitched-up ball which Pascoe stopped just short of the line, by which time the required three runs had been made. England had won two Tests in a row in a home series against Australia for the first time since Jim Laker demolished Ian Johnson's side in 1956 at Headingley and Old Trafford, and this was England's third win at Trent Bridge against Australia, the last being in 1930.

The crowd savoured the occasion, massing in front of the old pavilion as the players gave them a smile from the balcony, and gazing at the straw-coloured pitch upon which the victory had been won. It was a rare and wonderful moment for Englishmen, and for none more emphatically than Geoff Boycott, who may have created yet another record by batting on all five days of the match . . . in fact he was on the field for all but 1¾ hours of the match. There must have been some reluctance even about that brief absence.

So, the Ashes were within sight, and unless Australia could reverse the slide with a victory in the fourth Test, at Headingley, the Leeds crowd would, for the first time ever, witness the winning and losing of the tiny urn.

The match over, authors David Frith and Greg Chappell are photographed by Patrick Eagar before settling down to their reports

Greg Chappell writes:

The Trent Bridge pitch had a lot less grass on it than the one we had used in the county match, and there was some moisture in it. It was obviously not going to be as bouncy, and I had no hesitation in batting when I won my 11th toss out of 15 on the tour so far. Our target was

400 at least, and we began well. It was around 100 minutes before our first wicket fell, when Ian Davis played lazily at Underwood, neither going through with his shot nor holding back when he didn't get to the pitch of the delivery. I stayed with Rick McCosker till lunch, which made it a fairly good session for us all the same — in fact, the best beginning so far in the series.

Rick was beaten by a ball from Mike Hendrick that moved slightly away from him, and David Hookes and I then batted until drinks. I was in pretty good form, but the unexpected has a habit of happening in this game, and one from Ian Botham that kept slightly low, first ball after drinks, I dragged into my wicket. Australia could ill afford to lose a wicket at that stage, and it was a real setback.

A middle-innings collapse then followed, caused by some intelligent bowling and competent fielding — and some undisciplined strokeplay. Ian Botham was the main destroyer, picking up five wickets on his Test debut, and reminding me of Phil Edmonds' sensational debut at Headingley in 1975, when he took five wickets for little cost. Botham bowled not so much with any great venom, but he kept the ball well up, moving it either way, and was backed up by some good fielding. It was the old story: He'll probably bowl better in future Test matches and get nowhere near the same reward. It was a fine debut, and with his considerable ability Ian Botham should have a distinguished career ahead of him.

Kerry O'Keeffe, first with Jeff Thomson and later Len Pascoe, restored some face to the innings, but out total of 243 was still very mediocre.

We needed a quick breakthrough, and this came on the second morning, when we showed aggression and got results. Len Pascoe, in a fiery spell, got Brearley and Woolmer out, and then there was that unbelievable run-out of Derek Randall. Geoff Boycott was under tremendous pressure. Our bowlers had bowled tightly to him and added to the anxiety he must have felt upon returning to Test cricket after three years. He was patting back half-volleys, and seemed determined to keep away from the strike early in the innings. He saw hardly anything of Thomson while the ball had some shine on it. I believe he made up his mind to get away from Jeff with a single through mid-on, but the single was highly unlikely since Jeff was quickly across to field the ball. Boycott committed himself to the run, baulking briefly, and Randall had virtually no chance. The boos and jeers that sounded after the run-out of the local hero only added to the pressures on Boycott. Something must have been said to him during lunch, probably to the effect that the best thing for him now was to make as many runs for the side as he could; nothing could undo what was done.

He was still very slow indeed after the break, and he was almost out to a beautiful ball from Len Pascoe which left him and found the edge. Unfortunately Rick McCosker, moving to his right at slip, couldn't hold the catch. I felt sorry for him, for he had worked hard to find his batting form again and he had held some good slip catches recently as well. He must have felt now that the world had fallen in on him, and that he must have accidentally killed a Chinaman somewhere along the line for his luck to have turned so sour.

Soon afterwards Len Pascoe bounced one at Boycott, and his hook was hurried, lofting the ball. Sadly for us, Max Walker was late in picking up the flight of the shot against the dark background of the Council offices, and the ball dropped in front of him. Another close shave came when Boycott was rapped on the glove, and David Hookes at fourth slip was fractionally late in diving forward for the ball as it ballooned in his direction. All this confirmed my belief that when a batsman's destined to make runs the let-offs can come thick and fast. Geoff Boycott's run of luck was rubbing salt into our wounds, for we really had approached our job with spirit and aggression. England were 82 for 5, and could have been all out for something like 150. But it was not to be.

The game changed completely. Alan Knott batted with great exuberance, and Boycott was inspired by it. Their record partnership tore the game from our grasp, even though we bounced back at the end of the innings.

There were chances that went amiss, both catching and run-out, and I was guilty of two myself. One, from Ian Botham off Jeff Thomson, was a fairly regulation first-slip catch, but it came at me faster than expected and I got cramped up and spilt it. The other was when Underwood nicked one fine, and Rod Marsh moved — only to watch me take the catch — and I made a split-second adjustment which allowed the ball past, touching my thumb on the way.

The England lead of 121 was not disastrous, but it could have been so much less if one reflects on the scoreline of 82 for 5 at one point. We had to get out heads down well and truly this time, aiming for 400, which would put the pressure back on our opponents. A good start was essential. We didn't manage it. Ian Davis fell early, a victim of a straightforward slip catch, and after tea I was bowled by Mike Hendrick — a slightly short ball which didn't rise all that much, and came back some distance. For the third time running in the series I touched it into my wicket. The way things had been going for England, one of their batsmen might have got away with it! Two runs to long leg perhaps!

I felt very disappointed as I walked off. We needed a big partnership or two at the top of the order, and here was another chance gone begging. Rick McCosker and David Hookes dug their heels in now, though, and saw us through to the end of the day with some strong application.

That evening I declined an invitation to dinner with friends, feeling I would be poor company, Instead, I had a quiet drink at the Albany Hotel with my co-author, and slipped off for an early night. The Sunday was relaxing. I went with Rod Marsh, David Hookes, and Syd McRae, our masseur, to the home of Garth and Helen Pettit at Ashbourne. Garth, an Australian dentist, had been a great friend to my parents on previous visits, and today staged a lovely barbecue for us and Rod Marsh's parents and David Hookes's mother. We played records — too loudly, perhaps, for the parents — and had some superb chops and sausages before returning to the hotel to prepare for the big fightback.

The fourth day regrettably saw us blow all chance of getting back into the match. Rick McCosker apart, there was no truly worthwhile batting performance to speak of. Several got a start, but didn't go on to the big score we needed. Rick's determination was terrific. When he reached his century with a hooked six it was the culmination of many hours of endeavour since he had his jaw broken in the Centenary Test. He was late arriving in England (through no fault of his), and the weather for several weeks had been atrocious, making match practice elusive. He had trained hard and done all he could to get himself into top trim. Now he had his reward, and our faith in him through the thin times was fully justified.

No-one was able to get on top of the England bowlers. They held an ascendancy all the time, Mike Brearley using them in short spells, keeping the pressure on, with the catching again being first-class. Catching was the major difference between the sides. I said to Rod Marsh during Saturday's play, when we missed chances, that it seemed that we were being paid back for the previous five years, when everything that had gone in the air had been plucked safely out of it.

On the last day, when England needed a further 172 to win, we had by no means given up hope of pulling off a victory against the odds. There was even a possibility that a shower or two might upset England's poise. As always, a quick breakthrough was essential. But Boycott and Brearley survived the first hour, when the bowlers were fresh and the ball fairly new, and though they played and missed quite often, no chance was given.

Len Pascoe bowled well, and Jeff Thomson bowled with as much speed and bounce as at any stage of the match. Max Walker kept things tight, and we waited and hoped. England's safety-first policy helped us if anything, but we did need wickets. Our last hope of a breakthrough came with Kerry O'Keeffe, but though he got a couple to turn sharply and Brearley once swept perilously close to a fieldsman, it was not to be. The pitch was too slow to give any bowler much heart, especially with the batsmen cutting out all risks.

As in the first innings, Geoff Boycott made a huge contribution. I have seen him play innings of better quality, but for time spent at the crease and runs made, his comeback effort couldn't have been bettered. Alan Knott's 135, of course, was England's innings of the match. When Boycott was shocked almost runless early on, Knott provided the inspiration. His flair and sense of urgency set up England's win.

It was after the drinks break on the final afternoon that we got our first break. If it hadn't been for the threat of a thunderstorm I'm not sure we would even have got that. Phil Slocombe, England's acting 12th man, pulled Mike Brearley aside during drinks and told him that a storm only 25 miles away was moving towards Nottingham. It could well reach the city by teatime. There was now a decided urgency about the run tempo, and Mike Brearley finally chopped one on from Max Walker. We soon saw the advent and departure of Alan Knott and Tony Greig, but the target was soon polished off, and we were two-down with two to play. The thunderstorm seemed to have got lost.

After our loss the Press, particularly the Australian section, really gave the team a hiding — ''weakest Australian team ever'', ''the side has no ability'', ''no match for England'', and so on. What annoyed me most was that much of the criticism was shortsighted, and some of it was vitriolic. It seemed that the Packer affair was getting some of the reporters down even more than it was the players, and they needed to take it out on somebody. Quite unfairly, it seemed to me, they were leaning on the Australian side, which contained more Packer signatories than the English. This made us pretty good targets.

We had lost two Tests, but was this really so hard to understand when we were so short on experience? So many of our fellows had had no more than a couple of seasons of Sheffield Shield cricket, and were touring England for the first time. Compare any one of them with, say, Ian Botham, who, although only 21, had played over 60 first-class matches in three seasons and a bit, and had played club cricket in Australia last winter under a sponsorship scheme. Derek Randall, who might also be looked upon as a relative newcomer, had played in over 100 matches in the previous five years. This amounts to a lot of experience — especially, of course, in English conditions, which we're playing under at the moment.

It is easy to fall for the trap of comparing some of our present players with established Australian players of the recent past, but they all had to be launched, and not all of them hit the headlines straight away. I believe that all of the young players on this tour have learned a tremendous amount and have the ability to go on to become very good players. I have deplored the way they have been written off as no-hopers. Experience is something you can't buy. An experienced player can sit down and talk to an inexperienced player for hours, but once he's in the middle he's on his own.

I think we have bowled as well as England, but our batting and fielding have let us down. Fielding is a confidence thing rather than an experience thing. I wonder how much thought, too, is given to the ardours of travelling non-stop, living out of suitcases for five months when you haven't done this sort of thing before? Homesickness can be a problem, and even loneliness. You may be part of a group, with a good deal of laughter from time to time, but there are times when you're on your own, left with your thoughts — which, when things are going badly on the field, can become morbid. You can think of the future, and wonder what's going to happen to you. If you're going through a rough trot, especially if you're a young player who's never known such a thing in a short first-class career, you don't automatically know how to get out of a slump. You need to concentrate on doing the right things and playing sensibly, and you'll come out of it. To be too anxious to get runs leads to mistakes, and early dismissal.

The team had a long coach trip to Sunderland to play Minor Counties straight after the Trent Bridge Test. Rod Marsh and Richie Robinson missed the match because of finger injuries, Rick McCosker rested for the first time on tour, and I took the match off because my feet were troubling me again. It was a welcome break from the game, and found me looking forward to cricket again when I reached Manchester ready for the final month of the tour.

We lost the two-day match at Sunderland, after a couple of declarations. Conditions were not easy, and on top of everything Doug Walters, who captained the side, nicked a ball into his chin and had to have seven stitches. Kerry O'Keeffe took over on the last day after Doug had made the final declaration, but dropped catches together with Kerry's aim to keep on the attack in the hope of victory saw us run out losers in the end — something that added fuel to the flames for the journalists who had been giving us such a hiding. The defeat was no skin off our nose, maybe because we had just had the experience of losing two Test matches. If there was a benefit anywhere it must have been for Minor Counties, who had never had the pleasure of beating an Australian touring side before.

So we checked in at the Grand Hotel, Manchester for the third time this summer, and chose our side for the Lancashire game, which preceded the Headingley Test. Kerry O'Keeffe's spinning finger still had fluid on it, and Max Walker had a knee injury, so we included Geoff Dymock, who went on to bowl very well, as did all the bowlers, Ray Bright taking five wickets in Lancashire's second innings as we moved towards a winning position. I enjoyed the chance to bowl off-spinners for the second or third time on the tour. It helped break up the fielding routine, and the three wickets I took gave me extra pleasure, since I've bowled medium-pacers for a number of years now since starting out as a leg-spinner. We needed 170-odd in better than even time, and with Gary Cosier batting sensibly, picking off the loose balls and making 66, and myself scoring 70 not out, we reached our target. I hadn't batted in the first innings, giving my feet a further rest and allowing further opportunities to other batsmen to stake a claim for the last two Tests. Craig Serjeant had batted well, and Kim Hughes got into the eighties with a good display before being caught while trying to sweep. It was probably his best knock of the tour, and included some huge sixes, one off Jack Simmons going about 40 yards over the wide mid-on boundary.

Our morale was therefore revived during this three-day match, and we went into the fourth Test with hope restored.

THIRD TEST MATCH

Trent Bridge, July 28, 29, 30, August 1, 2

Paying attendance 87,000; takings £152,000

AUSTRALIA

		min	6	4			min	6	4
R. B. McCosker	c Brearley b Hendrick	51	143	—	8	c Brearley b Willis	107	366	1	10
I. C. Davis	c Botham b Underwood	33	91	1	3	c Greig b Willis	9	27	—	1
*G. S. Chappell	b Botham	19	83	—	3	b Hendrick	27	37	—	5
D. W. Hookes	c Hendrick b Willis	17	47	—	1	lbw b Hendrick	42	185	—	4
K. D. Walters	c Hendrick b Botham	11	27	—	1	c Randall b Greig	28	77	—	3
R. D. Robinson	c Brearley b Greig	11	25	—	2	lbw b Underwood	34	95	—	5
+R. W. Marsh	lbw b Botham	0	8	—	—	c Greig b Willis	0	8	—	—
K. J. O'Keeffe	not out	48	110	—	5	not out	21	121	—	4
M. H. N. Walker	c Hendrick b Botham	0	8	—	—	b Willis	17	53	—	4
J. R. Thomson	c Knott b Botham	21	36	—	4	b Willis	0	5	—	—
L. S. Pascoe	c Greig b Hendrick	20	59	—	4	c Hendrick b Underwood	0	5	—	—
Extras	(b4, lb2, nb6)	12				(b1, lb5, nb18)	24			
		243					**309**			

Fall: 78, 101, 131, 133, 153, 153, 153, 155, 196

18, 60, 154, 204, 240, 240, 270, 307, 308

Bowling: Willis 15-0-58-1, Hendrick 21.2-6-46-2, Botham 20-5-74-5, Greig 15-4-35-1, Underwood 11-5-18-1.

Willis 26-6-88-5, Hendrick 32-14-56-2, Botham 25-5-60-0, Greig 9-2-24-1, Underwood 27-15-49-2, Miller 5-2-5-0, Woolmer 3-0-3-0.

ENGLAND

		min	6	4			min	6	4
*J. M. Brearley	c Hookes b Pascoe	15	86	—	—	b Walker	81	261	—	13
G. Boycott	c McCosker b Thomson	107	420	—	11	not out	80	314	—	9
R. A. Woolmer	lbw b Pascoe	0	1	—	—					
D. W. Randall	run out	13	29	—	2	(5)not out	19	40	—	3
A. W. Greig	b Thomson	11	23	—	2	(4)b Walker	0	5	—	—
G. Miller	c Robinson b Pascoe	13	24	—	2					
+A. P. E. Knott	c Davis b Thomson	135	295	—	18	(3)c O'Keeffe b Walker	2	2	—	—
I. T. Botham	b Walker	25	94	—	3					
D. L. Underwood	b Pascoe	7	46	—	1					
M. Hendrick	b Walker	1	9	—	—					
R. G. D. Willis	not out	2	6	—	—					
Extras	(b9, lb7, nb16, w3)	35				(b2, lb2, nb2, w1)	7			
		364				3 wkts	**189**			

Fall: 34, 34, 52, 64, 82, 297, 326, 357, 357

154, 156, 158

Bowling: Thomson 31-6-103-3, Pascoe 32-10-80-4, Walker 39.2-12-79-2, Chappell 8-0-19-0, O'Keeffe 11-4-43-0, Walters 3-0-5-0.

Thomson 16-6-34-0, Pascoe 22-6-43-0, O'Keeffe 19.2-2-65-0, Walker 24-8-40-3.

Umpires: H. D. Bird and D. J. Constant

Toss won by Australia

ENGLAND WON BY 7 WICKETS

7. FOURTH TEST MATCH

HEADINGLEY, LEEDS, AUGUST 11, 12, 13, 15

David Frith writes:

FIRST DAY

After a brief absence between Test matches, summer returned, and the Headingley ground was radiant in morning sunlight as the practice nets were taken down from in front of the brick pavilion. The ground was full, and chattering, and then roaring as Boycott came down the staircase with Brearley, England having won an important toss. Yorkshire's hero had make his 99th century a couple of days earlier, and stood to become the first man to hit his hundredth hundred during a Test match. Since that Test match was on his home ground the prospect was such as the best fiction is made of — and something to add to the bookmakers' activities. They gave his chances at four to one.

There were two team changes: Bright for O'Keeffe for Australia, and Roope for Miller, a change which caused little surprise, with England needing only a draw. Brian Rose, the Somerset left-hander, had been asked to stand by as Woolmer's finger was still troubling him, but the Kent batsman reported fit, and Rose, fresh from his first double-century for his county, had to wait for his Test baptism after all.

There was absolute and intimidating silence as Thomson cantered in from the football end to bowl the first ball to Brearley, the sort of cathedral numbness that Hutton so disliked as he awaited Lindwall's opening salvo. Two balls were bowled without incident, and then England's captain touched one to Marsh, waited disinterestedly as the appeals rang out, and saw umpire Budd's finger raised. England one down for nought.

Walker, not Pascoe, bowled from the Kirkstall Lane end, erring twice for no-balls in his first over, in which Boycott opened his score with a two through point, to rapturous cheering. A three to square leg, and England's returnee was in charge again, aiming for a mortgage on this Test, as on the last. Woolmer opened his account with a fluent four off Thomson behind square leg. Soon he was square-driving a

Thomson full-toss to the boundary, and after nine overs England had 21. Pascoe replaced Thomson for the 11th over, and both batsmen took runs, picking up more at the other end off Walker, with the outfield now revealing itself to be fast as a billiard table. At drinks 42 had been made, Boycott 16, Woolmer 20.

The best stroke so far came from Boycott as he cracked a shorter ball from Walker straight to the fence through point, but soon he was beaten by the same bowler and Marsh dived desperately to his right but couldn't get to it as it touched the earth.

The fifty came up in the 15th over, but the ball was now beginning to beat the bat, and heads were being thrown back in disgust. It may well be that in sport one makes some of one's own luck, but there is surely more to it than will ever be understood by man.

Pascoe beat Woolmer with a pearl of a ball which swung in a little and cut away upon pitching, but the batsman, expectedly, remade his

A first-over breakthrough for Australia — Mike Brearley caught by Rod Marsh off Jeff Thomson — and for a brief moment Greg Chappell and his team are on top

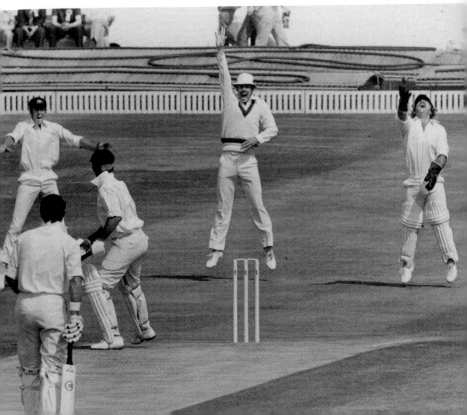

crease-mark and carried on as if nothing untoward had happened. The pitch and outfield were filled with runs — everyone knew — and the inevitable was starting to unfold.

Thomson relieved Walker, who had bowled nine tidy overs, and Boycott got four from a push through square leg which Robinson tried to cut off with a sliding tackle, and then Pascoe got the better of Boycott, Marsh and the slips shouting a confident appeal for caught-behind. As the batsman rubbed his forearm umpire Budd shook his head, and the Australians looked aggrieved.

There was no question that Thomson was bowling very fast here-abouts. Woolmer took a four off him to a vacant third man, but was beaten all ends up shortly after. When he glanced him fine and strongly, Pascoe made a tumbling stop to save two runs.

At the other end, Boycott dispatched a lifter from Pascoe cleverly over the slips for four to reach 30, and a classical Woolmer cover-drive off Thomson deposited the ball at the base of the pavilion. Walters was tried just before lunch, but Boycott simply waited for the overpitched ball and coolly on-drove it for four, and when a further over was squeezed in, Bright was given the ball, and during an animated over, Chappell broke the stumps from silly mid-off as Woolmer leaned forward, the only discomfort being caused Marsh as a bail flew into his face. In 28 overs England had advanced to 76 for the loss of Brearley, Boycott on 34, Woolmer 33. The sun still shone, and Yorkshiremen everywhere enjoyed their Scotch eggs and ham salads in the knowledge that their man was a third of the way to his illustrious target, and should therefore accommodate himself and themselves before tonight.

Boycott's achievement, the prospect of it, probably rested at the forefront of the people's consciousness, but there were other matters: the Queen's safety in Northern Ireland, the £9000 presented by David Evans' group of businessmen to the non-Packer players in the England team (the likelihood seemed to be that *all* would share the sum, in the interests of team harmony), and a possible further cut in the mortgage rate.

But there was no escaping it: the preservation of Boycott's wicket meant more to more folk than ever before. There was relatively little reaction to Woolmer's dismissal in the fourth over after lunch, except among the Australians. The batsman played defensively at a fairly straight ball from Thomson and edged low to first slip, where Chappell took it two-handed: 82 for 2, and Jeff Thomson now needed only four wickets for his hundred in Tests.

Derek Randall ambled to the wicket — how can he ever grow old? — and was soon flowing: a square-drive for three, leg thrust well out, off Thomson, whom he then "patted" to third man for four, glanced for two, and fended off through the gully area for another boundary. Walker beat Boycott with a ball that barely moved. It didn't need to; it pitched on the perfect length. Then Randall brought up the hundred with a three tucked past square leg. Shuffling right across his stumps, he may have mesmerised Pascoe (on for Thomson) into overpitching, and smacked the full-toss through cover for four. Pascoe then brought one back at him and hit his pads, and umpire Alley gave the Australians the response they craved. England, 105 for 3, were looking to have thrown it all away.

Greig entered, booed by some and perhaps less surprised by it now, though it cannot have been any less painful for that, and a no-ball from Walker produced an off-drive for three to open his score.

Boycott now had a scoring sequence that enlivened. A steer through slips for four preceded a businesslike three through mid-off off the back foot, and, after Greig had French-cut for two, he scored four runs for a tickle to long leg which fetched a quick two and the same again when Pascoe's alert throw to the far end bounced badly for the fieldsmen and ran almost to the line. This made him 48, and a beautiful cover-drive off Walker raised his half-century, in 175 minutes, with eight fours. The Boycott bat was raised high again in acknowledgment of the thunderous applause, most of the spectators rising.

Thomson came back at the Kirkstall Lane end, and got one through Greig's flashing stroke — nowhere near the bat, it seemed, although the captain and vice-captain appealed loudly. Greig off-drove the next uppishly for four, and drinks came on at 133 for 3, made off 42 overs.

Greg Chappell took up the attack, and bowled wide of off stump, with the occasional one seaming in. Twice he appealed for lbw against Greig, and once he dropped short, Greig hooking it high over Pascoe's upstretched right hand for six. The 150 came up with a single in the 50th over, and a quiet period ensued, the Australians, six of them at any rate, inscrutible under sunhats. Boycott straight-drove Chappell to the football stand, and at the other end Greig's big drive off Pascoe eluded the high dive to his left by Davis. Eventually Bright came on at the Kirkstall Lane end, and Boycott, leaning like a craftsman over his creation, sent the first ball though cover for four to reach 71 out of 171, and followed with an uppish cut wide of slip for four. While the ball was fetched, Greig came down to speak with Boycott as Chappell spoke with Bright. It was prelude to incident, for Bright's last ball went past Boycott down the leg side and Marsh felt he had made a catch. The appeal was excited and widespread, but Bill Alley dismissed it. Bright was thunderstruck, and snatched his hat from the umpire, who reprimanded him. Greg Chappell ran up and placed both hands on his shoulders, talking to him in an attempt to pull him out of his rage, and while the crowd rumbled disapprovingly, things slowly settled. When Alley no-balled Bright's first ball next over the tension returned, but fortunately passed on. Boycott, head over ball, stroked another four through cover, and with only one further noise — a piercing lbw shriek by Walker against Greig as he padded up to an off-cutter — the game reached the tea interval, England having reconsolidated to 185 for 3, Boycott 79, Greig 31.

I had to count the Australian fieldsmen as play resumed: it seemed they were a man or two short, so farflung was the field. Greig aimed some mighty blows at Thomson, not always connecting, but getting one away straight and another through cover. The 200 came up in the 62nd over, but two overs later the next breakthrough came as Greig was bowled by a ball from Thomson which came back at him. Graham Roope came in, a good season with Surrey behind him, and an innings of 77 against Australia at The Oval in 1975 in his last Test innings. He was beaten several — no, numerous — times by Walker, who received a word of consolation from the unquenchable Robinson. Roope's first real shot was a square-cut for four, and from then on his back-foot play seemed much more composed.

When Pascoe replaced Thomson, Boycott surprisingly pulled him for four, but when drinks were taken, the Yorkshire champion had managed only ten runs in the hour since tea.

He moved to 93 with two twos to long leg off Walker, and after a single to midwicket off Pascoe, he wasn't interested in turning Roope's square-drive into a two. Retention of the strike was all-important now.

Walker came off, having bowled 26 overs, 12 maidens, 0 for 55, and Chappell, having offered obviously heartfelt appreciation, took over. Boycott placed his sixth ball to point for a single to go to 95. Policemen were now observed taking up positions around the boundary. A single to cover off Pascoe took Boycott to within four of his glittering prize. His thoughts as he stood at the other end, sleeves up, cap off, mopping his brow, would have been worth monitoring.

The great moment arrived. In the 77th over Chappell bowled a leg-cutter well up, and Geoffrey Boycott moved into it and drove it to

Geoff Boycott's triumphant return to Test cricket, initiated at Nottingham, is crowned at Headingley as he drives Greg Chappell to the boundary to bring up his 100th first-class century, an innings that ensured that England would regain the Ashes

the football stand for four, Roope leaping over the flying ball. Pandemonium broke out. He raised his arms and held his head, and youngsters streamed onto the ground through the thin almost non-existent police cordon. For five minutes celebrations raged, the batsman lost in a seething scrum of worshippers. When he emerged he had lost his cap, and Yorkshire secretary Joe Lister sent out a selection of replacements, conveyed to the middle by a bearded policeman. Boycott chose one, only for a youth in green trousers to run back on with the original cap, and as the figures were announced — 320 minutes, 14 fours, including one all-run — Boycott composed himself as Chappell resumed — with a harmless, humorous bouncer. Seventeen great batsmen had trod this way before, John Edrich the most recent, but none had reached the century of centuries in a Test match. This, added to the drama of Boycott's return from the self-imposed exile, was almost too much to grasp on a warm summer's evening.

Boycott picked up another four, a repetition of the historic on-drive, and a further delay occurred when the scoreboard showed too many overs, and for a moment it seemed the new ball was due. In fact only 81 had been delivered with the old, so Bright and Walters came on, with Thomson being given a final chance as the sun went down on a memorable day, a day that will be spoken of by those who were present until the end of their time. A further cover-driven boundary by the immaculate Boycott, a free square-cut for four by Roope off Walker to raise the 250, and all was done. Boycott was mobbed again as he fought his way off, and Union Jacks waved everywhere, making a change from the triumphant Caribbean banners of the previous year. The hero did a quick TV interview on the balcony, saying it was all "magic" and sipping champagne while the insistent crowds massed below, wanting to prolong the ecstasy.

England 252 for 4 (G. Boycott 110 not out, A. W. Greig 43, R. A. Woolmer 37).

SECOND DAY

The papers gave Boycott acres of coverage, much of it on the front pages, and Friday came as an anticlimax. The first hour produced only 36 runs, though Roope tried to push it along, driving Walker twice to the boundary in his first over, the new ball having been taken the previous evening. Again Thomson and Walker bowled tightly and well, beating the bat from time to time with movement off the lightly-grassed pitch. Roope was looking settled when Thomson bowled three balls to him that grilled him, poached him, and eventually dropped him into the flames. The first ball flew high down the leg side off some part of Roope's person, the next went past his wavering bat, and the third found the edge for Walters at third slip to take a neat catch to his right. Roope's 34 had taken two hours, and had neither sealed his place in the side nor disappointed.

Boycott got two to long leg when Pascoe misfielded, but Thomson scored a point or two by beating him outside off stump before giving way to Pascoe, who looked lively from the start. Boycott edged him wide of McCosker for four, Marsh and Chappell looking agitated even though a full-length dive would probably have been inadequate. The penalty for Boycott was a bouncer, from which he withdrew his knowing head, and at drinks he was 126, having added 16 in the hour. His sights were clearly on a double-century, at least, and, given the strength and support, he could probably bat till Saturday afternoon in England's cause.

Knott was 25 minutes getting off the mark, and looked a different man from the twinkling, bustling artisan of Trent Bridge. When Bright came into the attack Knott swept him daringly for four to raise the 300, but raw pace from the Kirkstall end still came from Pascoe, who in one torrid over to Boycott, which included two no-balls, almost had him chopping into his stumps, hit his bat-splice, roared a couple of bumpers past his nose, and struck his pads. Thomson relieved him for the 35th over, and Boycott picked up a lucky two when a quick single was doubled after Davis's throw hit the stumps from side-on. When Knott dragged Bright to the midwicket boundary it was only the fifth boundary of the day. Others followed. Boycott drove Thomson nicely and then glanced him very fine — passing his highest score against Australia, 142 not out at Sydney in the 1970-71 series — and Knott went down the pitch to Bright and took four to midwicket, following it with a late-cut past Chappell's left ankle for another four. A Boycott on-drive off Thomson was worth three and ensured that the morning was merely thin on runs and not verging on the bankrupt. The crowd wanted Boycott's 150 before the interval, but he was content to lunch one short, with England, 339 for 5, moving ever closer to those Ashes.

Play after lunch was slow, verging on the boring. Boycott, batting on his seventh consecutive day in this Test series — probably a record — and embarking on his umpteenth session, passed 150 (490 minutes) with a two through gully, and with a three to cover off Pascoe he brought up the 350. Pascoe found the edge of Knott's bat, but the ball dropped short of McCosker, and after four leg-byes and a well-timed four by Knott to square leg, drinks were taken at 373 for 5, Walker's and Thomson's figures making interesting reading at this point: 41-19-82-0 for the toiling, luckless Max and 4 for 111 off 34 overs by "Thommo".

A thin cut by Knott off Bright registered the century stand for this sixth wicket, still with a long way to go if they were to challenge the 215 they made at Trent Bridge, and Walker surprised with a full-toss or two, one of which Boycott drove lipslickingly to the little white boundary pickets. Knott reached 50 with a swift single to silly mid-on, after batting for 170 minutes, and matters livened with a five for

Boycott: he tapped to cover, ran one, and Hookes's throw eluded Marsh and ran on for four more.

Bright commanded respect. Knott missed a sweep and got the benefit of a stumping appeal, and after the ball had lost its shape and given way to a replacement, Bright bowled a half-volley which Knott hit hard and high, and then induced a sweep, which he missed, and which cost him his wicket, lbw on the front leg. The stand of 123 had laboured on for three hours and had copper-bottomed the innings.

Botham now had a chance to exploit the situation. But three balls were his ration, the third intelligently bowled faster by Bright at the off stump, which it knocked backwards: 398 for 7, Boycott 171.

Boycott had the pleasure of making the 400th run, but soon Underwood was in trouble, edging Bright into Chappell's hands, low and to the left, and out again, the first identifiable miss of the match so far. It was not costly. Pascoe took his second wicket when Underwood was gloriously snapped up right-handed by Bright at gully. Pascoe greeted Hendrick with a bouncer, perhaps forgetting for the moment that it was not the eternal Boycott at the other end, and an edged four got the tailender off the mark just before tea, which was taken at 418 for 8, Boycott 179, having made 30 since lunch, nine fewer than in the pre-lunch session. Greater love hath no man than that he be prepared to lay down his life for 22 yards of his own land.

The Australians were not kept waiting long after tea for the last two wickets. Pascoe had Hendrick caught by Robinson at short leg and, just as the list of England batsmen who have carried their bats through Test innings was being perused, Boycott drove at Pascoe and Chappell took the slip catch. He had been in for just over 10¼ hours — the length of the innings, of course — and missed his double-century by a mere nine runs. His 191 was the highest ever for England against Australia at Leeds, passing F. S. Jackson's 144 not out in 1905. The total, 436, was there, defiant, bulky, almost smug, saying to the opposition, "Catch me if you can." The crowd, content as could be, reacted most phlegmatically to a bomb-scare announcement between innings.

Australia were soon in trouble. The second over, by Hendrick from the football stand, saw Davis out lbw, trapped by a ball well up to him before he had scored. McCosker, having glanced the first ball of the innings for four, repeated it once, and again, and after Chappell had taken a chancy run to cover, turned into two by an overthrow, and survived an lbw shout from Hendrick (examining his bat as if to emphasise the absurdity), and had essayed a square-cut without connecting, McCosker hooked a Willis no-ball courageously for six.

Then the big one fell: Greg Chappell, aiming a strongish drive at one from Hendrick that moved away, touched it rib-high to Brearley at first slip, and a roar went up to signify the demise of a principal Christian to the lions. Australia 26 for 2, and thoughts already turning to what would be required to save the follow-on.

The total was doubled by McCosker and Hookes before the next wicket went, the odd lbw shout and mis-hit stroke punctuating a period of hope and promise for both sides as young Hookes square-drove, hooked and sliced Willis for fours in one over and Hendrick was through his partner three times in another. Botham replaced Willis, and Hookes took one to bring up the half-century. Then Australia's third wicket fell, in strange fashion. Hookes played slowly to mid-off, and McCosker backed up a long way. Randall, who had been running in even before Hendrick had released the ball, pounced on it and threw from less than five yards as he slid along the ground. McCosker saw the danger too late. The wicket was broken, and the batsman walked off, utterly crestfallen. Hookes for his part threw his bat to the ground and looked as if he could have wept. 52 for 3 soon turned to 57 for 4 as Hookes himself, having cut Botham stoutly for four, was adjudged lbw next ball, playing half-forward and across the line.

Robinson made everyone nervous from the start, lunging at the ball with a left leg more a battering ram than part of a pair. Soon he lost Walters, caught at third slip, not for the first time, by the almost infallible Hendrick off Botham. Five wickets in the 85 or so minutes of the evening were more than most patriots can have hoped for or expected. Chants of "Easy, easy!" sprang up from one corner, and a banner displayed the morbid message, "Ashes to Ashes, dust to dust, bionic Thommo's turned to rust". As the Englishmen trotted eagerly from end to end it all had a touch of the Normandy landings about it — years of trial, tribulation and torture about to be avenged. At the close Australia stood limply on 67 for 5, a forbidding 369 behind, with Hendrick having taken 2 for 21 and Botham 2 for 9. The thousands looked as if they had feasted well as they wended their way out, and I saw two men waltzing, without, of course, relinquishing their beer-glasses.

England 436 (G. Boycott 191, A. P. E. Knott 57, A. W. Greig 43, R. A. Woolmer 37, G. R. J. Roope 34, L. S. Pascoe 4 for 91, J. R. Thomson 4 for 113); *Australia* 67 for 5.

THIRD DAY

An overcast day was lightened at the start by a charming ceremony when Geoff Boycott posed for photographs on the pitch with Sir Len Hutton and Herbert Sutcliffe, who was now 82 and confined to a wheelchair. These three Yorkshiremen had all made a hundred centuries, a generation apart, and the resulting pictures would make handsome companions to the one of Woolley, Ames and Cowdrey, who were photographed at Canterbury after Cowdrey made up a similar Kentish trio.

The questions were whether Australia could last out the day, and whether there would be any temptation not to enforce the follow-on. The first question remained seriously in consideration as wickets toppled, starting with that of Marsh, who broke what would have been his third successive Test duck with a two into the open spaces at cover, and was then victim of a glorious catch behind. He glanced Botham, and Knott flew to his right and took the ball one-handed, securing it with his left as he fell and rolled over. Robinson meanwhile had been looking for runs. He cover-drove Hendrick for four and played him high just out of Willis's reach at gully for another. An off-driven two followed, and then he edged and Greig took the catch at second slip at the second attempt. The score was 87, one of the devil's numbers.

Walker's policy was clear: to hit. He cut Hendrick for four, then swung three times without connecting before taking a single to bring up the hundred. At the other end he tried to thump Botham over cover and got an edge for Knott to take in front of first slip. Thomson, greeted fondly by the audience, was bowled second ball by a Botham leg-cutter, and Pascoe, his mate, also failed to score before Hendrick bowled him at 103, Australia's lowest total ever in a Headingley Test. Don Bradman, why did you have to grow old?

The innings had lasted, if that is the word, 130 minutes, and was an exercise in sheer misery for Australia. For England the honours hung thickly about Ian Botham and Mike Hendrick, two pleasant men, one 21, the other 28. Botham's figures, 5 for 21 off 11 overs, outstripped those on this debut at Trent Bridge, when it was thought that he might often bowl better for lesser rewards. This latest performance made one wonder. Has he that special knack? Certainly, when the pitch offered something for the seam he knew how to employ it.

For the first time since 1968, at Lord's, Australia were asked by England to follow-on, though Ray Illingworth could have done so —

A momentous photograph showing three generations of great York-shire batsmen, Sir Leonard Hutton, Herbert Sutcliffe, and Geoff Boycott, all scorers of a hundred centuries

and should have done so, in the popular view — at Adelaide during the 1970-71 series. Australia had followed on against England only five times previously since the war (how would we compartmentalise time had Hitler never been born?). The deficit was a symmetrical-looking 333, and would take a lot of working off.

Davis was 25 minutes getting off a "pair", cutting Hendrick to the scoreboard rope, having been struck on the pads a few times and playing not wide enough of fieldsmen. Randall once slid across, transferred the ball hand to hand, and tossed in a return when the batsmen might have been justified in taking off for an apparently safe single. But there was no sign of anxiety. McCosker played and missed a few times, again mis-hooked Willis, and played best of all of his pads

— which were deliberately placed behind an off-side delivery from Willis which cut back dangerously, though not enough to impress umpire Budd. Greig came on for Hendrick for the eighth over, and Davis stroked his first and fourth balls nicely off the back foot for four. Another four straighter next over was a model of timing and technique, and after innings of 34, 12, 33, 9 and 0 in the series, the question was whether this was to be Ian Davis's hour. An off-drive off Willis was stopped at the line, and they ran three, but after McCosker had played a controlled hook for two off Willis, Davis was out. He glanced Greig fine, and Knott, moving across, took the catch comparatively easily, two-handed. It was his 250th Test dismissal, 231 of them having been catches.

The ball had lost its shape by the 12th over, and was replaced with one that often swung quite violently. Botham, by now increased appreciably in stature, came on for the 13th over, and generated a resounding shout for lbw against Chappell. But Australia's tragic morning culminated in Greig's last over before lunch, when he got one through McCosker, only for the appeal to be turned down, and found the edge of McCosker's bat with his fourth ball. The catch was no formality this time. Knott hurled himself to his right and arrested the ball centimetres from the ground. Australia were 35 for 2, there was no sun, and there were signs that the crowd were growing just a little weary of the slaughter.

It was 20 minutes before Chappell got off nought, but Hookes found a gap or two, and was getting into his stride when he was given out leg-before, perhaps unluckily, for 21. He had stroked Greig for four through cover, and then a two and a three in the same over in which a noisy bat-pad appeal had been rejected. Lloyd Budd's raised finger cut short yet another of the fast-diminishing ration of opportunities for this young Packer signatory to make a hundred in a Test match. Walters was next, with as much faith invested in him right now as in the pound sterling before its late-summer recovery, though a pull off Hendrick — a typical Walters shot — was heartening. Just when it seemed that Chappell was settling down, he lashed at Botham and sent the ball high enough over slips to escape the ultimate penalty. When drinks were brought on for the first time, Australia were swaying at 85 for 3 in 33 overs, and journalists and others were worrying about maintaining their hotel bookings.

Chappell pulled Greig for a four that served as a reminder of better times, but Walters, having steered four through the expectant gullies,

Yet another half-chance taken by England fielders as Alan Knott catches Rick McCosker off Tony Greig for 12 in Australia's second innings. The ball wouldn't have carried to Mike Brearley, and Knott took the ball literally inches from the turf

missed one from Woolmer, who had replaced Greig from the football end, and was leg-before: 97 for 4, and Richie Robinson in, shaping, forward or back, like a samurai swordsman, the similarity needing only Max Walker's roar overdubbed to be complete.

A beautiful drive brought Chappell four off Botham and posted the hundred, and a while later his two to fine leg made him 28, the highest score for Australia so far in the match. There was time for Underwood's introduction, for the first time in the match, before tea, taken at 114 for 4 off 50 overs, Chappell 29, Robinson 6, and then the weather had its say, descending greyly during the interval, so that the umpires were satisfied that the light was unplayable during the first over upon resumption. Soon the rain came, and any in doubt about further play were quickly convinced that there would be no more until next week . . . until the weather cleared a little and play resumed at half-past-six, before a desultory number of people.

Robinson cut Hendrick's first ball for four through the armada of close fielders, and Brearley retained his faith in Greig at the other end, the tall man moving the ball outwards but getting very little bounce. Robinson sent for a spray for his painful finger, and there were delays while the unaware walked behind the bowler's arm. Then, as Willis embarked upon an over the umpires consulted again, and off they went, this time finally, even though the extra hour had been entered. *England* 436; *Australia* 103 (I. T. Botham 5 for 21, M. Hendrick 4 for 41) and 120 for 4.

FOURTH DAY

It rained during Sunday night, and Monday morning offered unhappy prospects, with rooftops wet and drizzle about. But it cleared as the morning wore on, and the mopping-up machines did their job, and after an early lunch play resumed at two o'clock. It gave us time to reanalyse the ''Test match'' on Sunday between English and Australian Press elevens. It produced Australia's one triumph so far during the summer — and the extraordinary scoreline of Lush caught Packer bowled Lord: TCCB spokesman dismissed by a combination of rebel organiser and (erstwhile) crusader for defection. It was a great pleasure to bat with Ian Chappell and something of a strain resisting the many imprecations to run Kerry Packer out when he came in for the final two overs. Equally distracting were the suggestions that Frith was playing for the wrong side. But birth qualifications are one thing, time spent in one or other country and affiliations of temperament another. Anyhow, the newspaper and TV cameramen were there in droves, and ''shot'' Mr Packer from every angle as he made two not out, held the slip catch, and kept wicket capably against Ian Chappell's sometimes wayward spin bowling. The moderate-sized crowd gave him a hot reception, but he was there simply to enjoy himself and relax, and I believe he succeeded.

Play in the ''other'' match began at two, and the guarantee that England would win the Ashes this day and not the next was strengthened when Greg Chappell was out in the seventh over. Two strokes which would normally have gone racing to the line brought only three runs apiece because of the damp outfield. Then, in playing indeterminately at Willis, he edged to Greig at second slip, his 36 having taken about three hours. It was Willis's first wicket of the match and 98th in Test matches.

Robinson was prepared to go after the bowling, as usual, though he didn't make contact all that often. A four through cover off Hendrick was followed by a huge swish at the air, and then Marsh came into the picture, sweaterless, warlike, aiming to break a dreadful run of Test failures, crashing a brutal straight-drive to the boundary, almost

As always the crucial wicket, Greg Chappell is caught by Tony Greig off Bob Willis for a second-innings 36. The expected result was now only a formality

cutting umpire Alley in two, and taking 11 off a Willis over with hearty blows through the off side. Then Roope put him down at the finer gully position, two-handed to his right. The error was so untypical that an air of disbelief surrounded it.

Marsh was risking injury in the vigour which he imparted to his strokes and attempted strokes. He missed with four almighty swishes at Willis and finished the over with a couple of cut fours.

Botham came on in place of Willis, and managed a wide, and Robinson pulled a ball from outside off for three. Sawdust was needed, and gave Hendrick sufficient foothold to send a nasty one to Robinson which he tried to leave alone but which hit his elbow and dropped into his stumps. That made it 167 for 6, and any anxiety towards the weather was being allayed by increasing periods of sunshine. For

Rod Marsh decided that Australia would go down with at least his guns blazing, and returned to form in the second innings with a hard-hit 63. Here Tony Greig lies prone having spilt a caught-and-bowled chance, up to now a rare England fielding lapse

Robinson, though, it was gloom — out for 20 for the second time.

Marsh off-drove Botham for four, sending Boycott leaping after the ball over the line and on top of the wicket-covers, which fortunately took his weight. Bright, having swished and missed a few times, played Hendrick to midwicket, where the ball this time just beat the fieldsman. It was needing a good hit to make a four, and after drinks Marsh kept making them. There was life in the pitch, attributable only to its basic nature and to the light covering of grass, which must have been helped by the damp atmosphere over the past 36 hours, and a lifter from Hendrick had Bright getting his beard out of the way in the nick of time. The next ball got him, caught by Greig at second slip, the snick going fast off a flailing bat.

An inside edge for four by Marsh took him to 37, his highest of the series. Botham bowled another wide, and Marsh, having hooked Hendrick for four, saw Walker make a cumbersome glance to the boundary to raise 200 at half-past-three. Greig relieved Hendrick, and Marsh on-drove for four, his ninth, and ran a single to gully to reach his half-century in 80 minutes. Shortly Underwood came on at the Kirkstall end, as Botham left the field with a sore tendon. Walker pulled a lifter from Greig for another boundary, there being no point in prodding and

Throughout the series Bob Willis was consistently fast and hostile, and his 27 wickets were a major contribution to England's success. Here he comprehensively ends Max Walker's stubborn eighth-wicket stand of 65 with Rod Marsh

poking, and soon after those who were within vision of it had espied Randall on the long-leg boundary scratching a four-letter word into the turf in three-foot letters (revealing, one can only imagine, some sort of interest in ornithology), Marsh was missed by Greig, right-handed, from a caught-and-bowled chance as he operated from around the wicket. Like the earlier Roope error, it happened when it mattered not so very much; this, throughout the series, was a significant feature.

Marsh ran Greig through gully for three and lofted Underwood for four to raise the fifty stand, and Walker amused as he edged and spun round and round trying to locate the ball. A stumping attempt followed: no shortage of animation.

As the new ball was soon available, Brearley gave Woolmer a short spell, and Ealham caught the eye as he scuttled round the boundary, like Alice's rabbit, and picked up left-handed on the run. With Greig fielding courageously close to Walker at silly point for Underwood, the big batsman hit a three to midwicket, and the new ball was taken, with as much expectation as ever. With it, Willis did the trick.

The Warwickshire giant — born in Sunderland and nurtured in Surrey — knocked out Walker's middle stump, sent down a no-ball to Thomson, and hit his off stump next ball, delivering him of a ''pair''.

It was also his 100th Test wicket, taken in his 28th Test and at a climactic moment. He was now bowling very fast, and Pascoe's chances were slim — but he held on stoutly. It was the other batsman, the robust Marsh, with 63 to his name, easily top-score for Australia in the match, who fell, putting a seal on the match, the series, and possession of the Ashes. He tried for a six back over Hendrick's head but caught the ball with the end of the bat and send it swirling to extra cover, where Randall caught it over his shoulder, tossed it away, and did a cartwheel. It was 4.40 pm, and England had the Ashes back 31 months after losing them so painfully at Sydney.

The crowd massed in front of the four-up-four-down pavilion and shouted for their heroes, who came out in small clusters, with Greig and Brearley making one notable appearance and the godlike Boycott another. There was barely an unsmiling face anywhere in that sea of festivity, and small wonder, for England have won back the Ashes at home not much more often than once per generation (and never at Headingley), and many of those at the ground and watching on television were not even born when Len Hutton's side pulled off an emotional victory in 1953 — Coronation Year as opposed to Jubilee Year — and not so very many others would have been able to recall Percy Chapman's triumph in 1926 (the year the Queen was born).

This was England's first 3-0 victory in a home series against Australia since 1886, when A. G. Steel's side drubbed H. J. H. Scott's Australians, Grace, Shrewsbury, Lohmann, Barlow, and Briggs, all long dead, doing similar things to Boycott, Woolmer, Willis, Botham, and Knott in 1977.

Midst the popping of corks and the football-style chanting and rhythmic clapping of the tireless gathering of youngsters, the interviews were held, and both skippers were polite towards the opposition, Greg Chappell congratulating England for a ''well-deserved'' victory in which they outplayed Australia, and Mike Brearley pointing to the catches held by his side and dropped by Australia — the most crucial of factors. He felt that England's best performance had been at Trent Bridge, where conditions had not been helpful, and that the greater depth and sustained fitness of his group of bowlers had been highly significant. He paid tribute yet again to Tony Greig, who had first sparked off the new England spirit, helping to pick the right people for the job, and encouraging all the players to offer their thoughts.

Chappell told Pressmen that he still felt there had not been a great deal of difference between the basic abilities of the two sides. He attached

The Ashes are won by England and Rod Marsh congratulates Mike Brearley, Geoff Boycott prepares to protect his cap against souvenir-hunters, three of the four Kentish men in the England team, Derek Underwood, Alan Knott and Alan Ealham (substitute), head for the safety of the pavilion, while the fourth, Bob Woolmer, looks to be off to the middle for more action, as the inevitable crowd invasion begins

a lot of importance to experience, and felt that youngsters like Serjeant and Hughes would not have benefited from playing in a losing side. One was tempted to ask whether the defeats would necessarily have been so marked had a player or two of identifiable class — even if inexperienced — been included. This would be something for posterity to argue about.

Then the bombshell: the Australian captain announced to the outside world that the Oval Test match would be his last. He had intended not to embark on another full-length overseas tour because of his desire to spend more time with family and in business, but the Packer developments made it unlikely that he would be chosen for Australia at home. Thus, he was resigned to ending his Test career at the end of this month. Again, Test match cricket was to be depleted by class it could ill afford, bringing back thoughts of McCabe, O'Neill, Simpson, Cowper, Sheahan, even Ian Chappell. The way had already been opened for a massive influx of new faces in Test cricket, but it was a depressing thought that so many would be forced into top-level representation too soon. The ideal way is to slip a newcomer into an established side, as happened only just over six years back, when, at Perth, Gregory Stephen Chappell first took strike in a Test . . . and made 108.

Greg Chappell writes:

We had a few problems just before the Headingley Test match. Max Walker and Kerry O'Keeffe had cortisone injections, Max for his knee injury, though X-rays had established that there was no bone damage, and Kerry to his index finger, in an attempt to break up the fluid. Both of them had been in a good deal of discomfort.

But the real low point came soon after the team had arrived late at night in Sunderland. Some of the players, sitting talking in the lounge, suddenly found themselves taking part in a ''hate session'', with the bitterness and frustration built up during past weeks now pouring out. Some of the younger players vented criticism of the more experienced members of the team, and Doug Walters copped the lot. When things aren't going well it seems that a person turns upon the nearest other person, and it was a pity that the whole team wasn't there, for poor old Doug became the target. The younger players had grown restless at the lack of consistent success, but seemed to forget that the more experienced players were also very unhappy at the losses in the Test matches. Probably it was a good thing in one way that the air was cleared, and that several players got something out of their systems, even if it would have been better done in private.

Most of us were keen to get some rest before the fourth Test, and I took it easy around the hotel, which was set in lovely rural surroundings just outside Leeds. I caught up on letter-writing and did some reading, keeping my feet up whenever possible to relieve the tendon strain in the arches of both feet. My cricket boots with new arch supports arrived from the manufacturer. I had had moulds made of my feet by the same people who had manufactured Mike Brearley's crash-helmet, and I took the chance of wearing them around, breaking them in. They felt comfortable at the net practice on the day before the Test, and it seemed that the team's morale was high again. We had an enjoyable team dinner on the eve of the match, having entertained the Press corps to drinks beforehand and read them a lighthearted preview, by David Hookes and myself, of the Australia-England Press XI match coming up on the Sunday. We used some of the Australian writers' favourite phrases, and hoped they would take our remarks with the same equanimity as we usually took theirs!

At the team meeting we spent little time talking about the England players individually. We had talked a lot about them in the past few weeks, and there didn't seem to be much point in discussing them further. Hope was not lost: if we played well we knew we could win this one, and I felt reasonably confident that we could pull one back here at Leeds.

Before the toss I went out to the wicket, where Rod Marsh was squatting on his haunches, and said to him, "Well, what do you think?" He said it was probably worth giving some thought to sending England in, with the greenness still in the pitch. I suppose every time you walk out to look at a wicket you have that thought in mind, if the conditions are likely to be helpful. But it was a huge gamble, with us two-down with two to play. If the weather could have been relied upon for the duration of the match that would have been one thing. But we couldn't depend on the weather. Even if the haze helped us, if England suffered little damage in the first session we would be likely to pay heavily for such a gamble. I felt that I was due to lose a toss, and that Mike Brearley would make the decision for us by batting. He said he was about due to win a toss, and when I called tails as usual, the coin fell heads-up, and England were batting. There was expectation and confidence among the bowlers in our dressing-room as we prepared to take the field.

Jeff Thomson bowled two balls, and Rod Marsh turned to me and said, "It's about time we had a wicket in the first over." I replied that it was overdue now, and Jeff's next ball, still more of a loosener, got a faint edge as Brearley played at it, hitting the ground at the same time, and we had a great early breakthrough, though the England skipper looked dumbfounded.

Max Walker bowled magnificently in this opening spell, and Boycott and Woolmer played and missed quite often. But they saw it through until lunch, though Jeff Thomson and Len Pascoe also bowled exceptionally well. I swung the fast bowlers around at both ends, though at times they had trouble with their run-ups, and they used the breeze and heavyish atmosphere skilfully. Len Pascoe bowled one marvellous over to Boycott, keeping the ball well up at first, then dropping three just short of a length. The third got what we thought was a touch to the glove and through to Rod Marsh, but as Geoff

Boycott pointed to his forearm umpire Budd gave it not-out, and we were very disappointed, for this was the most important wicket of the innings. Boycott had been our stumbling block at Trent Bridge, and it took little imagination to realise how we wanted to get rid of him. I have no objection to batsmen not walking if they feel they have a fair chance of being spared by the umpire (I've seen enough Australian batsmen wait), but, like Tony Greig earlier in the series, Boycott went to the length of making this sign, and I do object to that sort of thing. Standing your ground is one thing, but trying to influence the umpire is something else.

Unfortunately, in the afternoon session there was another incident, when Boycott tried to flick a quicker ball from Ray Bright down the leg side, and with bat some distance from body, he got what we thought was a fine touch through to Rod Marsh. Ray leapt into the air, confident that he had removed the prize wicket from the England line-up, and the entire team went up with him, thinking it was a legitimate catch. But one person on the field — umpire Bill Alley — was not so sure, and Boycott was reprieved. It was the last ball of the over, and Ray Bright, still in a state of shock, snatched at his hat as umpire Alley tossed it to him, and obviously muttered something. The umpire reprimanded him, and I had to intervene and calm Ray down, apologising to Bill Alley. I don't approve of this kind of reaction, though the umpire might have been partly to blame by not handing him his hat back. This probably served to incite the bowler to react.

It was another of those days when nothing seemed to be going right. Earlier Boycott had edged one just short of Rod Marsh, who made a great effort, diving forward and to his right, touching the ball just as it landed. It would have been an unbelievable catch.

We needed to get England out by lunch on the second day for as little over 300 as possible. We needed time as much as anything. Starting at 252 for 4, England were moving towards an impregnable position, and they lost only one further wicket before lunch, Graham Roope being very well caught by Doug Walters at slip. Boycott carried on as before, getting away with the odd mistake. It had me thinking that we had been putting catches down in the slips cordon probably because the pitches were so slow that many edged shots were not carrying. Consequently we had to stand nearer the bat than was ideal, and when a ball really took off it came at a hot pace. Not that it was dropped catches that were hampering us at this time. We simply could not find the edge. Max Walker must have averaged one-and-a-half balls an over where he beat the batsman without touching willow.

When I brought Len Pascoe back later in the day I had to remain wary of runs, and so put two men in the covers. What happens? Boycott nicks the first delivery waist-high to where third slip would have been! Every move that we made seemed to be the wrong one. Fate seemed to be running the show, taunting us at every turn.

Boycott was batting us out of the match, and it looked as if England may even be batting into the third day. But in the afternoon Ray Bright bowled particularly well, removing Knott and Botham, and we were into the tailenders, who didn't offer much resistance. Any thoughts I had of our not batting that evening were soon dispelled.

Geoff Boycott's marathon innings was a terrific effort of concentration, and deserved all the praise it received. By the time it ended the clouds were showing signs of closing in, and there were to be difficult times ahead for us. The first day had produced good conditions for batting, and even when we took the second new ball it didn't swing all that much, moving a little off the seam. Nevertheless, we were feeling disheartened as we set about replying to England's 436 in that final 85 minutes, after over ten hours in the field during which we had experienced every kind of frustration. England's bowlers would be able to throw everything into that last period and with this negative attitude we became victims of nothing less than a debacle.

In ideal bowling conditions, we first had the disaster of Ian Davis's dismissal in the second over, and I was the next to go, lunging at a ball from Mike Hendrick and edging to my opposing captain at slip. A ball from Hendrick just previously had probably been my undoing. It came back sharply from a similar length, and it was a close lbw call. I felt I had to get onto the front foot fairly early in order to avoid such a fate. This really meant that I was committing myself a fraction too early, and the ball that got me was not truly drivable. All I did was help it on its way to slip.

Rick McCosker's run-out was tragic. He didn't realise he was backing up quite as far as he was, and Derek Randall's smart piece of fielding did the rest. With the further fall of David Hookes and Doug Walters that evening it could be said that we were practically out of it.

On the third day Richie Robinson's downfall was a triumph for shrewd captaincy. Mike Brearley positioned a silly point for him, realising that with his strong forward movement he was likely to inside-edge a ball quite hard in that direction. Richie's reaction was to go for anything up outside off with plenty of blade. When he aimed to drive Hendrick he succeeded only in edging to slip. It was further evidence that this was not a pitch for strokemaking. Most of England's batsmen had played within themselves, taking the rank half-volley as the only ball from which runs could be taken with any kind of impunity.

Once again we were copping it from the Press. Yet we had been giving it everything we'd got in the field, knowing that nothing was really going our way. There was no avoiding a resignation now as it enveloped us. Ian Botham bowled well as our first innings folded, swinging the ball and using the moisture which seemed to stay in the wicket. On the third morning the groundsman had suggested we had the light roller, as the heavy one would bring up more moisture. But wickets fell all the same.

Mike Brearley had no hesitation in enforcing the follow-on, though I suspect there were those in the English camp who would have preferred him to bat again, shutting us out completely and making certain that England would not be embarrassed in a fourth innings on a crumbling pitch, by some near-miracle. Bowling conditions were still ideal, and Mike probably made up his mind without difficulty.

I didn't use any roller before our second innings, and things seemed to be going quite well as Rick McCosker and Ian Davis took us into the thirties. Then, just on lunch, Ian attempted a leg glance to a ball down the leg side from Tony Greig, and after it had brushed his pad it was taken by Alan Knott, and the appeal was answered in the affirmative. It was a very disappointed Ian Davis who made his way back to the pavilion. Again we had the bad break. It seems to me that when things are going well you don't notice the misfortunes anywhere near so much; when things are bad, the rotten twists and turns seem to multiply.

As I walked to the wicket I reasoned that we should try to play Boycott's game, making the bowlers bowl to us, and hope that by sound play we could build up at least one big partnership. The new ball hadn't swung much, but after a few overs the umpires decided it had gone soft and square, and it was changed. Unluckily for us the replacement did swing, and we lost Rick McCosker right on the stroke of lunch, caught behind as he tried to pull his bat away from an outswinger. The catch would not have reached first slip, and Alan Knott did very well to reach it at full stretch.

I was not at all happy about this replacing of the original ball with another. When we were in the field we had not felt it necessary to refer the soft ball to the umpires until the 35th over, yet here was England complaining in the eighth over and again in the tenth. It had not moved off the straight-and-narrow, but Tony Greig's first delivery with the replacement swung appreciably, and I saw it as a compounding feature of the adverse way things had been going for us. The umpires had not even shown the old or new ball to the batsmen, and when I asked Lloyd Budd what had gone wrong with the old ball, he said it had gone square and soft, and asked if the replacement was swinging. I put him in the picture by telling him that it had swung "square".

I thought the light after lunch was too poor for play to continue but the umpires decided otherwise. The main problem was the row of trees at the Kirkstall Lane end, which made it extremely difficult to see the ball out of the hand of a tall fast bowler such as Hendrick or Willis. A couple of times I failed to pick up the line of the ball and played at thin air. I tried to make it fairly plain to the umpires that I felt play should have been discontinued for the time being. It was not that the light was so very bad, but the dull background in the generally sombre conditions made batting a mighty difficult business.

So I was especially disappointed when David Hookes was given out lbw during this period. The introduction of Woolmer into the attack — perfectly understandable in the conditions — soon brought results when he cut one back some distance to Doug Walters and trapped him in front, and we were really struggling. Richie Robinson came in, and we played only at those we had to play at, some balls seaming and bouncing quite a lot. Survival was everything now.

After the tea interval we faced only a couple of balls, in terrible light, before the umpires decided it was too bad to warrant further play. As we sat in the dressing-room the rain began to intensify, and at 6.15 Bill Alley came to me and said, "Well, I think that'll be it for the day. We'll just wait till twenty past." I had the pads off by now, and was starting to get undressed. I was down to my singlet and socks when Bill reappeared.

"Ah, come on!" I said jokingly, "don't tell me you've changed your mind?"

"Yes," he said. "I think it's brightened up a bit and we're going to go back out there."

I said, "You must be joking?" — to which he replied, "No, we're not. You'd better get dressed."

We took the field again at 6.27 pm, the regulations stating that if more than an hour is lost during the day because of weather conditions an hour can be added to the day providing play is possible at 6.30. The light was still pretty poor, and the pitch had taken some rain — hardly ideal conditions. And when I lost one completely from Bob Willis as the ball came out of the background of trees, the umpires must have realised how awkward conditions were, and they conferred again, this time for us to come off for good.

My impression was that the umpires might have had thoughts that the match could be got over and done with that day, and may even have been encouraged to take the field again by some of the administrators. But perhaps I am too suspicious, from a position of pretty abject hopelessness. Only rain was likely to save us now, unless by chance batting conditions should drastically improve.

I had a long sleep-in on the Sunday morning, the rest day, and then went with David Hookes after lunch to watch a bit of the Australia-England Press cricket match at Harrogate. The Australian side made 220 in their overs allocation, Ian Chappell scoring 61, Dave Frith 58, and Peter McFarline 43, and in worsening light the English side made 147, with Peter Lush of the TCCB hitting 53. So Australia had some success on Yorkshire soil that weekend.

The fourth day of the Test was wet at the start, but play was eventually able to start at two o'clock, and in better light than on Saturday but on a pitch still offering the bowlers something we held out until nearly five o'clock, with myself out fairly early, Richie Robinson getting out unluckily, bowled off his arm, and Rod Marsh playing a fine attacking innings, full of defiance.

We lost the match by an innings and 85 runs, and with it the Ashes, which Australia had won so convincingly under Ian Chappell in the 1974-75 series. The reasons for our reversal were several, and I will go into them shortly. Meanwhile, I offered my congratulations to Mike Brearley and his team for a well-deserved victory, and at the Press conference that followed I announced by impending retirement from Test cricket. Headingley 1977 would always mean sadness for me.

It will also carry memories of a pretty unseemly incident that evening back at the hotel when two of the younger players decided to air strong protests to Rod Marsh and Richie Robinson at the way the Test teams had been chosen. The bar is hardly the ideal place to discuss internal matters such as this, but Kerry O'Keeffe and Gary Cosier, perhaps a little frustrated at their relative lack of success on the tour, took these two senior players to task. Rod Marsh was especially upset at some of the things that were said.

Some of the frustration was understandable. Almost the whole side felt that things had not turned out as well as they should have done. Results had not shown the true latent talent in the side, and nobody had done as well as he would have liked. The slow start to the tour, when the rain seemed to follow us everywhere, was a handicap that left its mark, and when opportunities occurred, the younger players were very often unable to grasp them by timely performances. Richie Robinson's enthusiasm and experience were, I feel, the right ingredients on the occasions when he was picked in the Test team. He made a smooth transition from wicketkeeping to fielding very well indeed at short leg or in the outfield. His second-innings 34 at Trent Bridge entitled him to a further chance at Headingley. Not everyone saw it that way.

Experience is vital at Test level. By that, I mean that a young player must weather the ups-and-downs outside Test cricket, not in it while he is virtually untried at the top level. I would illustrate my point by citing the case of Paul Sheahan, who entered Test cricket after a very short and successful period in first-class cricket at home and, when he suffered a few failures in international cricket, actually learnt to play first-class cricket at the Test level. It set him back for a long time. It was only when he retired, at a fairly early age, that he was beginning to reveal his true potential.

On this 1977 tour we were compelled to play one of the young newcomers in the Tests, and David Hookes was the lucky — or unlucky — one, depending on which way you look at it. He was thrown in at the deep end, to learn and develop his first-class cricket at Test level.

It's all very well for someone to sit down and, with hindsight, say "You did this wrong, and you did that wrong", but when you have to make decisions on the spot things can be a bit more difficult.

After the fourth Test we had a leisurely journey down to London, and in the afternoon those of us who had signed up with Kerry Packer were invited to his suite at the Dorchester. I had met Kerry twice before and Rod Marsh once, but the majority of the players had never met him. This was the chance for questions to be asked, and the players were able to clarify any doubts they might have had. It was a generally satisfactory get-together.

At Arundel we met a Rest of the World side in a one-day match in aid of the Queen's Silver Jubilee Fund. Recent rain had made conditions anything but ideal, but we did at least manage to play, on a pitch that was slow and keeping rather low, and in poor light. I won the toss and batted, expecting that the wet outfield would soon make the ball greasy. As it happened, we didn't get the ball off the square often enough to make it greasy! At one stage we were five down for 20, with three of the boys making ducks. David Hookes made a face-saving 33 and I got 29 batting at seven, and that was about it. We made the World XI work hard for their 107 runs, and it took them until the 48th over to get them. Not a brilliant cricket day, but the Appeal benefited by around £5000, and that was no bad thing.

The Middlesex game ought to have given everyone a chance to press claims for inclusion in the final Test match, especially Mick Malone and Geoff Dymock, since Len Pascoe's injured thigh, sustained in the Nottingham Test and aggravated at Leeds, was causing him concern. The doctor put him on tablets for five days, and though he was expected to be fit in time for the Test, he would not be match-fit. But the last of the county matches proved useless as a guide to form. The rain had restricted the preparation work on the wicket, and after the Middlesex tail had taken them past 200 on the second morning, their spinners had a field day on a dry pitch, dispatching us for 149. On the third day there was hardly any play because of rain, so it was something of a non-match, and left us in a quandary when it came to sitting down to choose the fifth Test team.

I had a very pleasant surprise on the day before the Oval Test when my wife Judy arrived. It had been a last-minute decision. She had decided to come earlier but the thought of travelling with two young children forced her to change her mind. Then friends of ours in Brisbane, Jim and Joan Sokoll, insisted that Judy go to see the last Test match while they minded the children. She arrived at Heathrow airport at 6.30 in the morning. It looked quite bright and promised to be a fine day, but by the time I had booked her into a London hotel and moved on to The Oval it was pouring with rain and there was no chance of practice. In fact the rain was so persistent that it was obvious that hopes of play on the opening day were extremely thin.

FOURTH TEST MATCH *Headingley, August 11, 12, 13, 15*

Paying attendance 77,500; takings £140,000

ENGLAND

		min	6	4
*J. M. Brearley	c Marsh b Thomson	0	2	—	—
G. Boycott	c Chappell b Pascoe	191	620	—	23+
R. A. Woolmer	c Chappell b Thomson	37	134	—	6
D. W. Randall	lbw b Pascoe	20	25	—	3
A. W. Greig	b Thomson	43	104	1	4
G. R. J. Roope	c Walters b Thomson	34	120	—	4
+A. P. E. Knott	lbw b Bright	57	180	—	7
I. T. Botham	b Bright	0	1	—	—
D. L. Underwood	c Bright b Pascoe	6	27	—	1
M. Hendrick	c Robinson b Pascoe	4	10	—	1
R. G. D. Willis	not out	5	14	—	—
Extras (b5, lb9, nb22, w3)		39			
		436	+ plus one 5		

Fall: 0, 82, 105, 201, 275, 398, 398, 412, 422

Bowling: Thomson 34-7-113-4, Walker 48-21-97-0,
Pascoe 34.4-10-91-4, Walters 3-1-5-0, Bright 26-9-66-2,
Chappell 10-2-25-0.

AUSTRALIA

		min	6	4			min	6	4
R. B. McCosker	run out	27	52	1	3	c Knott b Greig	12	65	—	—
I. C. Davis	lbw b Hendrick	0	8	—	—	c Knott b Greig	19	46	—	4
*G. S. Chappell	c Brearley b Hendrick	4	15	—	—	c Greig b Willis	36	180	—	4
D. W. Hookes	lbw b Botham	24	29	—	4	lbw b Hendrick	25	35	—	1
K. D. Walters	c Hendrick b Botham	4	19	—	—	lbw b Woolmer	15	48	—	2
R. D. Robinson	c Greig b Hendrick	20	52	—	3	b Hendrick	20	116	—	2
+R. W. Marsh	c Knott b Botham	2	23	—	—	c Randall b Hendrick	63	132	—	9
R. J. Bright	not out	9	34	—	1	c Greig b Hendrick	5	16	—	1
M. H. N. Walker	c Knott b Botham	7	7	—	1	b Willis	30	63	—	4
J. R. Thomson	b Botham	0	1	—	—	b Willis	0	1	—	—
L. S. Pascoe	b Hendrick	0	8	—	—	not out	0	4	—	—
Extras (lb3, nb2, w1)		6				(b2, lb3, nb18, w4)	27			
		103					248			

Fall: 8, 26, 52, 57, 66, 77, 87, 100, 100

31, 35, 63, 97, 130, 167, 179, 244, 245

Bowling: Willis 5-0-35-0, Hendrick 15.3-2-41-4,
Botham 11-3-21-5.

Willis 14-7-32-3, Hendrick 22.5-6-54-4,
Greig 20-7-64-2, Botham 17-3-47-0,
Woolmer 8-4-8-1, Underwood 8-3-16-0.

Umpires: W. E. Alley and W. L. Budd

Toss won by England

ENGLAND WON BY AN INNINGS AND 85 RUNS

8. FIFTH TEST MATCH

KENNINGTON OVAL, AUGUST 25, 26, 27, 29, 30

David Frith writes:

FIRST DAY

There was none. At Old Trafford in 1890 and 1938 not a ball was bowled in a scheduled Test match, and the same happened, more surprisingly, in Melbourne during the 1970-71 tour. These matches — or non-events — were recalled during the hours preceding the calling-off of the first day's play at The Oval, following days and days of rain. By mid-afternoon on the Thursday the sun shone leeringly down, as it often does, and the crowd, except that part of it which always waits to see the gods emerge from the dressing-room or exercise in a vaguely self-conscious way in the outfield, had wended its disappointed way home.

Thoughts of those three slushy washouts of bygone years had dawned at least a day before the scheduled start of this final Test match. The rain was so persistent that summer seemed to have been written off irrevocably for another twelve months. This was depressing far beyond the usual for The Oval, where traditionally the last Test of the season is played, with its farewells and sad backward-glancing. It was worse this year, since so many of the players seemed unlikely to play Test cricket again, swallowed up by the commercial octopus still described, for want of a better expression, as the Packer circus.

While hope remained that a prompt start could be made on the second day, I still harboured memories of the 1955 Test at Sydney — a match which still afforded more colourful snippets than any other — which did not get under way until two o'clock on the fourth day. Then, Graveney made a picturesque hundred, I saw Hutton and Compton batting for the last time, Wardle teased, to the sound of a boozy chorus from British sailors on the Hill, and there were farewells of many kinds, even if not recognised at the time. The most bizarre was Len Hutton's. He bowled Richie Benaud with the last ball of the match.

Here at Kennington in 1977, no teams had been announced and no toss made. Australia dropped Davis and Robinson and brought in Serjeant, Hughes, O'Keeffe and Malone to make a thirteen. For England, John Lever returned to the twelve, Ian Botham's foot injury having ruled him out for the rest of the season, which included Somerset's Gillette Cup semi-final against Middlesex, already rained off five times. Fixture problems abounded.

SECOND DAY

Play may have been called off at 2.30 pm on the first day — prematurely in the eyes of many, though they might have understood had they trodden across the stricken playing area — but on the second day play began on time, after a warmish early morning, the clouds, having broken up, now riding in split formation, not without the threat that they might mass again and drown us all.

Australia won the toss and put England in on a wicket of a deeper hue than is usually seen at The Oval. The story of recent Oval Test matches has been of big, slow scores made on straw-coloured pitches, with the follow-on the main question. Once avoided, both countries have been firmly set on course for a draw.

Miller was made twelfth man by England, and Australia left out O'Keeffe and made Pascoe twelfth, which presumed full fitness after all when so recently it had been doubted that a thigh injury would allow him to play again on the tour.

Thomson started from the pavilion end, and Malone, on Test debut, took the Vauxhall end, with Brearley and Boycott, the envy of Australia for soundness, aiming to get England away to another good start. Slowly, surely, they accomplished the first part of their mission. With a lush outfield and the long Oval boundaries making runs that much harder, it was an hour and a quarter before the first boundary was hit — a pull by Boycott towards the faded green gasholder. He repeated the stroke to Walker's next delivery and the score was suddenly racing at two per over overall. The momentum was building up noticeably, Brearley taking three off Malone through cover. The bowler switched to around the wicket, and occasionally worried both batsmen. He even managed a couple of bouncers, something scarcely seen, since Thomson had abandoned this weapon early in the series, reckoning it to take too much out of him on these placid wickets. In fact Thomson was now appearing appreciably less hostile, and his enthralling delivery action seemed somewhat restricted, the ball coming up from only his hip and not his hindquarters. We were, it seemed, seeing him in an English Test match for the last time.

The first incident of the match to stir the crowd was McCosker's missing of Brearley, who tried to withdraw his bat from a ball from Malone and sent it low to the slips fielder's left shoe. He got his hand to it, but spilled it, and the familiar gestures of disgust were adopted. Brearley was 19 at the time, and in the next over, the 25th, there was a spate of runs off Thomson, who had replaced Walker. Boycott square-drove powerfully for three, Brearley played a delayed drive to the third-man rope, his first boundary, and then took a single to raise the fifty. In his next over Thomson bowled a wide, and Brearley then took another four, steered through slip. Just before lunch Chappell tried Bright from the Vauxhall end, resting Mick Malone after 13 admirable overs for a mere 15 runs, and England reached lunch at 60 without loss, both batsmen 29. Perhaps the worst of the conditions had been weathered, but the thought was always there: what if the unprotected pitch should be flooded later, and Underwood were to have the ball tossed to him? It had not happened for a long, long time.

The bat was defeated fairly often after lunch as Walker, who, surprisingly, was smearing facial sunburn cream on the ball, pounded heavily in from the pavilion end and Malone from the other. The young, strong-looking, curly-haired Westralian, grandson of Irishfolk, purred in with an easy approach, hesitant only for a split-second as he turned his shoulders for delivery, which is not dissimilar to Mike Hendrick's. Red stains on his right buttock, left groin and left breast bore testimony to the work he put in on keeping the ball shiny.

The score crept up into the eighties, Brearley once losing his footing as he played Walker to leg, where islands of sawdust served as reminders of a wet week. The sun now shone, quite warmly, and from the distant Press annexe, high above the third-man boundary, the small figures of the players were starting to recede to mere silhouettes as the autumn sun came down. Hookes kept interest alive with a tumbling pick-up and throw as he rolled over, and run-making continued to be as difficult a process as finding parking spaces for cars in central London.

The opening stand had reached 86 when that rarest of events this series occurred: Boycott's dismissal. He played at a Walker inswinger, and the ball spooned via bat and leg to McCosker at slip. The Master was reluctant to leave, but umpire Constant's finger was unwavering, and for the first time in the '77 Tests Geoff Boycott had come close to

After a quiet tour, Mick Malone was given his Test debut at The Oval. He returned a remarkable performance, bowling 47 overs in England's first innings and taking 5 for 63, and then scoring 46 runs in a stand of 100 with Max Walker

failing, though he had done a responsible job in launching the innings and soothing any English brows that by chance might have been furrowed.

Slight anxiety arose very soon afterwards. With two runs added, England lost Brearley, who edged a Malone outswinger straight to Marsh. The captain had batted for three hours, and now it was turning into a cricket match after all.

Randall was received with noisy acclaim as he bounced through the gate before his captain was halfway off the field. He needed a big score now after a quiet series and a quiet county season. He perhaps had to reassure everyone, himself included, that he had earned a passage to Pakistan and New Zealand. At the other end Woolmer got off the mark with a hooked two off Walker, but was then hit on the pads, giving the Australians cause to shout loudly.

The hundred was eventually reached in the 56th over, celebrated, as they say, with a four to third man by Woolmer as he stood tall and cut Thomson. Runs, though, were still hard to find, and the bowlers operated in the certain knowledge that there was something in it for them. Malone kept at it, and soon his reward came again. Randall, after a most undistinguished innings of three in 45 minutes, one devoid of sparkle or convincing technique, offered a jabbing kind of cut at an off-side ball and touched it to Marsh. England were 104 for 3. And without addition, Woolmer fell, leg-before to Thomson, playing across the line. England were collapsing.

The slide continued when Greig attempted a square-drive at Malone and gave Bright a chest-high catch in the gully: 106 for 5, and Knott, preceding a tail of four prodders, came in and settled into his comical stance. He was hit on the pads first ball, and cricket once more seemed a difficult game, an impression lightened only by a whippy glance for two and a hearty straight-drive for four by Roope off Thomson just before tea, which was taken at 118 for 5 off 63 overs. Very much Australia's session — their finest of the series. Five prime English wickets for 58 runs in 32 overs was a gorgeous justification for putting the other side in.

Roope was beaten once or twice, Marsh showing clever thought and straight aim by underarming and hitting the stumps, with the Surrey man's foot just inside the crease. Knott had neither impressed with his immediate confidence, as at Trent Bridge, nor shown signs of being out of touch, as at Headingley. Much rested upon him now, and many had been the times that Australia had had to submit to his flailing bat. But not now. Malone, still pitching the ball well up and getting curve in the flight, brought him half-forward and found the edge, McCosker at second slip enjoying a happier moment as he clung to the low catch.

Malone had a chance of capturing his fifth wicket when Roope drove back a full-toss, but the catch, to his left hand, went begging. Amends of a kind were made when Lever was stranded across his crease and adjudged lbw. Malone, past 30 overs with hardly more than a run per over against him, thus picked up his fifth wicket, for 40 runs, on his first day in Test cricket, and once again one wondered if his earlier inclusion might have influenced the series, and once again one remembered Bob Massie, another wonderful Western Australian swinger.

The run rate seemed to have slipped irretrievably below two per over as Roope and Underwood opposed Walker and the gallant Malone — who must have been enjoying his toils, all the same, and feeling no pain. The applause for runs was a clue to the situation. There had been times this summer when runs were plentiful and the crowd response to them almost blasé. But now when Roope cover-drove Walker for three and Underwood did the same, and later Roope delightfully drove Malone for another three which would have been an automatic four on last year's brown and barren Oval outfield, the reception from the big crowd was as warm as their beer in its plastic cups. A four to long leg and a single by Underwood off the toiling Walker brought up the 150 in the 79th over, and though Malone showed signs of tiring — and *must* have been tiring, in his 40th over of the day — a change was made at the pavilion end, Thomson coming on.

Roope square-cut him for three, Walters' long throw almost touching the bails on the full. Roope soon tried again, and this time perfected his timing and found the boundary.

At five-past-six the new ball was taken. Chappell took it from David Constant and tossed it to Malone as if the thought had never occurred to him that the large 26-year-old should ever stop bowling.

The wicket, an important one since the 39 added was the highest after the opening stand, came when Thomson launched a yorker at Roope, and the tall man was beaten on the downswing. For Thomson there was extra satisfaction as it was his 100th wicket in Tests, a trail of devastation achieved in just 22 matches. He was to finish this Test, only his 14th against England, with the large haul of 72 English wickets.

Underwood's number now came up. After stout resistance and occasional handsome strokes, including a recent three through gully, he went for a largish drive against Thomson and was castled. This brought in England's last man, Willis, with the clock hands soon to meet at 6.30 and the light fading. He took four along the ground through slip off Thomson, and brought back memories of Richie Robinson as he thrust his angular legs all about the place and stretched his bat out, admittedly well angled turfwards.

Following his amazing recovery from a serious shoulder injury at Christmas, Jeff Thomson continued to trouble the English batsmen, and in bowling Graham Roope for 38 he took his 100th Test wicket in only 22 matches. By the end of this Test, his 14th against England, he had taken as many as 72 against the old enemy

The umpires consulted once about the light, and consulted again for some strange reason just as 6.30 showed, and, rather untidily, the day's play ended with England still alive at 181 for 9, and Australia looking something like their old selves.

England 181 for 9 (J. M. Brearley 39, G. Boycott 39, G. R. J. Roope 38, M. F. Malone 5 for 53, J. R. Thomson 3 for 65).

THIRD DAY

There was still rain about. It drizzled over Guildford at midnight, and it poured in Sussex in the morning. Nevertheless, the start of play was delayed only ten minutes as the light lifted and the air dried for the moment. The major distraction of the day was the announcement by the Cornhill Insurance Company of a one-million-pound plan to support English Test cricket and cricketers over the next five years. The details had yet to be sorted out, but one thing was known: a man playing for England would henceforth receive £1000 per Test, a decided improvement on the current fee of £210.

Malone bowled the first over, Thomson the second, Walker the third, and Malone the fourth. Having thus settled into their ends, Malone (for the first time from the pavilion end) and Thomson proceeded to fail to break up the last-wicket partnership instantly as expected. Rather, Hendrick drove Malone gloriously for four — as good a stroke as any in the match to date — and remarkably this was the first boundary hit off Malone in the match, in his 45th over. Pending examination of over 800 Test match scorecards, this was presumed to be unique.

Willis enjoyed an over from Thomson, taking ten from it, with a glance for four and a tuck behind square for another, Serjeant just failing to cut it off on the line. Hendrick brought up the 200, and then played the old-fashioned dog-stroke, and when Willis put Malone through midwicket for four it was noticeable how much faster the outfield was today. Hendrick got four through slip and then played a drive off Thomson's next ball which might have come from a right-handed Sobers. It was a zany business. The stand reached 40, second-highest of the innings, when Thomson penetrated Hendrick's back-foot defence, and the innings ended at 214, with Willis on the verge of exceeding his highest Test score.

Australia's innings was delayed by more poor light, and there was 42 minutes between innings. When it eventually got under way, Serjeant took strike to Willis, was beaten a couple of times, and was leg-before to the last ball. Another horrible start.

Greg Chappell came in, applauded warmly in this his last Test appearance. He touched the green cap on his close-cropped head and walked, erect as ever, to a fate at the crease which many hoped would be less grisly than that which awaited Don Bradman 29 years ago on his farewell to Test cricket. It happened to be The Don's 69th birthday today.

McCosker and Chappell each made two before the lunch break, and Willis got a couple of bouncers out of his system, but the gloom would not relent, and with the protective covers on an otherwise empty field, the crowd waited patiently well beyond the scheduled resumption, wishing perhaps that the band and marching girls would come back on until action recommenced. The umpires made occasional appearances, and though the light seemed to have improved barely at all a restart was effected at 3.35 pm. But only one over was possible. Chappell on-drove Willis's first ball for four, and at 11 for one wicket they all trooped off again, never to reappear. The darkness deepened and the spitting rain became a torrent, yet the umpires did not see fit to abandon play until half-past-five, by which time the pitch had absorbed a lot of rain. All the same, it was going to need some sensations on the remaining two days if a result was to be obtained.
England 214; *Australia* 11 for 1.

FOURTH DAY

The sun shone on Bank Holiday Monday, and a near-full house settled down to watch a prompt resumption. Lever began from the pavilion end, to Chappell in a sleeveless sweater, and in order to switch the opening bowlers round. The Australian captain took two through point straightaway, after being beaten by the fourth ball, edged for three, Brearley and Greig doing a double act on the boundary line. When Willis took up the attack at the Vauxhall end Chappell glanced him for four, and the runs were coming at a pleasing rate. Yet this was a deception. The game tightened up. McCosker, having been missed by Hendrick, by his left kneecap, at third slip off Willis, seemed to lose all interest in runmaking in his determination to keep out the probes of England's bowlers.

Chappell made progress, off-driving Willis for three and, after taking a painful blow on the thigh, winning five runs from a cover-drive which yielded four before the throw-in and another when Greig hurled past the 'keeper. Randall went off for attention to his hand after stopping the boundary, Surrey's Robin Jackman briefly taking his place in the field, and in the 18th over of the innings the ball was changed — almost a predictable feature of play nowadays. After McCosker had scored three from a glance wide of Knott's extended left

The end of a great Test career as Greg Chappell is caught-and-bowled by Derek Underwood for 39. Standing ovations from the Oval crowd summed up cricket-lovers' disappointment at the early retirement of such an outstanding cricketer

hand, Underwood came on for his first bowl at the Vauxhall end for the 19th over. The pitch had offered nothing unduly exciting for the faster bowlers, but McCosker was distinctly uncomfortable as the Kent left-armer went about his business to an aggressive close-field.

Lever relieved Hendrick at the pavilion end for the 20th over, and soon Chappell was smashing the bowler's stumps with a lovely, wasted drive. At drinks Australia had moved on to 47 for one, with Chappell 36 and McCosker a grim nine. At a quarter to one he got into double-figures at last, and a single by Chappell brought the fifty up. But Australia's main hope of running up something like 350 and pressuring England on the final day was shattered when Underwood induced an elevated stroke from Chappell back down the pitch, and caught-and-bowled him for 39. It was the tenth time Underwood had taken his wicket in Tests. The crowd, taking no chances on a second innings, gave Chappell a generous reception as he came back.

This brought in Kim Hughes for his first Test innings. He was beaten by Underwood's first ball, but killed the remaining two. McCosker, still cautious and tight, inside-edged Lever past Knott for four, and Hughes went on showing scant interest in making his first Test run, though it must have been the most pressing of needs. He had made a hundred in his first innings in first-class cricket. What awaited him in his debut at the very top? By lunchtime no-one was any the wiser. After half an hour at the crease he was still scoreless, if cool. In the two hours Australia had added only 49, McCosker making 17 of them. Underwood so far had one for six off nine overs, and the holiday crowd by now had the message: there was to be no holiday-style batting.

Resuming at 60 for 2, the Australian innings laboured on, in pleasant sunshine and before a patient crowd. Hughes spent another fruitless quarter of an hour before making a single — and that was his lot. He edged Hendrick and Willis, the former goalkeeper, made a remarkable catch at third slip, moving forward and sideways.

This brought in Hookes, batting in a manner of speaking on his 1975 home ground, for Surrey was where he played his season of English club cricket. His first worthwhile stroke was a splendid square-cut for four off Underwood, but he fanned often without getting a touch, and life seemed suspended on a thread. McCosker, rocklike, passed three hours in the middle, unleashing the occasional stroke of quality but only two boundaries came his way in the grim vigil, and one of them was unintentional, a fine inside-edge off Lever. He was a second Willis leg-before victim, the ball delivered from wide of the crease, the batsman playing to leg. Umpire Constant did not hesitate.

At 84 for 4 Australia were at a junction if not a crossroads, and Walters almost made it worse when he sliced Willis to Hendrick, an awkward, face-high ball which the usually reliable Derbyshire man could not hold. It was his second miss of the day, and, as it transpired, not expensive. Willis gave Walters the prescription bouncers, and he was quick to duck. But after a stirring cover-drive for four at the other end he was bowled by a beauty from Willis which came in sharply to knock the off stump down. The batsman puffed his cheeks out as he trudged off to the pavilion, his side half out and still not halfway to England's score.

David Hookes had been swishing and parrying and cutting and

driving, catching the eye with a fine glance and a couple of strong
square-drives off the back foot against Willis, all for four, the last
bringing up the hundred. After Walters' dismissal he found the fence
again with a perfectly-timed shot backward of point, letting the fast ball
come on. When Marsh joined him, there was the rare sight of two

*David Hookes played a fine cavalier innings of 85, and there was
general disappointment when he was out so close to a first Test
century in what might have been his last Test match*

left-handers facing two left-arm bowlers, Lever and Underwood. A huge shout for caught-behind against Marsh was to no avail, but England's next chance came when Hookes, on 42, edged Lever just in front of Knott, who failed to bring off what would have been a stupendous catch. The young batsman, still expressionless, got his head down and battled on, dominating the stand as it took root.

Marsh drove Underwood furiously to the pavilion, and the bowler was discreet enough to remove his hand from any likely contact with the screaming ball, but at the other end Hookes mesmericly thrust his right leg down the pitch and offered the bat a long way in front of him. It was a compulsive reaction, even though at times it had the efficacy of placing him in proper position against anything that propped. Several times against Underwood he was forward only to sway back and steer to point. Perhaps to have delayed the decision regarding movement until only a backward step were demanded might have led to a less precise remedy. One thing could be said of Hookes's method: in the manner of Sobers and Pollock, he was never dull, always offering a chance to the bowlers and slip fielders, always looking to drive and cut. He reached 50 in 100 minutes, with six boundaries, just before tea, which was taken at 143 for 5, off 66 overs.

Underwood was bowling into the bowlers' footmarks at the Vauxhall end, but Hookes continued to find the answers. An off-driven four took him past his highest Test score, 56 in the Centenary Test, and there followed an almighty swing at Underwood for four to midwicket. Interspersed with near-misses outside off stump, he put Australia on the road to revival, dominating the stand with Marsh, who was content to hold out while keeping an eye on the prodigy.

At ten-past-five Greig came into the attack, assuming now the role of partnership-breaker, with Willis, Hendrick and Lever getting through the bulk of the non-spinning work. The move worked. Soon after playing a glorious cover-drive for four off Underwood, Hookes fanned crossbatted at a widish one from Greig and was caught behind, the stand having realised a precious 80, of which the vice-captain had made only 21.

Greig put a lot into his bowling to Bright. The bearded batsman played him down off the splice and looked to the gully area for any runs. Gradually, Marsh took over. He thumped Underwood for six over long-on, taking a step to the pitch of the ball, and then cut him sweetly for four. The 200 came up in the 85th over, and at five-to-six the new ball was taken, England doubtless hoping to wrap up the innings in the brief time remaining. Willis, lion's mane flapping about his angular head, roared in, his recurrent injuries a dim memory, his series performance of 25 wickets so far a record for an England fast bowler at home against Australia. There were to be no more for him this evening.

Marsh placed him for two to fine leg to level the scores, and a single brought rather surprising first-innings honours — apparently at this point all that remained to play for in this rain-ruined game. Still there was much to see and admire. Hendrick brought one so far back from outside Marsh's off stump that Knott took it near to fine leg slip; and the bowler then brought off two magnificent stops in the gully next over, one of them as acrobatic as they come.

Lever came on five minutes from the end, when the shadows were four times the length of man, and in the final over Willis tried a short one at Marsh, who hooked it off his chin for four to reach 53 in almost three hours. It was by far his best innings of the series, his half-century at Headingley having been made with a breeziness permitted by the hopeless situation, rather like his 92 at Old Trafford five years before.

After four days, therefore, with more than ten hours lost, the match seemed dead and buried, the main motive for last-day attendance being the desire to see some of the greats on the Test match field for the last time.

England 214; *Australia* 226 for 6 (D. W. Hookes 85, R. W. Marsh 53 not out, G. S. Chappell 39, R. B. McCosker 32, R. G. D. Willis 3 for 55).

FIFTH DAY

When Marsh was out early, lbw to Hendrick for 57, the pattern of the day presented itself one way. When Australia were still in and 138 ahead at lunch after the 2½-hour first session things were different. The pitch seemed admirable, and even when England went in with a possible 175 minutes left and a deficit of 171, the match was likely to peter out.

Bright followed Marsh back to the pavilion soon afterwards, also leg-before, and Malone ought to have been sent packing before he had scored, edging Hendrick waist-high to Greig's left. He got both hands to it but it was grassed. It seemed not to matter much, but when Walker was missed at the other end by Brearley at first slip off Willis,

England were destined for much extra footslogging in the session ahead. Much of it was to come from boundary-fetching. The outfield was fast, the ball was finding the middle of the bat, which the batsmen were willing to swing hard.

Malone, in his first Test innings, struck a juicy square-cut off Hendrick, whom Walker off-drove also for four, using as little left arm in his batting as he does in his bowling.

Lever and Underwood replaced Willis and Hendrick, but it made no difference. The two big Australians, never the epitomy of elegance, picked off the odd ball and usually found the gap. Walker brought up the 300 with a top-edged hook, and when he swept Underwood for four he passed his previous best in Tests, 41 not out. Malone's boundary off the back foot off Lever was a breathtaking stroke.

Walker, making up for all his bad luck in the series as a bowler, reached his first — and presumably sole — Test fifty, and then passed his first-class highest of 53 with a drive to the pavilion which eluded Boycott's foot. A hold-up followed as Boycott lobbed the ball to an unsuspecting Lever and hit him on the head; he was not hurt, but Walker was in trouble with a split boot, and there was a longish delay while he left the field.

It is not often that Underwood is cut backward of point, but Malone did it twice in an over, both times for four. Walker asserted his leadership with a hefty pull off Lever to the gasholder boundary and a three to midwicket, and as lunch approached Greig was called up. A leg-bye brought up the hundred partnership, still a long way short of the record but supremely welcome for an ailing side nonetheless, and only the second century stand of the series for Australia. Then, on the stroke of lunch, Malone's fine effort was ended by Lever, who bowled him round his legs for 46, thus depriving him of the rare and wonderful feat of five wickets and a fifty on Test debut. It was John Lever's first wicket and it had taken him 22 overs to achieve it, rather as it had taken Malone a long time to strike his first blow with the ball.

At lunch Australia were a proud 352 for 9, beyond their previous highest of the series, and it was looking more like old times. And the defiance continued after lunch until the last wicket had added 33, 17 of them to Thomson, who threw all his weight into some robust shots while Walker perhaps entertained thoughts of a three-figure farewell to Test cricket. It was 2.35 pm before Willis sealed another five-wicket performance by bowling Thomson, leaving Big Max on 78, and England faced the unappetising prospect of batting for almost three hours, avoiding accident and humiliation. The first few overs were unsettling.

Brearley struck Thomson's first ball to long-on for four, and the next was a wide, but in the third over Thomson got one to lift and the England captain, having been appointed to lead his side to Pakistan and New Zealand during the winter, signed off for the series with a catch off the splice to Serjeant at short leg.

Boycott opened his score with a streaky single off Malone, and with two to mid-on and a jabbed two through forward square off Thomson he reached 5001 runs in Test cricket, joining only 13 others from England, Australia and West Indies. For him, at least, the afternoon had been worthwhile.

For Woolmer it wasn't. In the eighth over he nicked one to Marsh and was on his way for six, England 16 for 2.

The next scare came when Boycott, on nine, hooked Malone just backward of square. The ball stayed in the air a long time, and Serjeant, from conventional square leg, ran backwards, legs tangling as he picked up the difficult line of the ball, which dropped beyond him and ran for four. There was an lbw appeal two balls later, and with the wide platform of cloud now overhead the atmosphere of the match had changed completely.

Thomson, after giving way for Walker from the pavilion end for three overs, returned, and worked up a fair pace, but the light was poor and the umpires decided on an early tea. The light was little better upon resumption, but they played on, Randall being beaten every so often, once by a ball from Walker that brought an eruption of an appeal as Marsh took it. But umpire Spencer gave it "not out", and the Australians were left to collect themselves.

Bright was brought on at the Vauxhall end, but despite the puffs of dust that rose when the groundstaff tidied up at lunch, not a lot of turn was discernible, and the contest was taking on the appearance of an exercise to fatten Boycott's already large average and to rehabilitate in the short time available Derek Randall's dented image.

It came to an end at ten-to-five. The evening was dank and dull, and no-one seemed to wish to concentrate any further. In a marked air of anti-climax the players left the field, some possibly never to return to this particular patch of London greenery. The numbness following an England-Australia Test series was of a new kind. For some, the best thing to do was to hurry to the car park or the tube train and take the first reluctant step into the future.

Greg Chappell writes:

We named a squad of 13 for the fifth Test, keeping a number of options open. Kerry O'Keeffe could have been an asset if the pitch had been underprepared and broken up early; he could even perhaps have served as an opening batsman, as in the Centenary Test. Ian Davis and Richie Robinson of the fourth Test side missed out, but Craig Serjeant and Kim Hughes were in the 13, and in the final 11 when we chose it on the Friday morning, when the match got under way just a few minutes late — and Mick Malone, like Hughes, got his first Test cap. Len Pascoe and Kerry O'Keeffe were the unlucky ones to drop out of the 13.

When I won the toss I had no hesitation in putting England in. To win the game we had to bowl them out cheaply, and this seemed our best chance to do so, in conditions that must have been favourable for bowling. It was now a four-day match, and I felt the risk was justified. I didn't ask Mike Brearley what he would have done, but I suspect he would have put us in.

I opened with Jeff Thomson and Mick Malone, leaving Max Walker to first change. He never minds this, perhaps preferring a ball that has had some use. Whereas Mick uses the new ball for Western Australia.

The bat was beaten now and then in the pre-lunch session but England went in at 60 without loss, and my decision to put them in was not looking too good at this stage, though the feeling in the camp was that if we continued to bowl so well, a breakthrough could lead to a collapse. And that is exactly what happened in the second session.

Max Walker took the first important wicket, Geoff Boycott's, and then Mick Malone got his first wicket, having Brearley caught at the wicket. The clouds had broken up, but though it was a brighter day than many recently, it was still a good day for swing bowling. Mick Malone kept the ball well up to the bat, allowing it to bend on its way, and such was his great stamina that I was able to keep him operating from the Vauxhall end all day except for two overs. It was an excellent performance in his first Test.

Jeff Thomson struck with the second new ball and finished with 4 for 87 — a fine performance considering the lack of pace in the wicket. Three of his victims were bowled and one lbw. Ray Bright's three overs showed that there was very little spin in the wicket as yet.

We could have done without the tenth-wicket resistance on the second morning's play, but it did at least show how easy the pitch was.

I ordered the heavy roller between innings, and the wicket could only get easier — unless the weather interfered. Unfortunately this is precisely what happened soon after our innings had started.

We lost Craig Serjeant to Bob Willis in the first over, the sky now darkening and rain approaching, and when it set in heavily, wiping out further play on this third scheduled day, we were 11 for the loss of one wicket, and a draw seemed the most likely result.

On the rest day, with the sun shining tantalisingly, we had a relaxed time, lunching at Denham and playing a round of golf while the wives played nine holes. The warmth had helped dry the Test pitch, and it rolled out reasonably well on the Monday, when Rick McCosker and I restarted the innings, intent on a solid start.

The slight softness in the wicket made attacking batting difficult, and by the same token there was not a lot in it for the fast bowlers. After a few overs England complained about the ball, which was changed, but this made no difference this time to the degree of swing or bounce.

We went along fairly comfortably until Derek Underwood came into the attack. He made the ball "stop", and was his usual accurate self, so that batting became no picnic. He claimed my wicket, the ball not coming through as I tried to play him to the on side of the pitch, a fairly simple return catch resulting.

Kim Hughes kept his head down for a long time, staying cool as he searched for his first Test runs. He tends to commit himself to the front foot, and this was a stern trial for him, especially against Underwood. When Rick McCosker was dropped early in the day it was a vital let-off for us, just the kind of break we had been wanting all through the series. He batted till lunch and beyond, wearing the bowling down, but Kim Hughes fell to a magnificent slip catch, and David Hookes entered, to play some good square-drives and to flick anything well up to him through midwicket. He may have played and missed a few times, prompting some of the England fieldsmen, particularly Tony Greig, to tear their hair out, but it merely served to remind us of the countless occasions this summer that England's batsmen had played at the ball — not always attackingly — without making contact. It was their turn at last to know frustration. It emphasised what Mike Brearley and I had been saying throughout: that catching was the department of the game where matters tended to be settled. Here England put some on the floor — for once.

David Hookes's 85 was a very fine effort. At 22, this young man, with so little first-class experience, did so well in this Test series, and a brilliant future must lie before him. He doesn't always get his right foot to the ball as he drives, and his defence might need tightening up, but he has gained a very great deal from his tour.

Rod Marsh batted well after being lucky to survive his first ball, off which he probably gave the faintest of edges into Alan Knott's gloves. And Bob Willis had a good day, bowling the bouncer effectively and getting rid of Doug Walters with a superb delivery. Doug had not looked at all comfortable, and I think that his continued lack of success in England had by now resulted in a huge psychological barrier. He still has a tremendous amount of ability but he has probably lost belief in his ability to make runs in this particular country — a great pity, since he is a fine batsman and has given wonderful service to Australia for a dozen years.

The century stand between Max Walker and Mick Malone might have been unexpected, but it gave them — and the rest of the team — immense pleasure, and it also extended our lead on first innings to the point where, even though little time remained when England went in again, there was a slender chance that we could bring off a big surprise, and a greater possibility that we could fire a few parting salvoes at their batsmen. Two early wickets fell, but the weather had the final say.

As we left the field for the last time someone suggested that those who were joining the Packer camp be clapped off, but when we did a quick count we realised that eight players were concerned, so it really might have been simpler if we had clapped off the other three, Kim Hughes, Craig Serjeant, and Jeff Thomson!

FIFTH TEST MATCH   *The Oval, August 25, 26, 27, 29, 30*

Paying attendance 54,000; takings £125,000

ENGLAND

		min	6	4			min	6	4
*J. M. Brearley	c Marsh b Malone	39	177	—	2	c Serjeant b Thomson	4	12	—	1
G. Boycott	c McCosker b Walker	39	171	—	3	not out	25	103	—	2
R. A. Woolmer	lbw b Thomson	15	55	—	1	c Marsh b Malone	6	18	—	—
D. W. Randall	c Marsh b Malone	3	45	—	—	not out	20	69	—	2
A. W. Greig	c Bright b Malone	0	7	—	—					
G. R. J. Roope	b Thomson	38	110	—	3					
+A. P. E. Knott	c McCosker b Malone	6	23	—	—					
J. K. Lever	lbw b Malone	3	28	—	—					
D. L. Underwood	b Thomson	20	58	—	1					
M. Hendrick	b Thomson	15	62	—	3					
R. G. D. Willis	not out	24	54	—	4					
Extras (lb6, nb5, w1)		12				(w2)		2		
		__214__				2 wkts		__57__		

Fall: 86, 88, 104, 104, 106, 122, 130, 169, 174

5, 16

Bowling: Thomson 23.2-3-87-4, Malone 47-20-63-5,
   Walker 28-11-51-1, Bright 3-2-1-0.

Thomson 5-1-22-1, Malone 10-4-14-1,
Walker 8-2-14-0, Bright 3-2-5-0.

AUSTRALIA

		min	6	4
C. S. Serjeant	lbw b Willis	0	4	—	—
R. B. McCosker	lbw b Willis	32	201	—	2
*G. S. Chappell	c & b Underwood	39	113	—	3+
K. J. Hughes	c Willis b Hendrick	1	54	—	—
D. W. Hookes	c Knott b Greig	85	154	—	12
K. D. Walters	b Willis	4	18	—	1
+R. W. Marsh	lbw b Hendrick	57	196	1	4
R. J. Bright	lbw b Willis	16	109	—	—
M. H. N. Walker	not out	78	153	—	10
M. F. Malone	b Lever	46	105	—	6
J. R. Thomson	b Willis	17	25	—	2
Extras (b1, lb6, nb3)		10			
		__385__	+ plus one 5		

Fall: 0, 54, 67, 84, 104, 184, 236, 252, 352

Bowling: Willis 29.3-5-102-5, Hendrick 37-5-93-2,
   ˙ Lever 22-6-61-1, Underwood 35-9-102-1, Greig 8-2-17-1

Umpires: D. J. Constant and T. W. Spencer   *Toss won by Australia*

MATCH DRAWN

9. CONCLUSIONS

Greg Chappell writes:

I believed from first to last that there was not a lot of difference between the two sides in this Test series, but in trying to analyse the results, "ifs" and "buts" are liable to come into it, and there isn't really room for "ifs" and "buts". It's what actually happened that counts, and the underlying cause of our defeat, in my opinion, was experience — the experience under English conditions of the home players, and the experience which so many of our younger players still lacked.

Early in the series England had a few of the breaks, and this enabled them to play above themselves — or at least to a confident level of their expertise. We didn't get the breaks, and this kept the pressure on us, keeping us straining away at a level something below our true potential. Close catching was very important, England holding almost everything until the last Test match but Australia putting a number of vital catches down. The reasons for our blemishes were that the sighting on English grounds is generally more difficult than in Australia, and much of the 1977 series was played in poor light, making batting and fielding less easy. But, as I discovered in 1975, we tend to field a little too close at slip, because English batsmen, when they play defensively, usually have loose wrists, and the thicker edges don't carry too far. When a quicker ball bounces more and catches a thin edge as the batsman plays an attacking stroke, the ball flies fast, and we're probably not deep enough to ensure a safe catch. On the other hand, when we bat we tend to be stiff-wristed, and when we get a nick it invariably goes fast, with the English fieldsmen standing deeper and getting a better view of the ball.

Our three main faster bowlers bowled as well as their three counterparts, I believe, but England had more depth in their back-up bowlers — fellows like Tony Greig, Bob Woolmer, Geoff Miller. When his key bowlers needed resting, Mike Brearley was able to call upon second-line bowlers who get a lot of bowling in county cricket and were able to keep things tight. Our second-liners, like Doug Walters and myself, were not able to bowl much even in the county games, where our regulars had either to regain or retain form. This resulted in Australia being unable to sustain the pressure on the batsmen as an innings developed.

There is another important factor here. Bob Willis, Mike Hendrick, and Chris Old, England's fast bowlers, all fielded in catching positions and took some very fine catches throughout the series. This allowed for greater mobility in the outfield, and offered the advantage of a captain being able to talk to his fast bowlers between their overs.

England's batting was not really so terribly strong. Geoff Boycott played a couple of marvellous innings, but Bob Woolmer, after a great start in the series, faded a bit, and Derek Randall, an attacking player such as we're not used to seeing in the England side, didn't have all that much success. Mike Brearley often gave his side a solid start, and Alan Knott and Tony Greig chipped in with important innings, especially Knott's century at Trent Bridge, which helped put Boycott back on the road. Greig went for the bowling, and sometimes it came off and sometimes it didn't. By contrast, our middle batting, especially the two most experienced players, Doug Walters and Rod Marsh, to whom we looked for a number of important scores, came to our aid in a couple of Tests, but in the middle of the series, when we were really struggling, England's bowlers got the better of them.

During the tour we played against a lot of young English players of real promise. On previous tours it always seemed to be the older, experienced players who did well against us, and this was a noticeable feature of the '77 tour. The future for the game in England seems to be in good hands.

My Test career is over now. I have no regrets. I have enjoyed playing for Australia against England, West Indies, Pakistan, and New Zealand, and I have achieved almost everything I set out to do. It is time to look to the future once more. In doing so, I might just venture into choosing an Australian Test team to play against India, although by the time this book sees the light of day I appreciate that the series will be under way. With a large number of Australian players signing with Kerry Packer, I can see the new Test team shaping something like this: Bruce Laird (W.A.), Alan Turner (N.S.W.), Craig Serjeant (W.A.), Kim Hughes (W.A.), Gary Cosier (S.A.), John Inverarity (W.A.), Graham Whyte (Qld), John Maclean (Qld), Wayne Clark (W.A.), Jeff Thomson (Qld), Alan Hurst (Vic).

Six of the team have Test experience already, and I would have John Inverarity as captain. Laird and Turner have toured England, and

Maclean is a very experienced wicketkeeper. Thomson, Clark, and Hurst would be a fine fast attack, with Graham Whyte, the young Queensland off-spinner, Cosier and Inverarity as support bowlers. Other players could come into the reckoning, of course, bowlers like Wayne Prior (fast), Jim Higgs (leg-spin), Ian Callen (fast), Malcolm Francke (leg-spin), Geoff Dymock (fast-medium), Dave Colley (fast-medium), David Hourn (left-arm spinner of distinct promise), and batsmen such as Rob Langer, Graham Yallop, Paul Hibbert, Peter Toohey, and David Ogilvie. Steve Rixon of New South Wales could challenge for the wicketkeeping position.

I am sure the new side will do Australia justice, and perhaps a year from now Australia will be ready to win the Ashes back from England.

David Frith writes:

Victory can be blind. The winning is all that matters to most people. And who would argue with that, for if the *best available* play for both sides it is of no pragmatical consequence that Bill was unavailable because of injury or Bob was absent through financial distractions or Bert had to withdraw for undisclosed reasons. These omissions are buried in the small print in years to come, and it is the result which stands out boldly.

All the same, the turn of the Anglo-Australian wheel came rather suddenly this time and with surprising emphasis. Four-one it was two years ago, and three-nil the other way now. Lillee, Redpath, Ian Chappell, Edwards, Mallett — these were now shadowy memories beyond the boundary, as were some of the English players they had overwhelmed. It was almost a post-war type of series, with new names abounding — and one old and familiar: Geoffrey Boycott.

Boycott was almost, but not quite, the difference between the two sides. His average for the series (147.33) beat Bradman's record of 139.14 in 1930. Woolmer and he saw England's batting through the "business" phase of the series, with assorted assistants. Too much, on the other side, depended on Greg Chappell. For a while it seemed he could rise above it, but it was asking too much of any man.

Too much, it seems, has always been expected of Doug Walters, and reluctantly his admirers have to concede that a cricket pitch in England is no place for him. He is a touch player, and, like Garry Sobers, does not believe in net practice. Sobers got away with it, but it is hard to overlook Walters' aversion to extra-matchplay batting.

Perhaps the greatest example of courage seen not only in the series but in Test cricket history was Rick McCosker's fight against the memory and physical horror of a shattered jaw, pursued by failures in the first two Tests and some aberrations at slip. His Trent Bridge half-century and century were moving in their gallant determination. Unhappily for Australia, the perennial problem of finding a solid, dependable opening *pair* has remained.

Once more, Max Walker was expected to be a bowler ideal for English conditions, and once more his figures disappointed. In 1975 his 14 wickets in four Tests cost 34.71 each, and this series he took 14 in five Tests at 39.36. His bad luck in passing the bat was proverbial, but towards the end it gave cause to wonder if perhaps he was not bowling the right length.

Considering the recent shoulder damage and the loss of his joint-spearhead, Lillee, Jeff Thomson bowled magnificently. That attractive jog up to the crease and the awe-inspiring bowling action were almost as of old, but he had lost a little, there was no denying it. Yet he managed 23 wickets in the series, a total bettered only by Bob Willis, who was such an important member of England's winning combination.

Willis was now very fit, and remained consistently so, running four or five miles a time in training, and being able to bowl up to eight or nine overs at top speed in a spell, generating top pace even at the start. His captain paid warm tribute to him at the end, describing him as a "more versatile" bowler than ever before. With Hendrick, Willis was on the verge of adding another pair to the world's list of fearsome fast men.

Spin bowling, for the second successive English summer, was seldom seen in the Tests, and it was disappointing that Kerry O'Keeffe, the only wrist-spinner on view, should have had such a dismal series. The slow pitches and damp conditions deprived him of a propitious setting, and we were condemned to protracted periods of faster bowling, with the consequent slower over rate. In the final Test (where, incidentally, England's principal worry had been to combat a sense of anti-climax, which, Brearley recalled, contributed to their defeat in the fourth Test in India when they were three-up) each side had a pace attack plus only a slow-medium left-arm finger-spinner. This is one area in which the game has suffered grievously, and it is a problem which legislation can hardly expect to overcome since it lies in the heart rather than the book of regulations.

England rode the storm of Greig's disgrace well. No longer captain, he remained a vital component in the team, welcomed and indeed highly valued by Mike Brearley, who remarked more than once that, if anything, it was a good time to come in as captain since Tony Greig was one side of him at second slip and Alan Knott the other as wicketkeeper. The wars fought by those two assemble into a breath-taking catalogue. Brearley expressed the hope that they and Underwood would not be lost forever to Test cricket, saying that England ought to hold their own in Pakistan as that country had lost five players to the Packer organisation. When, several days afterwards, Bob Woolmer announced that he too was joining, the old trepidations came back — trepidations for the entire structure of cricket. If the two sides could work out a compromise, the game could advance. But this now seemed a redundant plea, and a compromise was looking more and more remote a possibility. Packer had his dates and grounds fixed by early September, and everything appeared to rest on the High Court hearing. If the proposed ICC/TCCB ban were allowed to be enforced, most of the world's top players would be lost to Test and all first-class cricket, to be seen only in the ''circus'' matches, still promoted optimistically as ''Super-Tests''. Whether or not the ban were deemed to be illegal, no-one could say for sure what would happen, although the expectation was that the depleted first-class game would lose revenue and impetus, would slump in playing standards, and yet would be required by the Packer organisation to serve as a recruiting ground. It was all stickier that a crushed box of jam tarts.

While Jeff Thomson was telling his radio listeners when he got home that the Australians had ''played like a bunch of schoolboys'', manager Len Maddocks admitted that the Packer business had had a disastrous effect on team morale. The topic had been inescapable. ''Everywhere we went the media were on the subject'', he said.

The Australian public are seldom in a mood to listen to excuses, and cricket's fascination in that great land went down a few points each time Australia lost a Test. Time after time the team's followers had been given cause to cringe as wickets fell cheaply or catches were floored. There is a fickleness about a certain type of sports-follower, and this type has flocked to the game by the thousand during the 1970s while Australia has ruled the cricket world. The authorities will be concerned about a possible drift away, and Kerry Packer probably hopes to win the affections of those newly disinterested parties. Whether their enthusiasm will revive if ''Australia'' beat ''West Indies'' or

"The Rest of the World" remains to be seen, as does the matter of whether the legitimate Australia-India series will draw the crowds.

An era has ended. During the Melbourne Centenary Test match we thought we were celebrating 100 years of Test cricket between England and Australia, but it was more than that. It happened to be marking the termination of an uncomplicated and time-honoured institution, now transformed, if not exactly in a state of collapse, by mammonism. Lost, for the moment, are the tender, now seemingly juvenile expressions of delight by players from the distant or recent past at their first call to represent their country — grown men who have slept with their England caps under their pillows, who have said they would play for their country for nothing, or even pay for the honour if need be. All soppy, dated stuff.

The summer of '77 will be remembered for its nuisance weather, for the Jubilee joy that swept the Commonwealth, for an exciting County Championship, for feats at international level by Boycott and Woolmer and Knott and Randall and Greig and Brearley and Willis and Botham and Underwood and Hendrick and Chappell and McCosker and Thomson and Hookes and Malone. It will be remembered for distinguished performances for their counties by Procter and Zaheer and Edrich and Illingworth and Radley and Viv Richards and McEwan and Eddie Barlow and Hopkins and Hayes and Greenidge and Old and Glenn Turner.

Most of all, though, it will be remembered as the year when the government didn't fall but England recovered the Ashes. Those Ashes, prepared in 1882 by Ivo Bligh's bride-to-be, were supposedly of English cricket. Now there were very real fears that the cricketers who had defected from the official international game would be playing for something which might well be described as the ashes of Test cricket.

FINAL TEST AVERAGES

ENGLAND BATTING

	M	I	NO	R	HS	Av	Catches
G. Boycott............	3	5	2	442	191	147.33	0
R. A. Woolmer........	5	8	1	394	137	56.29	2
A. P. E. Knott	5	7	0	255	135	36.43	12
D. W. Randall.........	5	8	2	207	79	34.50	4
A. W. Greig..........	5	7	0	226	91	32.29	9
J. M. Brearley........	5	9	0	247	81	27.44	7
R. G. D. Willis........	5	6	4	49	24*	24.50	2
D. L. Underwood	5	6	2	66	20	16.50	3
C. M. Old	2	3	0	46	37	15.33	2
D. L. Amiss	2	4	1	43	28*	14.33	2
M. Hendrick..........	3	3	0	20	15	6.67	5
J. K. Lever	3	4	0	24	10	6.00	2

Also batted — G. D. Barlow (1) 1 and 5; I. T. Botham (2) 25 and 0; G. Miller (2) 6 and 13; G. R. J. Roope (2) 34 and 38. (Botham took one catch; A. G. E. Ealham took two catches as substitute fieldsman).

Bowling

	O	M	R	W	Av
G. Miller...........................	24	7	47	3	15.67
R. G. D. Willis	166.4	36	534	27	19.78
I. T. Botham.......................	73	16	202	10	20.20
M. Hendrick.......................	128.4	33	290	14	20.71
D. L. Underwood	169.1	61	362	13	27.85
A. W. Greig	77	25	196	7	28.00
R. A. Woolmer.....................	16	5	31	1	31.00
J. K. Lever........................	75	22	197	5	39.40
C. M. Old	77	14	199	5	39.80

AUSTRALIA BATTING

	M	I	NO	R	HS	Av	Catches
K. J. O'Keeffe	3	6	4	125	48*	62.50	3
G. S. Chappell.........	5	9	0	371	112	41.22	6
D. W. Hookes.........	5	9	0	283	85	31.44	1
R. B. McCosker	5	9	0	255	107	28.33	5
K. D. Walters.........	5	9	0	223	88	24.78	5
M. H. N. Walker	5	8	1	151	78*	21.57	1
C. S. Serjeant	3	5	0	106	81	21.20	1
R. W. Marsh..........	5	9	1	166	63	20.75	9
I. C. Davis...........	3	6	0	107	34	17.83	2
R. D. Robinson........	3	6	0	100	34	16.67	4
R. J. Bright...........	3	5	1	42	16	10.50	2
J. R. Thomson	5	8	1	59	21	8.43	0
L. S. Pascoe..........	3	5	2	23	20	7.67	0

Also batted — K. J. Hughes (1) 1; M. F. Malone (1) 46.

Bowling

	O	M	R	W	Av
J. R. Thomson	200.5	44	583	23	25.35
L. S. Pascoe	137.4	35	363	13	27.92
R. J. Bright	72.1	27	147	5	29.40
M. H. N. Walker	273.2	88	551	14	39.36
K. J. O'Keeffe	100.3	31	305	3	101.67

Also bowled — M. F. Malone 57-24-77-6; K. D. Walters 6-1-10-0; G. S. Chappell 39-5-105-0.

AUSTRALIANS FINAL FIRST-CLASS TOUR AVERAGES

Batting	M	I	NO	R	HS	Av
G. S. Chappell	16	25	5	1182	161*	59.10
K. J. O'Keeffe	13	19	12	355	48*	50.71
R. D. Robinson	14	23	4	715	137*	37.63
C. S. Serjeant	15	22	2	663	159	33.15
D. W. Hookes	17	26	1	804	108	32.16
G. J. Cosier	12	20	1	587	100	30.89
I. C. Davis	13	20	0	608	83	30.40
K. J. Hughes	14	19	0	540	95	28.42
K. D. Walters	17	26	1	663	88	26.52
R. J. Bright	14	19	8	287	53*	26.09
R. B. McCosker	18	32	1	737	107	23.77
R. W. Marsh	17	24	2	477	124	21.68
M. H. N. Walker	15	17	2	250	78*	16.66
G. Dymock	10	6	5	16	8*	16.00
M. F. Malone	10	10	3	95	46	13.57
J. R. Thomson	16	17	1	130	25	8.12
L. S. Pascoe	11	9	3	44	20	7.33

Bowling	O	M	R	W	Av
Bright	333.5	114	794	39	20.36
Pascoe	323.4	79	893	41	21.78
Walker	514	154	1184	53	22.34
Malone	327	95	837	32	26.16
Thomson	383.2	84	1207	43	28.07
O'Keeffe	335.4	112	1035	36	28.75
Dymock	192	54	468	15	31.20
Chappell	106	28	304	6	50.67

Also bowled — Walters 17-5-30-0, Cosier 16-3-36-0, Hookes 4-0-18-1, Marsh 1-0-6-0, McCosker 2-1-5-0.

Centuries (11)
5 — G. S. Chappell 161* v Northants, 113 v Somerset, 112 v England, 2nd Test, 102 v Gloucestershire, 100* v Worcestershire; 1 — G. J. Cosier 100 v Notts, D. W. Hookes 108 v Somerset, R. W. Marsh 124 v Essex, R. B. McCosker 107 v England, 3rd Test, R. D. Robinson 137* v Warwickshire, C. S. Serjeant 159 v Notts.

AUSTRALIANS IN ENGLAND, 1977 SCORES

APRIL 27; ARUNDEL
Australians 186 for 5 (45 overs) (C. S. Serjeant 65, G. S. Chappell 44, R. A. Woolmer 3 for 17); *Duchess of Norfolk's XI* 166 (P. Willey 50, D. W. Randall 41, G. J. Cosier 4 for 18). *Australians won by 20 runs.*

APRIL 30, MAY 2, 3; THE OVAL
Surrey 327 for 8 (G. R. J. Roope 107*, J. H. Edrich 70, Younis Ahmed 40, M. H. N. Walker 3 for 70). *Match drawn (no play first and third days).*

MAY 4, 5, 6; CANTERBURY
Australians 240 for 7 dec (K. J. Hughes 80, C. S. Serjeant 55); *Kent* 33 for 2. *Match drawn (no play second day).*

MAY 7, 9, 10; HOVE
Australians 111 for 1 (C. S. Serjeant 55*, G. S. Chappell 34*); *Sussex* did not bat. *Match drawn (no play third day).*

MAY 11, 12, 13; SOUTHAMPTON
Match against Hampshire abandoned without a ball bowled.

MAY 14, 15, 16; SWANSEA
Glamorgan 172 (A. Jones 59, A. L. Jones 46, M. H. N. Walker 3 for 27, G. Dymock 3 for 30) and 164 for 4 dec (J. A. Hopkins 66, A. Jones 47, R. J. Bright 4 for 53); *Australians* 153 for 6 dec (G. J. Cosier 56, K. D. Walters 36, M. A. Nash 4 for 71) and 86 for 6 (M. A. Nash 5 for 32). *Match drawn (no play first day).*

MAY 18, 19, 20; BATH
Australians 232 (G. S. Chappell 113, G. J. Cosier 44, G. I. Burgess 5 for 25, J. Garner 4 for 66) and 289 (D. W. Hookes 108, C. S. Serjeant 50, G. S. Chappell 39, I. T. Botham 4 for 98); *Somerset* 340 for 5 dec (B. C. Rose 110*, I. T. Botham 59, P. A. Slocombe 55*, P. W. Denning 39) and 182 for 3 (I. V. A. Richards 53, I. T. Botham 39*, P. W. Denning 34). *Somerset won by 7 wickets.*

MAY 21, 23, 24; BRISTOL
Australians 154 (R. J. Bright 53*, K. D. Walters 32, B. M. Brain 7 for 51) and 251 (G. S. Chappell 102, D. A. Graveney 5 for 70); *Gloucestershire* 63 (M. H. N. Walker 7 for 19, M. F. Malone 3 for 44) and 169 (L. S. Pascoe 4 for 36, R. J. Bright 4 for 63). *Australians won by 173 runs (in two days).*

MAY 24; BRISTOL (special one-day match)
Gloucestershire 195 (44.5 overs) (M. J. Procter 52); *Australians* 196 for 4 (38 overs) (K. D. Walters 52*, K. J. Hughes 51, R. B. McCosker 46). *Australians won by 6 wickets.*

MAY 25, 26, 27; LORD'S
Australians 194 (K. J. Hughes 60, M. Hendrick 4 for 28, G. Miller 3 for 44) and 235 (R. B. McCosker 73, G. S. Chappell 44, M. Hendrick 4 for 32); *MCC* 136 (D. W. Randall 50, K. J. O'Keeffe 3 for 29) and 214 (G. D. Barlow 54, D. W. Randall 51, J. M. Brearley 47, K. J. O'Keeffe 4 for 56, J. R. Thomson 3 for 50). *Australians won by 79 runs.*

MAY 28, 29, 30; WORCESTER
Australians 358 (G. S. Chappell 100 ret ht, I. C. Davis 83, R. D. Robinson 44, K. D. Walters 37, R. B. McCosker 33, N. Gifford 3 for 77) and 210 for 7 dec (G. J. Cosier 44, I. C. Davis 41, R. D. Robinson 38, N. Gifford 4 for 65); *Worcestershire* 243 (J. A. Ormrod 73, G. M. Turner 69, R. J. Bright 5 for 91, L. S. Pascoe 4 for 40) and 169 for 4 (J. A. Ormrod 57, P. A. Neale 43*, L. S. Pascoe 3 for 37). *Match drawn.*

PRUDENTIAL TROPHY (three matches)

JUNE 2; OLD TRAFFORD
Australia 169 for 9 (55 overs) (C. S. Serjeant 46, R. W. Marsh 42, G. S. Chappell 30, D. L. Underwood 3 for 29); *England* 173 for 8 (45.2 overs) (G. D. Barlow 42, M. H. N. Walker 3 for 20). *England won by 2 wickets.* Man of the Match: R. W. Marsh.

JUNE 4; EDGBASTON
England 171 (53.5 overs) (D. L. Amiss 35, C. M. Old 35, G. J. Cosier 5 for 18, G. S. Chappell 5 for 20); *Australia* 70 (25.2 overs) (J. K. Lever 4 for 29). *England won by 101 runs.* Man of the Match: J. K. Lever.

JUNE 6; THE OVAL

England 242 (54.2 overs) (D. L. Amiss 108, J. M. Brearley 78, L. S. Pascoe 3 for 44); *Australia* 246 for 8 (53.2 overs) (G. S. Chappell 125*, R. D. Robinson 70). *Australia won by 2 wickets.* Man of the Match: G. S. Chappell.

Men of the Series: D. L. Amiss and G. S. Chappell.

JUNE 9, 10; RATHMINES, DUBLIN

Australians 291 (C. S. Serjeant 63, D. W. Hookes 58, R. B. McCosker 40, L. S. Pascoe 40, J. D. Monteith 6 for 97, S. C. Corlett 3 for 84) and 96 for 5 dec (R. B. McCosker 47); *Ireland* 200 for 4 dec (J. F. Short 80*, B. A. O'Brien 51) and 104 for 3 (J. Harrison 37*, I. J. Anderson 37). *Match drawn.*

JUNE 11, 12, 13; CHELMSFORD

Australians 274 (R. W. Marsh 124, K. D. Walters 38, G. A. Gooch 4 for 60, K. D. Boyce 4 for 90) and 206 for 4 dec (D. W. Hookes 69*, C. S. Serjeant 59); *Essex* 170 for 2 dec (K. S. McEwan 100*, M. H. Denness 34) and 59 for 4 (K. J. O'Keeffe 3 for 14). *Match drawn.*

JUNE 16, 17, 18, 20, 21; FIRST TEST MATCH (LORD'S)
Match drawn.

JUNE 23, 24; OXFORD

Oxford & Cambridge Universities 130 (V. J. Marks 46, R. J. Bright 3 for 8, G. Dymock 3 for 32) and 240 for 8 dec (P. M. Roebuck 77, C. J. Tavaré 60*, V. J. Marks 58); *Australians* 188 for 4 dec (D. W. Hookes 74, I. C. Davis 55*) and 150 for 5 (K. J. Hughes 54, R. Le Q. Savage 4 for 52). *Match drawn.*

JUNE 25, 26, 27; TRENT BRIDGE

Nottinghamshire 210 (C. E. B. Rice 38, M. J. Smedley 38, P. D. Johnson 37, R. A. White 33*, M. F. Malone 4 for 62, K. J. O'Keeffe 3 for 55) and 223 (C. E. B. Rice 59, B. Hassan 40, R. J. Bright 3 for 34, M. F. Malone 3 for 73); *Australians* 531 (C. S. Serjeant 159, G. J. Cosier 100, K. J. Hughes 95, I. C. Davis 72, G. S. Chappell 48, R. A. White 4 for 77, D. R. Doshi 4 for 135). *Australians won by an innings and 98 runs.*

JUNE 29, 30, JULY 1; CHESTERFIELD
Derbyshire 126 (A. Hill 45, K. J. O'Keeffe 4 for 21, L. S. Pascoe 4 for 23) and 136 for 4 (A. Hill 59*, H. Cartwright 35); *Australians* 380 (K. J. Hughes 92, R. D. Robinson 77, I. C. Davis 53, R. W. Marsh 47, K. J. O'Keeffe 39*, E. J. Barlow 3 for 46, C. J. Tunnicliffe 3 for 95). *Match drawn.*

JULY 2, 3, 4; SCARBOROUGH
Australians 186 (R. D. Robinson 54, K. J. O'Keeffe 48, C. M. Old 3 for 25, A. L. Robinson 3 for 25, G. B. Stevenson 3 for 76) and 215 for 7 dec (D. W. Hookes 67, C. S. Serjeant 55, R. D. Robinson 33*); *Yorkshire* 75 (M. H. N. Walker 5 for 29, M. F. Malone 4 for 39) and 233 for 5 (G. Boycott 103, J. D. Love 59, K. Sharp 30*). *Match drawn.*

JULY 7, 8, 9, 11, 12; SECOND TEST MATCH (OLD TRAFFORD)
England won by 9 wickets.

JULY 16, 18, 19; NORTHAMPTON
Australians 328 for 6 dec (G. S. Chappell 161*, D. W. Hookes 53, R. B. McCosker 34) and 238 for 4 dec (I. C. Davis 68, G. J. Cosier 54*, D. W. Hookes 47, R. B. McCosker 39); *Northamptonshire* 236 (Mushtaq Mohammad 37, A. Hodgson 35, G. Sharp 34, R. T. Virgin 30, L. S. Pascoe 6 for 68) and 115 for 1 (R. T. Virgin 66*). *Match drawn.*

JULY 20, 21, 22; EDGBASTON
Australians 260 for 6 dec (R. B. McCosker 77, R. D. Robinson 70*, K. D. Walters 47, R. Le Q. Savage 3 for 47, W. A. Bourne 3 for 61) and 320 for 6 dec (R. D. Robinson 137*, G. J. Cosier 56, K. D. Walters 53); *Warwickshire* 260 for 5 dec (J. Whitehouse 114, R. N. Abberley 72, K. D. Smith 31*) and 190 (A. I. Kallicharran 80, R. N. Abberley 35, M. H. N. Walker 4 for 36, J. R. Thomson 4 for 61). *Australians won by 130 runs.*

JULY 23, 24, 25; LEICESTER
Australians 229 (D. W. Hookes 59, R. J. Bright 43*, G. J. Cosier 32, P. Booth 4 for 42, J. Birkenshaw 3 for 38) and 148 for 1 (I. C. Davis 65, R. B. McCosker 59*); *Leicestershire* 178 (B. F. Davison 44, M. H. N. Walker 7 for 45). *Match drawn.*

JULY 28, 29, 30, AUGUST 1, 2; THIRD TEST MATCH (TRENT BRIDGE)
England won by 7 wickets.

AUGUST 4, 5; SUNDERLAND
Australians 170 (K. D. Walters 42, B. G. Collins 4 for 42, S. J. Wilkinson 4 for 49) and 169 for 6 dec (I. C. Davis 55, D. W. Hookes 51, P. J. Kippax 3 for 46); *Minor Counties* 133 for 4 dec (M. D. Nurton 40, P. N. Gill 39) and 207 for 4 (P. N. Gill 92, R. Entwistle 33). *Minor Counties won by 6 wickets.*

AUGUST 6, 7, 8; OLD TRAFFORD
Lancashire 215 (J. Lyon 34, H. Pilling 31, R. Arrowsmith 30*, C. E. H. Croft 30, J. R. Thomson 3 for 37, G. Dymock 3 for 58, M. F. Malone 3 for 60) and 202 (B. Wood 80, J. Simmons 35, J. Abrahams 30, R. J. Bright 5 for 67, G. S. Chappell 3 for 45); *Australians* 251 for 5 dec (K. J. Hughes 89, R. D. Robinson 52, C. S. Serjeant 32) and 167 for 3 (G. S. Chappell 70*, G. J. Cosier 66). *Australians won by 7 wickets.*

AUGUST 11, 12, 13, 15; FOURTH TEST MATCH (HEADING-LEY)
England won by an innings and 85 runs (in four days).

AUGUST 18; ARUNDEL
Australians 106 (44.4 overs) (D. W. Hookes 33, R. G. D. Willis 4 for 19); *Rest of the World* 110 for 7 (47.2 overs). *Rest of the World won by 3 wickets.*

AUGUST 20, 21, 22; LORD'S
Middlesex 207 (J. M. Brearley 46, M. W. W. Selvey 41*, N. G. Featherstone 41, J. R. Thomson 3 for 41, M. F. Malone 3 for 63) and 18 for 0; *Australians* 149 (D. W. Hookes 34, W. W. Daniel 4 for 27, P. H. Edmonds 3 for 29, J. E. Emburey 3 for 44). *Match drawn.*

AUGUST 25, 26, 27, 29, 30; FIFTH TEST MATCH (THE OVAL)
Match drawn.